CREATION GOD and HUMANITY

Engaging the Mystery of Suffering within the Sacred Cosmos

CATHERINE WRIGHT

Foreword by Gloria L. Schaab

Paulist Press
New York / Mahwah, NJ

Cover image (background) by Nikki Zalewski / Dreamstime.com
Cover design by Tamian Wood
Book design by Lynn Else

Library of Congress Cataloging-in-Publication Data
Names: Wright, Catherine (Assistant Professor of Religion and Philosophy), author.
Title: Creation, God, and humanity : engaging the mystery of suffering within the sacred cosmos / Catherine Wright ; foreword by Gloria L. Schaab.
Description: New York : Paulist Press, 2017. | Includes bibliographical references and index.
Identifiers: LCCN 2017026189 (print) | LCCN 2017002689 (ebook) | ISBN 9780809153176 (pbk. : alk. paper) | ISBN 9781587686603 (ebook)
Subjects: LCSH: Ecotheology. | Nature—Effect of human beings on. | Human ecology—Religious aspects--Christianity. | Suffering—Religious
Aspects—Christianity. | Catholic Church—Doctrines.
Classification: LCC BT695.5 .W745 2017 (ebook) | LCC BT695.5 (print) | DDC 231/.8—dc23
LC record available at https://lccn.loc.gov/2017026189

ISBN 978-0-8091-5317-6 (paperback)
ISBN 978-1-58768-660-3 (e-book)

Published by Paulist Press
997 Macarthur Boulevard
Mahwah, New Jersey 07430

www.paulistpress.com

Printed and bound in the
United States of America

IN DARKNESS GROWS THE GREEN

A soul cornered by Death's
unwelcome visit to the mind
cowers in darkness;
illusions gathered as gold
purchase denial.
A friend sold on the auction block;
faithful Wisdom goes with her.

Death sings to the rising sun
reminder to live
dance,
dream,
hope,
extend a hand beyond
a casual, passing reach
through the edge of one more day.

Despised gypsy
rattles bones in fleshy cages
where we do not welcome ourselves
as who we are,
but as what we do
and do, and do and do
forgetting to live,
becoming the stranger.

An intruder is defined
by a locked door;
welcome,
embrace,
devour what comes,
what will come;
within a dark womb
the first howl awaits.

Be still
Be still
Be still

Seek the eyes of Death
as Lover,
bestowing compassion;
as Prophet,
foretelling the uselessness
of anything less
than love.

—Magdalena Gómez

CONTENTS

CONTENTS

FOREWORD

The inspiration to compose this foreword comes from Catherine Wright herself in her book *Creation, God, and Humanity: Engaging the Mystery of Suffering within the Sacred Cosmos*. As I look out my window, I witness the tropical storm force winds and rains of the first major hurricane to threaten my home state of Florida in more than ten years. The winds and rains are the warning signs—the feeder bands—of Hurricane Matthew, a Category 4 storm that has already wreaked havoc in the Caribbean on its way to the Bahamas and the central coast of Florida. It has brought death and destruction in its wake to Cuba and to Haiti, whose people and lands have certainly borne, by any reasonable standard, a disproportionate measure of suffering wrought by this evolutionary world. And yet, as Wright fittingly points out in her expansive work, the visage of nature in an evolving cosmos is cruciform and this reality prompts us to reexamine how we envision and interpret Earth; its inhabitants, both human and nonhuman; and God in the midst of inherent and inflicted suffering.

Clearly, the mystery of suffering has demanded a reasonable and authentic theological response in every era. Impelling theological debates about retribution and atonement, about the relationship of God to suffering, and about the possibility of suffering in God, the ecological and human scope of suffering in the twentieth and twenty-first centuries has often driven these debates to an acute pitch. In response, Wright offers us the lens of "ecological theological anthropology" through which to conceive and interpret suffering. This is a lens grounded by a scientific Earth literacy, enhanced by theological and spiritual insight, and emergent as ecotheology with implications for individual, communal, and planetary travail. To accomplish this task, Wright has marshalled a remarkably wide-ranging collection of sources—traditional, historical, and contemporary—from science, theology, spirituality, and literature to "construct a Christian anthropology based on the wisdom of our blossoming Earth literacy." A particularly rich source—and one frequently overlooked in works that engage in the dialogue between theology and science—is the witness of the saints and the desert mothers. These wisdom figures establish the very foundations on which the four pillars—eschatological hope, the intrinsic worth of creation, the sacredness of cosmic communion, and the kenotic-kinetic dynamic—that form Wright's ecological theological anthropology (ETA) stand. By rooting her research in the fertile soil of its earliest religious wisdom, Wright demonstrates that the perspective on creation, its creatures, and its Creator that shapes this ETA is not only the product of contemporary scientific and theological investigation, but truly of the essence of the Christian Tradition.

By grounding her first pillar in a retrieval of the wisdom of Irenaeus, Wright makes a critical move in establishing eschatological hope. Irenaeus counteracts the interpretation of suffering as divine retribution that spawned from Augustine's doctrine of original sin. For Augustine, suffering stemmed from the evil that was either sin or punishment for sin, borne not only by human beings but by creation, itself. In contrast to a humanity and universe perverted by sin from its origin, Irenaeus's understanding of creation in dynamic movement from immaturity to fullness of union with God is essential to the pillar of hope. For Irenaeus, neither humanity nor the natural world could be both created and perfect, since to be created is to be finite, subject to corruption and, ultimately, to death. Nonetheless, creation could be perfected through the processes of change, growth, and maturation that we now know to be the essence of an evolutionary cosmos.

Hence, for Irenaeus, the world is a vale of soul-making or of soul-breaking—indeterminate, unpredictable, and chaotic, while, at the same time, full of potential and possibilities. For Irenaeus, a human existence free of difficulties, perils, and hardships would never allow human beings to develop into the likeness of God, for moral and spiritual growth comes through facing and overcoming challenges like those faced by Teilhard de Chardin and Audre Lorde upon whom Wright focuses her last chapter. Perhaps the same is true for the cosmos as well, since, as Teilhard himself stated, the process of creation "is no picnic but an adventure, a risk, a battle, to which [God] commits himself unreservedly." It takes place through *tâtonnement* or "groping," into which God enters, "step by step by dint of billionfold trial and error."[1]

While eschatological hope grounds the ultimate value of all creation in its dynamic movement toward union with God, Earth and its creatures have inherent value in and of themselves as created by God in a multitude of wondrous, purposeful, and irreplaceable life forms. As Maximus the Confessor points out in support of Wright's second pillar of the intrinsic worth of creation, "all things, in that they came to be from God, participate proportionally in God."[2] Thomas Aquinas also spoke of a relationship of "participation" between God and creation. According to Aquinas, everything that has being participates in the Source of all being, which is God whom Aquinas called "Being Itself." Moreover, not only do all things participate in God, but "God is in all things....Therefore as long as a thing has being, God must be present to it....in all things, and innermostly" (*Summa Theologica*, I.8.1). Pope Francis echoes this in *Laudato Si'* in the context of contemporary science. He states, "In this universe, shaped by open and intercommunicating systems, we can discern countless forms of relationship and participation. This leads us to think of the whole as open to God's transcendence, within which it develops" (no. 79). Truly, a profound relationship, a kinship, exists among all members of creation and makes plain that God's creative intention extends not only to the flourishing of humanity, but also to Earth. Emphasizing our common source and participation in God, as does Wright's second pillar, can foster in us a spirit of humility, a sense of interdependence, and an ethical stance that protects, sustains, and enhances the environment, all elements essential to an ecological theological anthropology.

The characteristics of interconnectivity and interdependence suggested by Wright's second pillar come to fruition in the notion of sacred cosmic communion. This third pillar emerges from an Earth literacy and Christian anthropology that stresses the inherent relationality that is constitutive of all that exists within and beyond the universe—nonhuman, human, and divine alike. It is rooted in the relational Being of the Christian God, as well as in the relations that constitute the very nature of human and nonhuman beings studied and described by the physical and social sciences. Rather than a hierarchy in creation based on a distorted notion of dominion and configured by use-value, a recognition of sacred cosmic communion fosters a deep sense of relationality and interdependence that in turn promotes the vitality of Earth and its inhabitants.

As Wright indicates, the cosmos is a graced reality and this is articulated by Hildegard of Bingen in her notion of *viriditas*. In this reality, God encompasses and permeates the entire created world, human and non-human alike, and humanity's role in this world is one of mutuality and care. According to Pope Francis, "We must forcefully reject the notion that our being...given dominion over the earth justifies absolute domination over other creatures." Rather there must be "a relationship of mutual responsibility between human beings and nature" (*Laudato Si'* 67) with "the priority of *being* over that of *being useful*" (no. 69, emphases in original). What is the nature of this "being" to which Francis calls us? Insights from contemporary cosmology, evolutionary biology, and quantum physics; from sociology and psychology; and from classical and contemporary theology essentially affirm the same truth concerning the "being" of which Francis speaks—to-be is to-be-in-relation. And to-be-in-relation is to exist within the web of life constituted by a kenotic-kinetic dynamic—death and birth, suffering and joy, pain and pleasure, cross and resurrection—Wright's fourth pillar of an ETA.

Wright's interpretation of kenosis as sacrifice is key to an evolutionary worldview. Both Arthur Peacocke and Teilhard de Chardin, whom Wright cites throughout her book, acknowledge the necessity of sacrifice in the emergence of novel forms of life in the universe. In *Science and the Christian Experiment*, Peacocke indicates that "new life can only emerge if other forms of life are, as it were...sacrificed on behalf of, the higher forms." Consequently, in the evolutionary process, "there is a cost when new forms of life emerge which are dependent on simpler forms for their continued existence."[3] However, such sacrifice is not only characteristic of creaturely existence. Sacrifice for the sake of new life is inherent in God who, out of abundant love, risks the creation of free creatures in a freely evolving cosmos. Sacrifice for the sake of new life opened St. Clare and the desert mothers to the revelation of God in creation and enabled them to live in harmony, balance, and abundance with Earth and its inhabitants. Moreover, in a unique manifestation of sacrifice, the kenotic-kinetic dynamic focuses our vision on God's kenotic choice to enter fully into the material world in incarnation. What unlimited value creation and its creatures have to God, for in the fullness of time, God entered into material existence in the person of Jesus of Nazareth, the Word-made-matter itself.

This incarnational vision of the kenotic-kinetic dynamic produces a profound reinterpretation of the God-world relationship, reminding us that, in the words of *Laudato Si'*, "The ultimate purpose of other creatures is not to be found in us. Rather, all creatures are moving forward with us and through us towards a common point of arrival, which is God" (no. 83). At one level, the kenotic-kinetic dynamic of incarnation enables us to contemplate the grandeur of creation, while, on another level, it moves us in the direction of a compassionate identification with those incarnate ones who are vulnerable, suffering, needy, and oppressed, demanding fullness of life. In view of the suffering of Earth and its inhabitants, the vulnerable, suffering, needy, and oppressed, demanding fullness of life, must include nonhuman beings and Earth itself. These poor ones call us to conversion and to recognize, as does Wright in the fourth pillar of the ETA, that Earth itself participates in the way of the cross.

Throughout her book, Catherine Wright constructs a vision that is as ancient as the Scriptures, as traditional as the lives of the saints, and as contemporary as systematic theology, evolutionary theory, and quantum physics. In creative and engaging ways, she orchestrates a chorus of voices that challenge and urge us to "embrace a distinctly ecological theological anthropology that reconnects sufferers with their ecological dwelling space and with their Creator and Redeemer." Engaging Wright and this stimulating chorus of voices has the capacity to move the heart toward contemplation, the mind toward insight, and the will toward social justice. Moreover, it will whet the reader's appetite to explore more deeply their mystical and scholarly refrains.

—Gloria L. Schaab, SSJ

ACKNOWLEDGMENTS

To the many wise and passionate, fellow sojourners
open to the sacred cosmic adventure,
Thank you.

To all those who have sustained, encouraged, challenged,
and loved me and my project into existence,
Thank you.

Know that I am, and always will be, immensely grateful.

INTRODUCTION

In the last century, adventures in science and technology, as well as expressions of creativity and innovation in art, economics, literature, music, sociology, and many other disciplines, have let us imagine our world, ourselves, and our Creator in new ways. When we turned our attention to the heavens, we discovered that life emerged from a singular moment of great cosmic exuberance and the subsequent primordial furnace crafted the elements hydrogen, helium, and a smidgen of lithium. Later, this material formed stars, which ultimately gave birth to the elements—such as calcium, oxygen, iron, and carbon—that would eventually make the physical face of Earth, help build human societies, and provide the materials that course through our veins, comprise our genes, fill our cells, and fabricate our bones. Humanity learned that we and all that we see around us is stardust.[1] When we looked deep into Earth's mantle and examined the diverse flora and fauna on its surface, we discovered that life forms have transformed over vast periods of time, all creatures are in fact related, all living bodies are powered by sunshine that is produced by photosynthetic plant life, and humanity was just one (but a fascinating one) of Earth's many magnificent bursts of creativity. When the subatomic level sparked our curiosity, we discovered order in chaos, interconnectivity, uncertainty, and mystery. Thus, at every level of reality we were offered scientific images to use as analogies and metaphors to help us reimagine how the Creator and Redeemer of this world and ourselves can be both transcendent, yet intimately involved in and concerned for this unfolding, good creation. In her book *Quantum Shift*, Heidi Ann Russell bases her approach to science and theology in a similar fashion: "The new images of reality taken from a contemporary scientific worldview gives us new images for thinking about God, humanity, sin, grace, and other theological concepts."[2] So, as we discovered new things about Earth, we asked new questions and are finding new answers.

Nevertheless, as our acuity of our beautiful and dynamic world improves, so too does our appreciation that this evolutionary world is perfused with incalculable levels of suffering, violence, and death spanning 13.8 billion years. How do we make sense of the painful aspects of creation if God is Love? The predominant answer that is given (or perhaps believed by sufferers) is that suffering is divine punishment for sin or wrongdoing. However, this cannot explain diminishment, suffering, and death occurring before the emergence of humans (the only organisms we know who are capable of sin) if creation is truly good. Thus, a "simple" way to explain this was to see creation as initially good in a state of grace but now it is fallen due to human sin. Suffering, therefore, is the ongoing result of this transgression. However, the broad application of the premise that suffering is punishment for sin is not questioned in the story of the Fall. How can other-than-human creation sin (or be affected by the sin of a species that was not present at the birth of the world) and thus be in need of punishment? The popularity of uncritically applying the idea of "punishment for sin" to explain many forms of suffering tells us that Christian imaginations are still laboring under the classic story of a static, fallen cosmos. The attractiveness of this "simple" answer is generated by the overemphasizing of God's transcendence in the minds of believers (which overshadows God's immanence), the false belief that we are radically distinct from (and thus innately superior to) creation, and the distorted conception that Earth is merely the stage where the human–God drama plays out (which relegates Earth to a machine comprised of inert objects to do the bidding of its human technician watched over by God).

Due to these misguided ideas, few believers have had the theological ideas or tools to imagine adequately faithful ways to engage with the mystery of suffering in light of evolution. This text invites readers to dislodge the pervasive idea of "suffering as punishment for sin" and to rediscover underappreciated interpretations of suffering. It will also remind us that our evolutionary world has much to teach us about engaging, describing, and responding to suffering. But beware, this is not a panacea for those in the grips of immediate suffering;

telling a friend who has just been diagnosed with liver cancer that her suffering is just part of the universe's costly creative impetus will hurt more than help. However, if she embraces an Earth literacy as she journeys through the ups and downs of her life and has her theological imagination fed by the analogies and metaphors offered by science, perhaps when she is in her darkest hour she will feel a divine presence to comfort and carry her—rather than a distant God who seeks to punish her. She also may experience the power of her inspirited but broken body to sustain her transformation in spite of her diminishment and death.

To begin, this book tells the story of many scientific and theological discoveries that can shape our imaginations as Christians and this new Earth literacy enables believers to see new ways of describing the relations among God, creation, and humanity. Part 1 is a narration of how scientists and theologians became more literate of Earth as a subject (not an object) and a witness of divine revelation. The description begins with how human mindscapes shifted from seeing the world as Mother (who nurtures), to nature as a seductive temptress (to be controlled because she cannot be trusted), to Earth as machine (to exploit for human betterment). Every shift was caused for specific reasons: a deep fear of human frailty, philosophies that emphasized a separation of mind and body, an exaggeration of scientific objectivity and precision, an over-emphasis of divine transcendence, an overstating of other-worldly salvation, and a very practical need—humans needed unlimited access to Earth's resources to feed industrialization. This story also tells how these shifts in patterns of thinking about creation impacted how the Christian faith was lived. For example, these shifts cultivated a passive, spiritual interiority that detached believers from the world, developed a purely transcendent understanding of God (i.e., Divine Watchmaker) and neglected the Holy Spirit, promoted an apathy towards the material needs of those deemed "other," bred indifference toward our religious duty to care for Earth, nurtured a false belief that all suffering can and should be avoided (via technology), and eroded any sense that a Christian way of life makes sense in an evolutionary world.[3] But it is not all bad news. The emergence of scientific Earth literacy in the twentieth century signaled another shift in consciousness to Earth as a dynamic communion of compassionate subjects where Christians can discover divine revelation.[4] This shift foretold the beginning of an ecological conversion and its development and incorporation in Christian thought is still sorely needed.

We are at a turning point in history, and if we do not choose abundant life for all, we will have chosen death. A very astute theologian, Douglas John Hall, has indicated that no Christian community of the past has had to sort out what it would mean to be a Christian in a world in the grips of the problems facing people today: the technological manipulation of life and death, globalism, the frightening power of terrorism, the immense and growing disparity between rich and poor, the unprecedented destabilization of our planet's life systems.[5] These are not just "secular" problems nicely insulated from the lives of churchgoers; these problems are also indicators of a crisis of faith. In his recent groundbreaking encyclical *Laudato Si'*, Pope Francis indicates that the physical degradation of Earth's ecosystems and human society indicates a deterioration of our spiritual lives: "The external deserts in the world are growing, because the internal deserts have become so vast" (no. 217).[6] Thus, for Earth's sake and our own, Christians need to address our estrangement from Earth as an invaluable source for physical, social, economic, and spiritual well-being. The only way to dislodge the firmly entrenched idea that humans are superior to Earth, which is destabilizing our planet and inhibiting life-giving relations with each other and God, is by reimagining creation, God, and humanity. We need to fall in love again with our planetary home so that our atrophied Christian imaginations can become more robust and inspire "vigorous and creative" reflections about God and our sacred cosmos, including the role of humanity in this grand narrative.[7] Pope Francis concurs:

> An inadequate presentation of Christian anthropology gave rise to a wrong understanding of the relationship between human beings and the world. Often, what was handed on was a Promethean vision of mastery over the world, which gave the impression that the protection of nature was something that only the faint-hearted cared about. (*Laudato Si'* 116)

This book presents an Earth-literate Christian anthropology, namely, an ecological theological anthropology (ETA). Its construction takes place in part 2 and is achieved by deep excavation into the roots of the Christian Tradition as well as by harvesting the fruits of modern ecotheological thought. It is this new relational framework that will enable believers to look anew at the suffering inherent to our evolutionary reality as well as to that which is inflicted by humans—the task of part 3.

For many Christians it is hard to see the connections among the disintegration experienced by supernovas, the experience of Christ on the cross, climate change, and their own suffering. This is especially true for Christians who have had their theological imaginations molded by both a mechanical worldview and a belief that God is apathetic, far from this fallen world, and not present in our world. An ETA allows people of faith to see creation, God, and humans differently, and thus, awakens us to the beautiful and yet painful cadence that animates our evolutionary world. The universe is teaching us that great moments of creativity and innovation come from disintegration, suffering, and death. The violent collapse and destruction of first-generation stars created the building blocks of all life that followed; the violent convergence of tectonic plates in the Pacific "Ring of Fire"[8] gave birth to the Japanese Archipelago and Galapagos Islands; monarch butterflies, if they are not allowed to engage in the struggle to emerge from their chrysalis, are unable to sustain flight, leaving them crippled and doomed; the sacrifice of independence by an ancient predatory species of bacteria brought forth mitochondria, the powerhouse of all complex cells.[9] Thus, from the smallest to the largest dimension of our sacred cosmic story, creation, fecundity, sacrifice, and destruction are inextricably intertwined.

Christians can relearn these lessons on suffering if we do two things: have a "critical remembrance" of classic wisdom[10] and ask the beasts for their wisdom, as Job 12:7 reminds us. When we do this, the sacrificial moments of great transformations spanning from the galactic to the microscopic levels of life, including the resurrection, can be appreciated as moments of grace. In spite of the darkness, they speak prophetically of new life emerging from death. Embracing our evolutionary reality as a source of wisdom concerning suffering is not *the* solution to the problem of suffering; the tendency of Earth's evolutionary processes to be wasteful (e.g., mass extinctions and evolutionary dead ends) can never be adequately explained away. Nevertheless, what is possible is the awakening of believers to new ways of interpreting their own experiences of suffering and death in light of our evolutionary reality. The world we encounter can teach us to take seriously the immense amounts of degradation, diminishment, suffering, and death that is inherent to the creative processes of the universe, most of which has existed for millennia prior to humanity's emergence. Fortified with this knowledge, people of faith are able to differentiate more adequately between unavoidable suffering inherent to Earth's creative processes and inflicted suffering caused by human sin. Perhaps we can also respond anew with hearts filled with hope and gratitude. This discernment, however, requires scientific and theological Earth literacy, and it is not easy. But much is promised if believers immerse themselves into the ocean of creation and witness anew our "creative, redemptive and all loving" God even in our darkest hour.[11] This has been affirmed in my own experiences of suffering. I have looked into the abyss of darkness in myself, my family, my social communities, and in Earth's ecosystems where I dwell, and there I have witnessed the "green" growing in the darkness as Magdelena Gómez offers in her poem "In Darkness Grows the Green." Her last stanza poignantly reminds readers of God's powerfully transformative and yet vulnerable and loving, sacred presence in suffering: "Seek the eyes of Death as Lover / bestowing compassion; as Prophet / foretelling the uselessness of anything less than love."[12] This divine presence in the darkness promises life in spite of death, not a life devoid of suffering and death. This is both the message of the cross and the cosmos, and it needs expression in Christian anthropologies.

Consequently, the ideas in the following pages concerning suffering are *rooted* in the suffering, compassionate heart of God (divine suffering) and attend to the suffering *of* the ground (suffering inherent to creation) and *on* the ground (human suffering). Thus, being literate of our biospiritual universe story and embracing an ETA can enable sufferers who courageously choose to follow God of the cosmic cross to be authentic witnesses to the green growing in life's darkest moments.

PART I

SCIENTIFIC EARTH LITERACY

1

THE EMERGENCE OF SCIENTIFIC EARTH LITERACY

To enhance the imaginations of Christians living in an evolutionary world, humanity must meaningfully reconnect to Earth and the cosmos. This demands a robust scientific Earth literacy to appreciate our many Earth neighbors and the sacred planetary communion of which we are a part. Thus, it is important to understand what is meant by the terms *Earth literacy* and *scientific Earth literacy*.

EARTH LITERACY: A DEFINITION

Literacy is not just learning terms and putting sentences together. The United States Department of Education indicates that "literacy is the ability *to use* printed and written information to function in society, to achieve one's goals, and to develop one's knowledge and potential."[1] This illustrates that the ability to understand and then apply knowledge in everyday life to develop one's potential is key.

Earth literacy is about becoming knowledgeable regarding our other-than-human neighbors and incorporating this knowledge into how we live and love together in our planetary home. Environmentalist and educator David Orr is a good starting point for understanding

Earth literacy. Orr uses the term "ecological literacy" to indicate the shift toward a truly "ecological consciousness" and affectivity that allows an individual to merge their physical "landscape" with their interior "mindscape."[2] The Greek root of *ecology* is *oikos*, meaning "household"; hence, ecology is the interdependent web of life—organisms and their physical surroundings—that makes up our planetary home. Orr indicates that students are being taught that "ecology is unimportant for history, politics, economy, society." As a result, we are forming "ecological yahoos" who envision Earth as a commodity for their personal use and they have no appreciation of natural or moral limits. Orr writes,

> The result [of a malformed consciousness] is a generation of ecological yahoos without a clue why the color of the water in their rivers is related to their food supply, or why storms are becoming more severe as the planet warms. The same persons as adults will create businesses, vote, have families, and above all, consume. If they come to reflect on the discrepancy between the splendor of their private lives in a hotter, more toxic and violent world, as ecological illiterates they will have roughly the same success as one trying to balance a check-book without knowing arithmetic.[3]

Hence ecological literacy, as Orr envisions it, reminds us that we are deeply connected to, and dependent on, Earth. This new way of understanding and interacting with the world should be driven by an aesthetic sense of wonder, an affinity for the living world, and a delight in life. Orr indicates that ecological literacy requires three aspects: (1) knowing about Earth and Earth's life systems (the "what" and "how" of Earth's life systems); (2) caring about the constituents of this planetary web of life (empathy or compassion); and (3) having a practical competency in how to know and care about creation. Without these you cannot have a healthy, sustainable world. Thus, the well-being of our planetary household requires a "radical change in the institutions and patterns that we have come to accept as normal…a change in metaphors from mechanical to organic, industrial to biological. This demands a re-envisioning to what human well-being means and how this is measured."[4] This is a good first step toward an ecological conversion all people, including Christians, are being invited to, so that "prudence, stewardship, and the celebration of Creation" can be cultivated.[5] However, Orr's ecological literacy is insufficient in two areas: Orr does not address specifically the ancient, dynamic universe story out of which Earth's ecologies emerged, nor does he address the sacred dimension of our evolving world. Hence, the term *Earth literacy* has more depth than *ecological literacy*.

The first inadequacy of Orr's vison has to do with the scope of his vision; ecological literacy concerns the planet's ecosystems while Earth literacy appreciates the entire 13.8-billion-year universe story out of which our planet emerged. This broader vision from the galactic to the quantum levels of life through an immense timeframe adds depth to Orr's purely Earth-centered perspective. A good question to ask at this point is how can we know that Earth is a microcosm of a greater universe and follows the same guiding principles? Isn't Earth very different from the moon, or ancient stars, or the planets in the ten thousand other galaxies the Hubble telescope captured in our universe?[6] The answer is yes, Earth is different, but also, no, the forces that enable Earth to be different are the same as the forces working throughout the cosmos. For example, Venus is hotter and devoid of biotic life because it is closer to the Sun, not because the forces working on Venus are different from those that affect Earth.

The reason this text can connect Earth's ecologies with the universe as a whole is thanks in part to Albert Einstein. This German-born American physicist developed his general theory of relativity in 1931, which states that "all places are alike,"[7] or more specifically, that the laws of physics apply to all that constitutes the cosmos. This means that Earth's ecologies are governed by the same rules by which every other galaxy—past, present, and future—are governed. This also means that there is an order to creation that scientists can figure out. Theologian Thomas Berry and mathematician Brian Swimme contributed more nuance to Einstein's vision by indicating that the evolution of the universe is "ordered by *differentiation*," "structured by *autopoiesis*" (subjectivity), and "organized by *communion*."[8] Consequently, our cosmos, which we thought was a static universe, is more aptly described as cosmo*genesis*—a universe of structures that are evolving or being created through time. Our universe is an ordered and dynamic 13.8-billion-year family history that speaks of its (and our) birth and its continual unfolding.[9] Earth is a part of this story and represents a *microcosm* of the macrocosm that is this energetic universe. However, Earth is also a *macrocosm*, a holistic *oikos*, or household, in itself. Our planetary home is a web of life where individual organisms live, love, and interact with one another. Thus, Christians require an appreciation of Earth as a macrocosmic household and as a microcosm of a bigger, older, unfolding universe story. This is offered by the term *Earth literacy*.

The second deficiency with Orr's ecological literacy is its lack of attention to the sacred dimensions of our Creation story. Christian imaginations must appreciate this aspect of the world we are encountering. Ursula King, a renowned scholar on spirituality, attends to the spiritual dimension of Earth in her preferred nomenclature, "earthing spiritual literacy." King asserts that when our spirituality is rooted in Earth, we can discover "the *zest for life* that fosters the flourishing of people and planet."[10] King employs the terms *earthing* and *spiritual* to represent a coupling of the spiritual and biological in her understanding of Earth literacy that compares to the term *biospiritual* used earlier. Hence, Earth literacy can affirm that the universe, Earth, and all of Earth's planetary citizens are a result of God's initial creative efforts (*creatio originalis*), a manifestation of God's ongoing creative efforts (*creatio continua*), and are participants in God's new creation at the end of time (*creation nova*).[11] For Christians, Earth can be understood as a complex, interdependent, ancient, evolving, *biospiritual* communion of subjects in an ancient, holy, unfolding universe story. This sacred cosmic story is the new context for making sense of the world we encounter, including the presence of suffering.

Therefore, Earth literacy is a way of knowing what leads to ways of acting or doing. Our biospiritual Earth is a key source of wisdom for understanding our world and ourselves. Earth literacy demonstrates a shift of consciousness from seeing Earth as a machine (an object) to seeing Earth as a biological and spiritual communion of subjects within an ancient, sacred universe story. People with a robust Earth literacy make our biospiritual planetary communion an important source and measure for determining what is valuable. They also make use of knowledge offered by many disciplines, including science and religion, to make sense of their encounters with creation. However, since the Earth literacy of Christians today is due in part to scientific discoveries not available to classic theologians such as St. Francis or Thomas Aquinas, then there must be space made for imagining the relationship between God and creation in new ways. This does not mean that we must throw away the Canticle of the Sun or the *Summa Theologica* as irrelevant in an evolutionary world; rather, it means that we need to appreciate ancient sources of wisdom with new eyes and hearts thanks to our Earth literacy. It also means that space has been made for new descriptions and interpretations of suffering.

SCIENTIFIC EARTH LITERACY

The rest of this chapter tells the story of how scientists awoke to a new planetary consciousness. Science, in the most basic sense, can be understood as a person's way of knowing and thinking about the material world that he or she experiences. However, as famous astronomer Galileo Galilei reminds us, without learning the dialect of the universe, we will not be able to make sense of what we see, hear, touch, smell, and feel: "But the book [of nature] cannot be understood unless one first learns to comprehend the language and read the letters in which it is composed."[12] It was the scientists of the eighteenth and nineteenth centuries who started to figure out Earth's language that told the story of the universe. The questions they asked and the answers discovered when they encountered creation was a creative activity; they used their imaginations and intellects that were formed by the communities in which they dwelled.[13] Class, gender, politics, religion, and other cultural factors all played a role in the science that was done. Consequently, scientists were participants and interpreters in their scientific endeavors, not radically separate observers discovering disembodied truths.[14] Many, such as Albert Einstein or Marie Curie, honed their faculties of observation, interpretation, and critical thinking to penetrate deeply into the inner workings of our universe, and we are the benefactors of their efforts. We now examine the dawning of scientific Earth literacy that was the result of a shift in how scientists in the eighteenth and nineteenth centuries imagined the world in which they lived.

A GREAT ADVENTURE: REAWAKENING TO EARTH

In *The Death of Nature*, Carolyn Merchant argues that, from the sixteenth to the eighteenth centuries, the human imagination shifted toward seeing Earth as a machine.[15] Merchant recounts the many changes occurring in how the world was understood by humanity that facilitated this shift. First, thanks to Copernicus (1473–1543), it was proven that the Earth rotated around the sun and not the other way around. This made many experience a feeling of homelessness and insignificance, which resulted in some, such as Francis Bacon (1561–1626), to acclaim fervently humanity's divinely charged mastery of creation to the detriment of the natural world. Another impetus that helped shift human mindscapes was the invention of powerful new technologies, such as nautical navigation tools, which allowed more ambitious maritime voyages to places beyond the narrow geographical boundaries of Europe. Documents written by Christopher Columbus (1493), Jean Ribault (1563), and Baltasar de Obregón (1584) expressed how these men marveled at the riches of the New World that could be taken and used to fuel the blossoming Scientific and Industrial Revolutions in resource-poor Europe.[16]

When Bacon's attitude of divinely sanctioned domination and the explorers' exploitative tendencies were linked with René Descartes's (1596–1650) ideas, (e.g., the mind is separate from, and more valuable than, the material body and the world is run by mechanical principles), it took only a small nudge to shift human minds to imagine Earth as a machine. This nudge came from British physicist Isaac Newton (1643–1727), who not only discovered the invisible forces (e.g., gravity) that caused the world to work the way it does (thereby offering the empirical data for Descartes's mechanical principles), but also formulated the potent analogy of the Divine Watchmaker. This idea distanced God from creation, conflated the living world with a machine (i.e., a watch), and placed humans in charge as the technicians of this machine. Throughout her beautifully constructed text, Merchant explores how the machine metaphor entranced human imaginations and caused the tenor of scientific discourse to become so human-centered (and male-centered) that Earth's voice was progressively drowned out. Humanity had rendered Earth all but invisible in their mindscapes. This "death" of nature was captured for all to see in the art, literature, economic patterns, and philosophical concepts of that time period. Scientists from the sixteenth to the eighteenth centuries absorbed the machine metaphor into their imaginations, which affected the questions they asked and the results they discovered. Thus, scientists stopped being artisans giving voice to Earth's truths and became technicians hungry to extract the secrets of how this machine worked to augment human power over nature.

The Adventurers of the Eighteenth Century

At the dawning of the eighteenth century, scientists were still enthusiastically accumulating and categorizing data about this elaborate machine, Earth. The scientific mindscape bequeathed to eighteenth- and nineteenth-century scientists was fairly atomistic, fragmentary, and "chiselled to perfection for controlling, for distancing, for calculating, and for dominating."[17] This thinking reached new heights in Europe as industrialization intensified and then percolated through the scientific mindscape of the United States in the 1880s with the rise of petrochemical and electrical industries. Similarly, on both sides of the ocean, scientists were asked to find ways to extract from Earth whatever was necessary to meet humanity's ever increasing need for energy. This is a provocative plot development but there is a twist; it was humanity's entrancement with collecting vast amounts of fragmented data about our mechanical world that ironically revealed to scientists that our world was more ancient, wild, vast, interconnected, and unpredictable than we could ever have imagined. These discoveries then cultivated scientists who were dissatisfied with the machine metaphor and yearned for a more intimate understanding of our own birth, place, and purpose in a dynamic universe.

The process of moving scientists from imagining Earth as a dead machine to envisioning Earth as an evolving, planetary web did not happen overnight. The shift took two centuries, demonstrating that a shift in consciousness is a complicated path that requires time and several crucial preemptive steps. The first step of this shift was to diminish humanity's fear of nature. One example of nature's cruelty is the Black Death (bubonic plagues), which terrified Europeans in the Middle Ages. It is hard to imagine the horror felt by people who saw entire families and communities suffer horrible deaths. To get a sense of this fear, one needs to remember the scares brought by SARS, Ebola, and now, the Zika virus. Imagine the intensity of fear felt by those who saw two-thirds of the population of Europe wiped out by an unknown and seemingly incurable sickness. This feeling of helplessness cultivated a belief in a capricious God, and people desired to live in a world where nature's cruelty was controlled.

It was the blossoming field of science that offered respite and security. For example, Giovanni Morgagni of Padua (1682–1771) helped to diminish humanity's fear of nature when he began to perform regular autopsies and discovered empirically based answers as to why individuals became sick and died. Previous to Morgagni, autopsies were considered sacrilegious (and even a crime); therefore, diseases or pathologies were thought to be punishments caused by the invisible, unpredictable forces of a malicious Mother Nature. However, when diseases were shown to be malfunctions of the body, then competent technicians of the body, physicians, could fix these biological problems and offer salvation. Thus, discoveries like Morgagni's lessened human anxiety and fear of nature and placed the people's hope for healing in the hands of scientists. His work, however, also presumed the body was like a machine that became sick when it malfunctioned, further embedding a mechanical worldview into the human psyche. Nevertheless, this first step did confront the error in envisioning creation as malevolent and nature's Creator as intentionally cruel. Hence, a small space was made in human imagination for a new way of envisioning Earth, humanity, and God.

The next in a series of important cognitive steps came when Swedish botanist and zoologist Carl von Linné (1707–78), better known as Carolus (or Carl) Linnaeus, laid the foundation for the modern system of identifying and comparing the varieties of living species of plants and animals on Earth. His work offered the linguistic tools to name and study Earth's many organisms—present and past. The ability of all scientists to have a common way to communicate about the organisms they encountered enabled long-term relations among these beings to be unveiled. For example, humanity started to understand how living organisms in the eighteenth century were similar and different from those buried far beneath Earth's surface thanks to the discoveries of ancient fossils by Louis Leclerc (1707–88). Humanity's dawning appreciation of Earth's old, tangled webs of life was also cultivated by James Hutton's (1726–97) contributions concerning the advanced age and uniform nature of Earth's rocks, and those of his predecessor, geologist and bishop Nicolas Steno (1638–86), who advanced the idea of the stratification of soil over time. Thus, a larger, more dynamic family history was being articulated and proved that Archbishop James Ussher's (1582–1629) date of creation (i.e., the night preceding Sunday, October 23, 4004 BC) was not accurate.[18]

Another important contributor who moved scientific imaginations in new directions was Georges Louis Buffon (1707–88), who challenged the prevailing theory of preformationism, which claimed that all things were static and came preformed—or "as is." His insight that Earth had a longer history than was thought at the time, and his observations of differences in plant and animal structure in differing geographic locations, showed that there were inherently creative forces at work in the world. These ideas were groundbreaking and affected many in the following century, including Darwin, who indicated that Buffon was "the first author who in modern times has treated it [evolution] in a scientific spirit."[19]

Consequently, at the twilight of the eighteenth century, scientists were no longer afraid of Mother Nature and were confidently unravelling the secret workings of this planetary machine. They could do so because they had a comprehensive language for conversing about the many creatures of Earth and they had a new timeline for their investigations. What was now needed was the time and energy to apply these new tools and techniques to the exploration of Earth's many frontiers. This was the task of nineteenth-century star gazers, fossil hunters, traveling naturalists, budding ecologists, and cellular biologists.

The Adventurers of the Nineteenth Century

There were many discoveries in the nineteenth century that helped shift Western mindscapes toward imagining Earth as an interconnected and dynamic world rather than a static machine. Not all of them can be outlined here but this section will offer a generous narrative that explores the contributions of those who looked to the heavens, the ground, the dynamic web of flora and fauna, and the minutia of cellular life to begin the process of becoming Earth literate.

Star Gazers

The great advances in physics and chemistry in the first decades of the nineteenth century allowed for a more detailed study of the stars. This, in turn, revealed a new level of interconnectivity inherent to the cosmos beyond the boundaries of Earth. Early in the nineteenth century, Bavarian optometrist and physicist Joseph von Fraunhofer

(1787–1826) invented the spectroscope (1814), which allowed him to study light sources with remarkable precision. Using this instrument with the larger, more sophisticated telescopes he invented and the improved optical gratings he constructed, Fraunhofer was able to study the dark absorption lines in the spectrum of sunlight. With the tools he invented and the data offered by other scientists such as John Herschel (1792–1871), Robert Wilhelm Bunsen (1811–99), Gustav Robert Kirchhoff (1824–87), and William Huggins (1824–1910),[20] nineteenth-century scientists were able to demonstrate that Earth's chemical composition was the same as that of the sun and stars. Hence, human star gazers revealed a vital truth: the entire universe is connected.[21]

Fossil Hunters

Other key contributions to reawakening us to Earth came from those studying our planet's rocky face. Geologists William Smith (1769–1839), Charles Lyell (1797–1875), and John Phillips (1800–1874) demonstrated many things: fossil discoveries showed a wonderful order to nature; the forces shaping Earth in the past are still at work; and the fossils in Earth's many layers of rock reveal that Earth's history can be classified into geological time periods that they called the Paleozoic, Mesozoic, and Cenozoic eras.

Lyell, in his *Principles of Geology* (written between 1830 and 1833), observed that geologic changes were the result of a steady accumulation of infinitesimal physical changes over immensely long spans of time. Lyell's vision of dynamism and connectivity had a significant impact on nineteenth-century scientific thought; Charles Darwin was so taken by Lyell's ideas that he chose to take his book with him on his five-year journey on the HMS Beagle.[22] However, Lyell was not able to offer an intermediary "transition" organism that showed a definite transition from one form (e.g., a fish) to another (e.g., a lizard). It was Mary Anning (1799–1847), a self-taught, working-class, underappreciated geologist, who provided this proof.[23] One particular transitional specimen she found in 1811 was named Ichthyosaurus, the "fish-lizard." Later she discovered the "flying-dragon," Pterodactylus, in 1828, and the Squaloraja in 1829, which was an intermediary between a shark and a ray. Her discoveries of intermediate forms vividly showed how seemingly different species were connected, and this inspired the imaginations of many who followed. Thus, the fossil hunters of the nineteenth century revealed astounding truths: Earth was very old, innately connected, geologically organized, and quite creative.

Traveling Naturalists

What was missing thus far was a way to describe why species change from one form to another. No one knew how this dynamism actually worked. Interestingly, partial answers to these questions were offered concurrently by Charles Darwin (1809–82)[24] and Alfred Russel Wallace (1823–1913)[25] after their adventures studying the flora and fauna in the Southern Hemisphere (Darwin) and in the South American and Malay Archipelago (Wallace). At a meeting of the Linnean Society of London in 1858, their copious amounts of meticulously gathered data were first discussed and the theories they developed from the data were debated at great length. A year later, Darwin formally published his theories of adaptation and change in *The Origin of Species by Means of Natural Selection or The Preservation of Favored Races in the Struggle for Life* (1859), and Wallace's article "On the Tendency of Varieties to Depart Indefinitely from the Original Type" was published in the same year. Both these men presented the idea that organisms change because certain traits are more favorable in their specific environments, which allows the organism possessing these traits to produce more offspring (who then have this trait). Hence, the favorable traits are "naturally" selected for and those with less favorable ones are selected against. Why is one trait more favorable than another? Thanks to an essay on the principles of human population by Thomas Robert Malthus (1766–1834) that outlined how human populations are curtailed by competition for limited resources, Darwin (and Wallace) imagined that communities of other organisms worked the same way; the favorability of the trait is based on how well they enabled an organism to outcompete others for limited resources.[26] If a finch has a strong beak that is very efficient for eating seeds, it will outcompete its weaker-beaked fellow finches and consume more calories and produce more viable offspring, hence passing on the strong-beak trait. This formidable work of Darwin and Wallace (who stood on the shoulders of many other scientific giants) significantly challenged the coherency of a static, mechanical worldview. They had hard evidence that organisms changed through time (due to environmental conditions), and they had logical theories as to how this change occurred.

What was missing from Darwin's work was a way of describing how the selected traits were transmitted from generation to generation. This part of the evolutionary puzzle was offered by Austrian monk Gregor Mendel in 1865. From experiments spanning from 1856 to 1863, this Augustinian friar discovered how pea plants transmitted characteristics to their offspring and gave a viable explanation of how all physical traits were transmitted to future generations. He even gave the mathematical likelihood for the distribution of different characteristics. Scientists soon recognized the importance of Mendel's data; it helped to explain the transformation in beak sizes in finches or shell attributes of Galapagos tortoises—two of Darwin's famous research subjects. Therefore, nineteenth-century naturalists offered a new truth: all life on Earth evolved through small changes to environmental conditions over immense time spans. Building on his *Origin of Species*, Darwin wrote *The Descent of Man* in 1871, which was an imaginative portrait of humanity's emergence from Earth. It sparked both controversy and intrigue but irreversibly caused humanity to reimagine how human life originated and hinted at a bigger cosmic story that was unfolding long before we arrived.

Blossoming Ecologists

As the idea of evolution was beginning to mold the imaginations of scientists in the nineteenth century, others were revealing similarly important truths at the ecosystem level. Biologist Ernst Haeckel coined the new term *Oecologie* (ecology) in 1866 and defined it as

> the economy of nature—the investigation of the total relations of the animal both to its inorganic and its organic environment; including, above all, its friendly and inimical relations with those animals and plants with which it comes directly or indirectly into contact—in a word, ecology is the study of all those complex interrelations referred to by Darwin as the conditions of the struggle for existence.[27]

This term, *ecology*, was further refined in 1875 when Eduard Suess coined the terms "biosphere," "hydrosphere," and "lithosphere" to describe specific parts of Earth's ecosystems.[28] Pioneers in the fledgling field of ecology observed that habitats were organized in a holistic manner and revealed how community members related and depended on one another. This approach to science emphasized a holistic comprehension of Earth's webs of life rather than the atomizing and dissecting of Earth into isolated categories or fragments. For example, industrial and environmental chemist Ellen Swallow Richards (1842–1911)[29] fleshed out the interconnectivity of human and ecological health; zoologist Clinton Hart Merriam's (1855–1942) holistic approach to research in Arizona in the 1880s revealed that each bioregion had unique features that needed to be taken into account when studying the flora and fauna; botanist Carl Georg Oscar Drude (1852–1933) emphasized the interdependence of animals and plant life; Andreas Schimper (1856–1901), a French-born botanist, blurred the boundaries of ecology, physiology (the way organisms function, including the way the many parts work together), and morphology (the way organisms are structured). His groundbreaking work documented the impact of adaptations of individual plants on the whole community of flora; botanist Eugen Warming (1841–1924) wrote *Plantesamfund* (1895) and offered a creative way of describing interdependence in the "social" world of plants.[30] Thus, budding ecologists offered human imaginations a vital truth: Earth was a holistic ecosystem comprised of dynamic webs of life characterized by connectivity and interdependence. This way of encountering our planetary home challenged an atomistic and mechanical understanding of Earth. It reinforced what was being revealed at the galactic and planetary level (e.g., Darwin's theory of evolution) and helped shift human consciousness.

However, scientists were not the only ones imagining Earth as a web of life in the nineteenth century; the imaginations of these budding ecologists were being fed by the work of artisans of literature, poetry, and art whose minds, hearts, and spirits were being molded and nurtured by a nonmechanical understanding of Earth. For example, essayist Ralph Waldo Emerson's book *Nature* (1836) became the accepted manual for one branch of American environmentalism due to its interconnected, organic, and prophetic vision of reality.[31] His insight lay in how he saw Earth as a book that reveals truths upon close inspection of its entirety: "Nature is a language and every new fact one learns is a new word; but it is not a language taken to pieces and dead in the dictionary, but the language put together in a most significant and universal sense."[32] Emerson wished to learn this planetary language not because he desired to know a new grammar or control a machine, but because it enabled him to read more proficiently the great holistic book that is Earth. Similarly, poet Henry David Thoreau (1817–62) sustained Emerson's vision of nature and extended his idea of physical and spiritual connectedness to human social spheres. He believed that in the preservation of wilderness is the preservation of the world itself.[33]

The idea of Earth's wild, expansive frontiers as places of value for human flourishing also resonates in the work of several of Emerson's and Thoreau's contemporaries including author James Fenimore Cooper, painter Thomas Cole, and nature writer Richard Jefferies. James Fenimore Cooper wrote two novels, *The Pioneers* (1823) and *The Prairie* (1827), both of which offered insights from his Native American protagonist Leatherstockings concerning conserving, respecting, and protecting the natural world. Thomas Cole painted realistic and detailed portraits of the American landscape to highlight humans' peaceful cohabitation with nature while Richard Jefferies's famous autobiography *The Story of My Heart* (1883) is an almost mystical description of how he intertwined with the universe around him. Similarly, John Burroughs (who will also be highlighted in the next chapter) extolled the beauty and intricacies of nature and encouraged people to experience the natural world.[34] These are just a few of the nineteenth-century artisans who offered visual and literary ways of envisioning Earth's interconnectivity, nondualism, beauty in wilderness, and intrinsic worth of nature. Thus, at an ecological level, expressed in both science and literature, Earth was beginning to be imagined as an interdependent, holistic, and valuable reality.

Cell Watchers

Because the art of microscopy had sufficiently evolved by the twilight decades of the nineteenth century, this field of science was helping to remold human imaginations by revealing how all life is intimately connected, even at a microscopic level. For example, in 1839, Czech anatomist Johann Evangelist Purkinje (1787–1869) used the term "protoplasm" to describe the fluid that all cells possessed. Concurrently, Scottish botanist Robert Brown (1773–1858) described how the more complicated cells (eukaryotic cells) possess a nucleus or central command center. Hence, all cells share important structural features, giving more nuances to Earth's connectivity.

Embryologists in the nineteenth century added even more detail to this story of kinship; biologist Walther Flemming (1843–1905) described the process of ordinary cell division (mitosis) in 1882, and this cell-splitting adventure is shared by all multicellular organisms. Biologist Oscar Hertwig's (1849–1922) observations of sea urchin reproduction in 1876[35] paved the way for understanding meiosis, which is the way organisms in the animal kingdom make sperm and eggs. This demonstrates even at the cellular level that organisms across a wide spectrum of life share many vital processes and structures.

SUMMARY

These are just a few discoveries that have allowed scientists working at the galactic and microscopic levels of life to reimagine Earth. Thus, at the twilight of the nineteenth and the dawn of the twentieth centuries, artisans of science were beginning to employ metaphors, imagery, and language that reflected what they were discovering in the world about them: our world was ancient, evolving, interconnected, and interdependent. These are the basic building blocks for scientific Earth literacy, and they helped to cultivate new questions, to inspire new scientific discoveries, and to stimulate innovative ways of understanding Earth and ourselves. In the twentieth and twenty-first centuries, the more isolated, individual voices of the preceding century, who spoke of dynamism and interconnectivity, became a sophisticated choral ensemble that signaled a more robust Earth literacy in science.

2

THE DEVELOPMENT OF SCIENTIFIC EARTH LITERACY

At the dawn of the twentieth century, the enthusiastic collection of scientific data was still ongoing and influenced by a mechanical and human-centered worldview. This meant that the fragmented data had yet to be incorporated into a larger universe story. But as the century progressed, there was a perceptible shift of human consciousness toward an Earth literacy that appreciated cosmic transformation rather than changelessness, interrelationship over atomization, interdependency instead of radical autonomy, ambiguity as an alternative to rigid order, and organic growth rather than mechanistic processes. This shift in mindscape prompted scientists in the twentieth and twenty-first centuries to discover different answers to ageless questions, such as the following: When and how was the universe created? Where did Earth and ourselves, come from? Where do humans belong? What is our purpose? Thus, since our scientific encounters with the cosmos were changing, how we told our Creation story was also adapting. The ability of scientists to help narrate the emerging universe story signaled the growth of humanity's scientific Earth literacy. This development of a robust planetary consciousness was not achieved by one scientist; many voices contributed to our scientific Earth literacy; however, not all of them can be heard in this chapter. Therefore, highlights that span from the galactic to the quantum levels of the universe as well as from Earth's more familiar ecosystems will illustrate the development of scientific Earth literacy that today's believers have been bequeathed.

FROM THE GALACTIC TO THE QUANTUM LEVELS OF LIFE

From the largest, most radiant galaxies in the universe (i.e., IC1101) to the energetic yet immensely tiny fundamental particles (e.g., electrons, quarks, and Higgs boson), our universe is teaching us about both itself and ourselves. There are many who desired to discover what the "inarticulate but not silent"[1] physical universe was communicating and augment humanity's budding scientific Earth literacy. One significant contributor at the turn of the century was theoretical physicist Albert Einstein. He effectively, albeit begrudgingly, undermined the static and purely mechanical vision of nature via his groundbreaking theory of relativity in 1915 that offered a new way of understanding the universe. The term *begrudgingly* fits because at the time he was publishing his data, a static worldview had entranced most imaginations, even Einstein's, which made him question his empirical data that pointed to a dynamic universe. As a result, he altered his findings by inserting a cosmological constant, "lambda," into his field equation so he could achieve a static model of the universe.[2] Later, the work of physicist Alexander Friedmann in 1922, the data collected by astronomer Edwin Hubble in 1924, and the work of Monsignor Georges Lemaître convinced Einstein of the error of his ways.[3] All of these scientists found evidence proving the dynamic nature of the cosmos. This new way of envisioning the cosmos inspired scientific imaginations and led astronomers to an exact age of the universe and a novel description of the birth of the universe. Data collected during this time showed how the four hundred billion galaxies (visible to the Hubble telescope) were rapidly moving away from our galaxy in every direction, and they were traveling at a speed that was directly proportional to their distance from Earth. This could only be explained if there was a single birth moment with a central focal point. This concentrated locus created the material and energetic impetus to disperse this newly formed matter in an outwardly fashion. Also, prior to a half a million years, radiation and matter were too intimately interconnected to be distinct entities revealing a primordial coupling of matter and energy that challenges the radical dualism offered by René Descartes and others. However, it was Abbé Georges Lemaître, a Belgium priest and mathematician, who offered a coherent model of the universe's origin and expansion in 1931. His model of the birth of space and time, as well as of matter and light, from an infinitely dense singularity of energy (that was 10^{-5} times the size of a proton)[4] became known as the Big Bang—a name that stuck after a cynical critic called it that during a radio broadcast in 1950.[5] These new concepts, namely the age, dynamism, interconnectivity, and birth story of the universe, are key features of a robust scientific Earth literacy.

Many other interrelated threads in theoretical physics further corroborated and augmented our understanding of the universe story,[6] but we had to wait until after the midpoint of the twentieth century to learn how precarious the emergence of life really was. In the 1950s, the astronomer Sir Bernard Lovell (followed in the 1970s by the physicist Stephen Hawking) told humanity that if the expansion rate had varied even an infinitesimal amount, the universe would have either collapsed back into chaos or expanded too rapidly for particulates to coalesce into atoms, molecules, or larger conglomerations such as stars, planets, oceans, trees, or even the human body. Thus, our world developed on a razor's edge of possibility, urging our imaginations to look anew at the meaning and purpose of life that could easily have not happened.

Scientists who followed in the twenty-first century have also contributed much to the telling of the universe story from a galactic perspective. For example, approximately a billion years after the Big Bang, the cosmos cooled enough that stars began to form and hence, our universe burst into a new level of radiance; the birth of our sun 4.5 billion years ago only added to this brightness. As larger stars ran out of fuel, their cores collapsed, causing explosions that created—then hurtled—vital elements into space. These new materials became planets, stars, living systems, and individual beings.[7] Consequently, the iron in our blood, the calcium in our bones, and the oxygen in our lungs connect us to the moment life began billions of years ago. As one of the universe's youngest species, we are participants in this dynamic, still unfolding story. As a result of our Earth literacy, we know that we are stardust—and unto dust we shall return.[8]

Contributions to a robust scientific Earth literacy were also derived from data discovered on a supermicroscopic scale: "a millionth of a millionth of an inch."[9] There were many scientists working at the dawn of the twentieth century at the level of the atom, such as John Dalton, J. J. Thompson, and Niels Bohr, among others. However, their work was still greatly influenced by a static worldview that allowed them to envision more static representations of an atom. For example, Dalton offered a billiard-ball model of an atom, which saw atoms as solid indestructible entities,[10] Thompson envisioned a raisin pudding model of an atom (atoms were the solid pudding and electrons the "raisins" in the pudding),[11] and Bohr's shell model had electrons in fixed orbits around a nucleus like planets orbiting the sun.[12] The invention of better technology in the twentieth and twenty-first centuries allowed scientists to actually "see" atomic and subatomic particles, which revealed a much more dynamic subatomic world. Scientists realized that particles, such as electrons, "no longer had separate, well-defined positions or velocities" as depicted in earlier models.[13] Instead, the many elementary particles possess a blend of both position and velocity (e.g., a quantum state). This caused complexity, uncertainty, and interdependency to become integral parts of how the universe works at the atomic level and further eroded the hold of the machine metaphor.

Another principle, discovered in the twentieth century, added more nuance to our scientific Earth literacy. In 1925, Wolfgang Pauli crafted the Pauli Exclusion Principle[14] that told the story of how the totality of an atom cannot be understood by the laws concerning individual electrons. Our subatomic world was telling us what Aristotle had said so long ago, namely that the whole is greater than the sum of its parts. The twenty-first century only added to the universe story; some scientists have compared the rate of expansion of the universe between galaxies of very different ages, and they have learned that galaxies are moving away from each other much faster now than they were. The reason for this, they think, is the enigma that is dark matter and energy. Others have *detected approximately one thousand planets outside our own solar system, some of which may sustain life*. Another fascinating revelation was made by François Englert and Peter Higgs (who won the Nobel prize in physics in 2013) for discovering *the way subatomic particles originally gained mass*. Their theories were confirmed with much fanfare on July 4, 2012, when the Higgs boson particle (part of the mechanism that enabled this mass gain) was discovered at CERN's Large Hadron Collider.[15] This *new* particle finally offered scientific imaginations a visible glimpse at how the universe unfolded and is continuing to unfold; Higgs boson is the link between a time when particles had no mass (very early in our 13.8-billion-year history) to when there were particles with mass (which includes particles existing today).[16] Thus, from its galactic immensity to its subatomic particulate, our imaginations have been formed by many scientific discoveries in the twentieth and twenty-first century, and this is deepening our understanding of the universe as a dynamic, complex, immensely old, unpredictably ordered, interdependent, evolving planet. Dynamism and stability, uncertainty and order, and particularity and relationality are built into every thread of the fabric of life.

EARTH'S ECOSYSTEMS

From the eighteenth and nineteenth centuries emerged the intellectual footing and aesthetic depth that would motivate twentieth- and twenty-first-century ecologists to encounter Earth in new ways. For example, marine biologist Rachel Carson (1907–64) recalls how poet Emily Dickinson helped her articulate the sensory and emotional impressions of the sea that were lying dormant in her imagination long before she learned specific empirical facts about marine life in her profession. Emily Dickinson wrote of an intrinsic, emotive knowledge of the sea that resonated with Carson. She found a kindred spirit in Dickinson's words: "I never saw a moor, I never saw the sea; Yet know I how the heather looks, And what a wave must be."[17] This is one example of the linguistic expressions and formative ideas (e.g., dynamism, interconnectivity, cooperation, and fragility) that were bequeathed by eighteenth- and nineteenth-century artisans to those who cared to listen.

Since the imaginations of scientists studying Earth's ecosystems are part of the general mindscape of the human communities where they dwell, then some formative aspects of human history need exploration. Human ecology (e.g., the web of human social, political, and economic interactions) in the twentieth century saw many unprecedented developments, including the rise of the modern city. Historian and social anthropologist Tim C. Wieskel offers some staggering statistics: in the 1700s, less than 10 percent of the global population of 700 million lived in cities; by 1950, 30 percent of the global population of 2.5 billion lived in cities—in North America, urban dwellers consisted of 64 percent of the population, and in Europe, that figure rose to 56 percent.[18] Hence, by the middle of the twentieth century, there was a huge demand for telephones, cars, phonographs, radios, and a multitude of other manufactured products. This demand coincided with a rapid housing boom; a growing requirement for waste, water, and transportation systems; and a diminishment of arable farmland to feed these growing urban populations.[19] This was a time when solutions to these problems came in the form of nonrenewable, polluting energy sources and the indiscriminate dumping of chemical pesticides and other deleterious wastes associated with industry into our ecosystems. A chilling but catchy dictum captures the approach to waste at this time: Dilution is the solution to pollution.

People living in the twentieth century were also deeply affected by the devastation of the First and Second World Wars. The magnitude and scope of science and technology's ability to inflict human and nonhuman suffering was demonstrated on August 6, 1945, when a uranium fission bomb, "Little Boy," was detonated over Hiroshima and again on August 9, when another fission bomb called the "Fat Man" exploded over Nagasaki, Japan. In mere moments, approximately 200,000 Japanese people died while untold damage was done to the planet's biosphere. The unprecedented scale and scope of destruction by the nuclear bombs during World War II affected how all people, including scientists, encountered the created world. The new awareness of how one species has the ability to disrupt all Earth's life-systems was captured in the statement uttered by J. Robert Oppenheimer after watching the detonation of the first atomic bomb: "I am Death, the shatterer of worlds."[20] Humanity had crossed an unprecedented threshold of history; "the bomb that fell on Hiroshima cut history in two. Before and after are two different worlds."[21] Scientists were not immune to the anxiety the general population had concerning the Cold War (1947–91), the very real threat of global nuclear annihilation, the Vietnam Conflict (1965–75), and the feminist and civil rights movements in the United States and abroad.

In addition, the people living in Western urban populations, including scientists, were becoming more and more insulated from nature in all its forms. According to Stephen Wheeler and Timothy Beatley, this separation was accomplished via "central heating, electric lighting, air conditioning, long-distance food transportation, or huge dams and pipelines bringing water from hundreds of miles away."[22] Even sickness and death were being banished from normal everyday life and institutionalized (e.g., hospitals, funeral homes). Humanity was also becoming more acutely aware of global power agents, militarism, political corruption, and the scope and magnitude of human suffering thanks to the rise of globalized information and communications technology. The people in the field of science were not immune to these events; scientists in the twentieth and twenty-first centuries were the first of their trade to be fully immersed in the technocratic mindset that saw no limits to human ingenuity and technological innovation. They were also being entranced by a consumption economy (take-make-waste way of living).[23]

However, there were many in the twentieth and twenty-first centuries—including scientists—who were disenchanted by the high cost of the "triumph of progress"[24] but at the same time were spellbound by the world they were encountering. Many reminisced about the thrill of the dawning of the space age in 1961.[25] North Americans appreciated Earth and the cosmos in a whole new way after hearing Genesis recited on Christmas Eve (1968) from "the heavens" (narrated by the astronauts of Apollo 8) and watching American Neil Armstrong and Buzz Aldrin walk on the moon on July 16, 1969.[26] But our understanding of Earth changed forever when humanity saw "the Blue Marble" from Apollo 17 in 1972. This was the first time human eyes saw Earth as a whole, interconnected, finite, and fragile planet from space—a gift no previous generations had experienced. With this new sight, humanity realized how artificial political borders really were, and in a concrete way, they could visualize a powerful truth: we are one planetary family. Scientists in the twentieth and twenty-first centuries are the beneficiaries of this new sight, which further invalidated the machine metaphor. Their new acuity affirmed the intricate interdependency of our living and evolving world at every level of scientific inquiry. This new enchantment with Earth as a dynamic web of life extended even to our human bodies, which came to be understood as "joint property of the descendants of diverse ancestors."[27]

Historian Carolyn Merchant offers a purview of some of the twentieth- and twenty-first-century scientists who uncovered dimensions of scientific Earth literacy within our planet's ecosystems.[28] Some saw nature as the context for human ecology (industrial and environmental chemist Ellen Swallow Richards [1842–1911]);[29] whereas, others focused on Earth as holistically connected yet with specific plant and animal patterns unique to specific regions (zoologist and naturalist Clinton Hart Merriam [1855–1942]).[30] Others, still, discovered that Earth was organic in character (plant ecologist Frederic Clements [1874–1945]),[31] economic in organization (zoologist and animal ecologist Charles Sutherland Elton [1900–1991]),[32] and made up of a multitude of stable interconnected ecosystems (botanist Sir Arthur George Tansley [1871–1955][33] and ecologist Raymond Laurel Lindeman [1915–42]).[34] Some spoke of Earth as an interdependent, dynamic, and holistic ecological household (*oikos*) with organized patterns of succession (biologist Eugene Odum [1913–2002]),[35] and chaotic, unpredictable, and contingent processes (mathematician Edward Lorenz [1917–2008], human ecologist William Drury [1921–92], and environmental scientist Ian Nisbet).[36]

Voices in seemingly incompatible disciplines, spoke passionately about a symbiotic model of community life that includes aspects of cooperation and intimacy. This cooperative vision challenged the "survival of the fittest" principle as the only way to understand how Earth's communities function. For example, American entomologist William Morton Wheeler did not just focus on the struggle for existence as expounded by Darwin to understand insect communities. What he found was that cooperation and altruism were primary ways of organizing communal life in ant colonies and that the entire colony could be seen as a communion of particular individuals dedicated to the perpetuation and reproduction of the colony as a whole.[37] On a much larger scale, nature writer and fruit farmer John Burroughs (the essayist from chapter 1) echoed this in his studies of cooperation within the Hudson River bioregion.[38]

Voices from within the fledging field of genetics also spoke of a deep physical interconnectivity of all living things through the commonality of natural, dynamic processes acting on all organisms to ensure that life continues. When Maurice Wilkins and Rosalind Franklin took "snapshots" of DNA (that led James Watson and Francis Crick to build their now-famous DNA molecule in 1953), they offered a visual representation of the basic building block of all life: a spiraling genetic ladder of purine-pyrimidine base pairs. The existence of this molecule concretely speaks of the consanguinity of life.

Social and animal activists in the early decades of the twentieth century also spoke adamantly of the consequences of humanity's growing blindness to the intrinsic value of indigenous natural ecosystems. They professed that these ecosystems were not just deposits of natural resources to feed industrialization. For example, Missouri-born zoologist J. Howard Moore's text *Universal Kinship* (1906) and revolutionary German socialist Rosa Luxembourg's *The Accumulation of Capital* (1913) spoke prophetically to the inextricable intertwining of human and natural economies as well as about the problems caused when we forget this fact.[39] British travel writer and essayist H. M. Tomlinson's 1925 essay "Lost Woods" critiqued humanity's destructive military and industrial tendencies through his portrait of haunting bluebells—a symbol of the stubborn vitality of Earth's ecosystems to withstand even our most powerful engines.[40] Tomlinson inspired many subsequent nature writers who followed, including Rachel Carson. H. J. Massingham, a British writer and poet, was greatly influenced by parson-naturalist Gilbert White (who will be outlined later as a pioneering theologian with a robust Earth literacy) and critiqued the prevailing industrial understanding of progress. John Seymour offered the following about how H. J. Massingham was a twentieth-century visionary:

> He wanted to go forward; forward to an England where the countrymen and countrywomen would come into their own again; where the countryside would no longer suffer the weight and oppression of the city; where civilisation should be the flowering of a culture based on the soil. He realised that a human being is a creature of the soil—exactly the same as an earthworm is! That if we cut ourselves off from our origins, we are doomed to sterility and ultimately death.[41]

Clair Cameron Patterson, an American geochemist, was able to determine the accurate age for the Earth, but he also proved how our dependency on lead-based products was causing significant changes to our ecosystems. Furthermore, he realized that the high levels of lead in our ecosystems were having dire health ramifications to humans.[42]

So, despite fierce resistance, Patterson helped to change public perceptions concerning lead-based products that led to their ban.[43] Canadian storyteller and environmentalist Farley Mowat's great nature narratives, such as *People of the Deer* (1952), *Never Cry Wolf* (1963), and *Sea of Slaughter* (1984), gave a prophetic and poetic warning; the blatant disregard for wisdom concerning Earth's ecosystems offered by indigenous peoples, wolves, and the teeming life in the North Atlantic by those entranced with industrialization will have dire consequences.[44]

Consequently, by the middle of the twentieth century, there was a talented ensemble of scientists and activists who were helping to develop a robust Earth literacy from truths discovered in Earth's many ecosystems. The latter half of the century saw the emergence of celebrated international ecological leaders whose maturing Earth literacy led them to continue the work started by preceding activists. Some memorable media figures include French conservationist Jacques Cousteau, Jane Goodall, a British primatologist, and David Suzuki, Canadian geneticist and host of the award-winning television show *The Nature of Things*. These figures (and those who tirelessly worked to protect Earth with much less fanfare) were forming human imaginations within a frightening new context: Earth's life systems are in peril due to human activities. A prime example of the efficacy of Earth literacy to move scientists to new behaviors as activists is Rachel Carson. Her intimate understanding of Earth's marine ecology led her to see herself as both a scientist and a planetary citizen who needed to protect Earth's many subjects from harm. Her love of the sea (and meticulous research techniques) drew her to discover Earth's aquatic wisdom, but her rising anxiety at the destruction of marine life due to war and the dumping of nuclear waste into the ocean moved her to act. She knew that the death of the ocean will be the death of humanity. Linda Lear echoes this:

> Carson could not be silent. She had peered into the fairy caves and tide pools of her beloved Maine coast and had seen the fragility and tenacity with which even the smallest creatures struggled for life against the relentless ocean tides. Her flashlight had captured the unforgettable spectacle of the solitary crab on the rocky beach at midnight, vulnerable yet unassailably resilient. She could not stand idly

> by and say nothing when all that was in jeopardy, when human existence itself was endangered. That was the message that brought her to the Senate hearing room. That was what had sustained her.[45]

Carson could inspire all of humanity in every profession to cultivate a robust Earth literacy in order to fall in love with our planetary home and cultivate planetary citizenship. She reminds us that we can never think of the physical environment as a separate entity from ourselves.[46] One cannot exaggerate the effect one person's scientific Earth literacy can have; when *Silent Spring* was published in 1962, "DDT measured in human tissue was 12.6 ppm and sixteen years later it had fallen to 4.8 ppm and today it is under 1 ppm."[47] Thus, our children and our children's children are the beneficiaries of the fruits of Carson's scientific Earth literacy.

Carson, however, was not the only voice helping to cultivate Earth literacy. In 1989, Gro Harlem Brundtland, a Norwegian physician and former chair of the World Commission of Environment and Development, outlined the threat we are living under and how it came to be:

> When the 20th century began, neither human beings nor human technology had the power to radically alter the global ecosystem. Today, 1987, as the century draws to a close, human beings in ever-increasing numbers have that power, and as a result of their activity on the planet, major unintended changes are taking place in the atmosphere, the biosphere, and the hydrosphere. These changes outstrip our present ability to cope: the world's financial and political institutions are *out of step with the workings of nature*.[48]

Humanity is out of step with the workings of nature and the only way to change this is to listen to those who are trying to cultivate a robust Earth literacy. We must appreciate each of the contributions made by so many: the women of the 1970s Chipko movement in India who put the life of the trees they protected above their own as a way of proclaiming how indispensable they were to their survival; American geneticist Barbara McClintock, who developed a keen intuitive sensitivity and intellectual appreciation and kinship with other-than-human organisms as subjects; Vandana Shiva, a physicist from India, who founded a women-centered movement to protect biological and cultural diversity via the preservation of native seeds; Katsi Cook, a Mohawk Native American midwife who brought attention to how toxic waste materials were contaminating the breast milk of Native American communities located in close proximity to dumping sites; mathematician Brian Swimme's efforts to tell the universe story to the wider audience; American farmer, writer, and activist Wendell Berry, who engaged in nonviolent civil disobedience against nuclear power plants, which were destroying the land, especially Kentucky farmland. These are just a few of the many voices dictating Earth's many lessons. Their messages are clear; we must reject dysfunctional worldviews that atrophy our imaginations and hurt our planetary community. Instead, we need to embrace Earth's many truths: our planet is a self-regulating, evolving organism over 4.5 billion years old; Earth must be appreciated as a whole entity with specific bioregions and particular ecosystems; our planet's ecosystems can be characterized by a series of relations that emphasize interdependency and cooperation; humans have emerged from the Earth, which widens who our kin are and what rights other-than-human ought to have; and Earth's ecosystems teach us that sacrifice and pain is coupled with growth and life—they are two sides of the same coin.

SUMMARY

To be in step with nature means being scientifically Earth literate. We need to know how nature works and understand that our well-being is predicated on the well-being of the ecosystems in which we dwell. Many scientists in the twentieth and twenty-first centuries have contributed valuable insights to enable a new planetary consciousness, but they are not the sole contributors as anthropologist Claude Levi-Strauss illustrates. In 1969, he mused whether humanity's self-destructive poisoning of the biosphere will mimic the pattern of self-annihilation seen in certain insect larvae communities.[49] He concluded that we will only save ourselves via a profound spiritual transformation—not merely an intellectual one. Thus, being literate of the "what" of creation is not enough; we also need to engage the "why" questions, for example, why we should care. This is beyond the domain of science, but it *is* the domain of theology. Therefore, the content of the next two chapters tells the story of how theologians have cultivated a robust Earth literacy, which has allowed interconnectivity, uncertainty, continuous creativity, interdependence, and risk to become part of the way they understand creation, God, and humanity.

3

SCIENTIFIC EARTH LITERACY IN THEOLOGY

On June 22, 1633, ecclesial authorities publicly condemned a scientist named Galileo as a heretic because he promoted Copernicus's idea that the sun, not Earth, was the center of the universe.[1] This was a highly visible severing of the long-standing relationship between scientific thought and Christian beliefs. After this point, many thought that science and Christian religion would be perpetually at odds and could never work together to describe the world believers were encountering, much less be able to critique each other. Thus, at the time of Galileo, this alienation set science and Christianity on separate paths; science was eagerly learning about our human origins and uncovering a new story of how the universe emerged, evolved, and sustained itself with little input from Christians. Alternatively, theologians cloistered their creative scholastic efforts almost exclusively to the human dimension of the Christian story, namely the personality of Jesus, Augustinian Fall/Redemption theology as human salvation *from* the natural world, church structure, and the conflicts within and between Christian churches. The spiritual significance of humanity's new encounters with creation was ignored to a large degree during this time. As a result, the faithful were led to believe that God was unchanging, static, and radically transcendent. God's perfection as an Unmoved

Mover was not tarnished by the dynamism and decay, nor by the joy or pain of the finite world. The consequence of this belief was the creation of an absentee God; our radically transcendent Creator and Redeemer was not intimately present to, nor involved in, the world, and certainly was not "passionately caught up in its destiny."[2] This separation of science and religion that fostered an absentee God also helped to maintain the static machine metaphor in the Christian imagination since the more modern scientific consciousness, which embraced dynamism (e.g., an evolutionary world), was either unknown or rejected as heretical. Another consequence was that believers came to see God only as a distant, all-powerful male. He was an unconcerned mechanic of a clock-like cosmos, and hence, humans became the divinely appointed technicians of this created machine in place of the divine mechanic or clockmaker. It was clear that without fruitful dialogues, the dynamic worldview offered by the emergence of scientific Earth literacy was falling on deaf ears in the Christian church, and the dysfunctional understanding of humanity's dominion over creation remained unchallenged.

But this is not the end of the story. This chapter offers many voices in theology, spanning from the twilight of the eighteenth century to those in the twentieth century, who brought science and theology into dialogue to describe Earth's intrinsic worth, articulate God's immanence in the world, and address humanity's treatment of the world. These investigations allowed a planetary consciousness to blossom in theology; new language, images, and metaphors were unearthed to articulate the sacred universe story. This emergence of Earth literacy in theology allowed for a more authentic and faithful interpretation of humanity's place, worth, and purpose within this unfolding narrative, and offered a viable alternative to the anthropocentric and mechanical worldview offered by previous Christian voices. It also laid the foundation for the emergence of ecotheology in the 1980s. It is noteworthy that these ecotheological forerunners were standing on the shoulders of theological giants who offered a profound understanding of creation's worth and humanity's connectivity to Earth. Many of these ancient contributors are discussed in part 2.

This chapter begins with eighteenth-century British parson Gilbert White (1720–93) and nineteenth-century Jesuit poet Gerard Manley Hopkins (1844–89). In the twentieth century, many voices were heard, albeit briefly: French paleontologist and Jesuit Pierre

Teilhard de Chardin (1881–1955); German Lutheran theologian Albert Schweitzer (1875–1965); American Lutheran theologian Joseph Sittler (1904–87); American process theologian John Cobb (born in 1925). All these voices have cultivated particular nuances within a distinctly theological Earth literacy. It is important to note that each voice made valuable contributions but did not perfectly articulate the form of theological Earth literacy that ecotheology enjoys today—nor could they. Earth literacy is an interactive, evolving encounter and response to creation, God, and humanity that defies permanent tethering in any one word, image, or description. Nevertheless, this chapter presents a rich matrix of ideas within a crucial period of history in order to understand the roots of ecotheology and where it may develop in the future.

FORERUNNERS

Parson-Naturalist Gilbert White

Environmental historian David Worster calls British parson and naturalist Gilbert White "one point of origin, representative if not seminal, for the modern study of ecology" and a foundational figure in establishing the standard for natural history essays in England and America.[3] He penned many letters from the 1760s to the 1780s on the wildlife, seasons, and artifacts of Selborne in his text *Natural History and Antiquities of Selborne* (1789).[4] This text was a compilation of White's meticulous observations on nature's exquisite systems: "Nature is a great economist," for she "converts the recreation of one animal to the support of another!"[5] This journal was the culmination of many years of observing his surroundings, and it illustrates his intense attachment to his immediate ecosystems. It also resonates with his deep reverence for Divine Providence that orchestrates this beautiful living, harmonized whole. The way he saw his own region of the world and how he recorded his thoughts set him apart from his theological contemporaries, as did his enthusiasm for nature's balance and economy. Unfortunately, his strong utilitarian and anthropocentric vision locates him squarely within seventeenth-century scientific and theological thought.[6] As a man of a higher level of leisure and comfort, he was insulated from the chaos of industrialization and political-economic upheaval occurring at this time in England, yet he still felt the progressive alienation of humanity from creation. Parson White longed with a special "rural felicity" to reestablish interior peace or harmony by reconciling with the outer world.[7] For White, this meant forming a peaceful order or harmony between humanity and nature. The shortcoming of his vision was that this peace was designed and enforced by humans who were to control nature for the benefit of the human community, and anything deemed useless, annoying, or noxious by humans needed eradication.[8] The work of White was appreciated by scientists like Charles Darwin (who, because of Gilbert White's popularity, made a pilgrimage to Selborne in the 1850s) and impacted the imaginations of nature writers like James Russell Lowell and John Burroughs. The writings of White inspired a fond, romantic nostalgia for a return to the original, peaceful state, not unlike the original paradise in Eden.[9]

White's great contribution to theological Earth literacy was his meticulous documentation of the world wherein he dwelled and of his understanding of an intelligible and stabilizing order within the myriad of interrelationships he observed. He also communicated in his writings a sense of reverent peace within his ecological microcosm of rural Selborne—something others may find in their own local regions if only they looked. White's *The Natural History of Selborne* became the symbol of a paradise lost and spoke of humanity's yearning to regain our ecological and spiritual bearings.

Jesuit Poet Gerard Manley Hopkins

Fifty years later, and in a starkly different context, British poet and Jesuit priest Gerard Manley Hopkins offered the world the "symbolic energy" of his nature poetry that intimately coupled creation and revelation.[10] He was not the only theological voice responding to Darwin's theory of evolution (*Origin of Species* was published in 1859); however, Hopkins strikes out in creative new directions. Hopkins's lyrical prose and poetry, and his unconventional responsivity to the awe-inspiring aspects of creation, characterizes his mature literary work. His theological Earth literacy flourished as the physical beauty of nature he encountered revealed God's self-communication:

> First saw the Northern Lights. My eye was caught by beams of light and dark very like the crown of horny rays the sun

> makes behind a cloud. At first I thought of silvery cloud until I saw that these were more luminous and did not dim the clearness of the stars in the Bear....This busy working of nature wholly independent of the earth and seeming to go on in a strain of time not reckoned by our reckoning of days and years...was like a new witness to God and filled me with delightful fear.[11]

His writing vibrates with a level of "tactile, physical" intimacy with nature and a sheer intensity of perception where "what you look hard at seems to look hard at you."[12] Hopkins is able to blur the boundary of the observer and observed reverently whereas White cannot, remaining forever the observer who meticulously recorded nature. For example, in the following, Manley moves the reader easily from the perspective of the water to that of an external observer:

> Yesterday it was a sallow glassy gold at Hodder Roughs and *by watching hard the banks began to sail upstream*, the scraping unfolded, the river was all in tumult but not running, only the lateral motions were perceived, and the curls of froth where the waves overlap shaped and turned easily and idly.[13]

Hopkins's work often articulates the grand hymn of creation, a joyful reading of the Book of Scripture and the Book of Nature. This is characterized in some of the sonnets he wrote while in the countryside of North Wales (during his training to be a Jesuit), including "God's Grandeur," "As Kingfishers Catch Fire," and "The Starlit Night." He was enchanted with moving waters and their possession of ancient, transcendent wisdom, and he was in awe "of mutable beauty masquerading as permanence, and, conversely, of form transcending decay."[14] His love of Earth's great beauty and his artistic sensitivity to the peace inherent in the landscapes and waterways sustained him later in life when he struggled with unrequited love, depression, uncertainty, illness, loneliness, rejection, spiritual weariness, and misery. Examination of the joyful as well as of the painful dimensions of creation and his own life are inextricably intertwined in his poetry, especially his *Sonnets of Desolation* penned around 1884–85.[15]

His work also resonates with the same laments uttered today by ecotheologians: Hopkins laments the willful besmirching of Earth by urban industrial development. This is clearly seen in his poem "Ribblesdale" (1882), where Hopkins appeals to humanity to become advocators and protectors of creation who "has no tongue to plead" to God to intervene.[16] In "The Leaden Echo and the Golden Echo" (1882), he is intensely aware of the squandering of Earth and the death of beauty.[17] He was deeply concerned with the encroachment of industrialization on rural Oxford, typified by the railway that he describes as "snorting, noisy, dangerous, above all ravenous in devouring rural land."[18] He was also aware of the bleakness of a manufacturing city, the crushing misery of the Victorian slums, and the intense degradation of nature for the sake of industry, which included the felling of trees in Well Walk (where Keats had lived) just to make "shoes" for locomotives.[19] Looking at the last stanza from "Inversnaid" (1881), one can see the imperative to move humanity from our destructive ways:

> What would the world be, once bereft
> Of wet and of wildness? Let them be left,
> O let them be left, wildness and wet;
> Long live the weeds and the wilderness yet.[20]

Hopkins's Earth literacy grew as he learned more about his physical landscape. However, his receptivity to the intrinsic worth of creation "for its reflection of Divinity" makes his Earth literacy distinctly theological.[21] He was able to articulate the sanctity of creation, the immanence of God in the world, and the harmony of all created life alongside astute observations of the ecosystems with which he came into contact.[22] This is artistically rendered in his poem "As Kingfishers Catch Fire" (1877):

> As kingfishers catch fire, dragonflies dráw fláme;
> As tumbled over rim in roundy wells
> Stones ring; like each tucked string tells, each hung bell's
> Bow swung finds tongue to fling out broad its name;
> Each mortal thing does one thing and the same:
> Deals out that being indoors each one dwells;
> Selves—goes itself; *myself* it speaks and spells,
> Crying *Whát I do is me: for that I came.*

Í say móre: the just man justices;
Kéeps gráce: thát keeps all his goings graces;
Acts in God's eye what in God's eye he is—
Chríst—for Christ plays in ten thousand places,
Lovely in limbs, and lovely in eyes not his
To the Father through the features of men's faces.[23]

Hopkins often blurred the distinction between human and nature, "self and sky,"[24] because all aspects of created life are elements of one divine creation. He balanced this homogenizing unity by paying attention to the particularity of his many subjects via what he coined as a personal "Inscape." This inscape was an "inherent coherence of the individual that distinguishes it from all others." Hopkins appreciated both what was particular and what was universal in creation.[25]

Another vital part of Hopkins's theological Earth literacy is his appreciation of the dynamism, darkness, and transience of this created world: the changing seasons of the landscape, the fluid beauty of God's waterways, the tenuous harmony of decay and resistance, the balance of transience and continuity. All of these elements characterize earthly life. Arguably, Hopkins's unconventional poetry[26] is a gift he left to modern ecotheologians because in his unfamiliar patterns, strange imagery, implied subjectivity (for Earth's elements), and novel language, he breaks through humanity's entrancement with the machine metaphor and shocks readers into new ways of perceiving Earth. Thus, his poetry became the raw, literary precursors to modern ecotheological conceptions such as the unity in diversity, communion of subjectivity, and planetary consciousness.

TWENTIETH-CENTURY CONTRIBUTORS

In the twentieth century there was a *crescendo* of theological voices that followed White and Hopkins. These included paleontologist and priest Pierre Teilhard de Chardin, Lutheran theologians Albert Schweitzer and Joseph Sittler, and process theologian John Cobb. All these voices offer a rich matrix of ideas during a crucial period of history that helped give birth to ecotheology.

Jesuit Paleontologist Pierre Teilhard de Chardin

During the latter part of the nineteenth century, scientists were telling the world that the birth of our universe, including Earth, was extremely different from what was popularly held. In the early twentieth century, Pierre Teilhard de Chardin told this new story not via prose like Hopkins, but through the fossils he unearthed and studied. His Earth literacy manifested in his ability to integrate his research with his theological training and had several vital results: a unique biospiritual understanding of the unfolding, evolutionary world; an employment of new language and images in theological reflection; and a special way of expressing a deep love of creation.

In Teilhard's *The Phenomenon of Man* (penned in 1938; published after his death in 1955)[27] and his mystical meditation, *The Divine Milieu* (penned 1929; published 1957), he saw matter and spirit united, he connected the past and present with the future, and he offered the one God as present in all the many parts of creation. All of these are central features of a theological Earth literacy. For Teilhard, God is the "cosmic eddy"[28] of animating force that influences everything from the atom to the vast mountain. Hence, God is the intangible at the heart of the universe.[29] God, however, is also a very personal being for Teilhard: "I can feel God, touch him, 'live' him in the deep biological current that runs through my soul and carries it with it."[30] God is not a fixed end point but rather the "Prime Mover, Gatherer and Consolidator, ahead of us"[31] and the eternal God above, connecting the entire evolutionary process as one unified sacred story of growth and development. As a result of this connectivity, Teilhard never extricates his Christian theology from the sacred universe story. He placed theology in a fruitful dialogue with science (articulating in new ways the dynamism and creativity inherent in the cosmos), and this cross-pollination required the use of new terms to describe our encounter with the biospiritual Earth—*cosmogenesis*, *geogenesis*, *biogenesis*, *psychogenesis*, and *noogenesis*. In each of these terms, "genesis" means the development of whatever prefix precedes it (e.g., cosmogenesis is the development of the cosmos; biogenesis is the development of all biological life). Teilhard indicates that noogenesis is the development of the self-consciousness by the human mind, which he believes is the crowning achievement of creation: "...when for the first time in a living creature instinct perceived itself in its own mirror, [and] the whole world took a step forward."[32] These, he indicates, are ultimately processes of *Christogenesis*—the movement toward the living, risen Christ that is the final Omega or final point of all development. Thus, his scientific understanding of our evolving universe helped him articulate to believers how we can understand creation, God, and humanity.

As a priest, Teilhard desired to reconcile his deep love for God (and adoration of the Sacred Heart of Jesus) with his yearning to better understand the empirical world. This is why he dedicated *The Divine Milieu* (1957) to those who love the world; in this text he described how at the heart of the universe, each soul exists for God.[33] The reason we can fall deeply in love with the world was due to "the diaphany of the divine at the heart of a glowing universe, the divine radiating from the depths of matter a-flame."[34] Consequently, for people of faith to come to know God, we must "bathe [ourselves] in the ocean of matter"[35] and never become alienated from the material universe. This does not mean God is trapped in the world (pantheism), for God is always infinitely more than all created life. But our unfinished, finite world is always moving toward higher levels of complexity. For Teilhard, this complexity revealed itself in more self-conscious and "spiritual" beings (e.g., those capable of interiority). He saw our world eternally converging "towards a personal transcendent God" who is the center and apex of our universe and this divine center is always "loving and worthy of being loved."[36] Teilhard's vision, however, is not without flaws. His "ascending axis of hominization" is how he justifies labeling humanity as the penultimate apex of the evolutionary process and accordingly, all of Earth's energies are leading to the "Ultra-human" (a purely spiritual, conscious being).[37] This assertion reflects his anthropocentrism and is not well-founded in either science or theology. Also, his insistence on a final, purely spiritualized "Omega Point" (the glorified Christ who is pure spirit)[38] suggests an antimatter bias to his thinking. This is reinforced when he claims that when we achieve the final spiritual state, the "material vastness of the universe will disappear" into "the nothingness of consciousness."[39] Despite his anthropocentrism and biases, Teilhard's deep love and reverence of creation and his fruitful reconciliation of science and Christian thought are cornerstones of his theological Earth literacy.

Lutheran Theologians
Albert Schweitzer and Joseph Sittler

Teilhard was not the only voice in the Christian Tradition in the twentieth century that contributed to the emergence of Earth literacy in theology. Two highly influential Lutheran theologians were Albert Schweitzer and Joseph Sittler. Both are vital not only because of their academic contributions, but also because of the audience they addressed—that is, the international and scientific communities. Schweitzer believed that ecology was "the study of the architecture of creation"[40] yet lamented that an overemphasis on the human had tainted our understanding of this science and its moral applications: "The great fault of all ethics hitherto has been that they believed themselves to have to deal only with the relations of man to man [*sic*]."[41] His groundbreaking work critiqued anthropocentrism and the nature-human dualism in *Reverence for Life* and earned him a Nobel Peace Prize in 1952. He also garnered the attention of formidable scientific minds, including Rachel Carson.

Joseph Sittler was an influential theologian who developed a "theology of the earth" that he took to the international stage in order to address wide-scale ecological degradation and human devastation.[42] He had lived through the devastation of both World Wars in the natural world and in human communities and desired to change the way people of faith saw and cared for our Earth. On November 21, 1961, he addressed the Third Assembly of the World Council of Churches (WCC) in New Delhi, India, and lamented the "doctrinal cleavage" of grace and nature that was impacting our disregard for creation.[43] He also committed himself as a man of faith to rectifying this wrong. He recognized how "for fifteen centuries the Church has declared the power of grace to conquer egocentricity, to expose idolatry, to inform the drama of history with holy meaning" and now, he asserted that our historical moment was requiring something unprecedented: recognition of the sacredness of all of creation.[44] His now-famous statements to the WCC reflect his theological Earth literacy: "The mathematization of meaning in technology and its reduction to operational terms in philosophy has left no mental space wherein to declare that nature as well as history, is the theatre of grace and the scope of redemption."[45] He knew that for many centuries, Protestant imaginations saw creation as a stage where only the relationship of humans with God was important. Earth had no intrinsic value or worth. Sittler was not satisfied with this; he saw how devastating human actions can become when we forget that our sister Earth has intrinsic value:

> This radio-active earth, so fecund and so fragile, is [God's] creation, our sister, and the material place where we meet the brother in Christ's light. Ever since Hiroshima the very term light has ghastly meanings. But ever since creation it has had meanings glorious; and ever since Bethlehem meanings concrete and beckoning.[46]

Sittler believed that a Christian's responsibility to care for Earth is firmly grounded in a cosmic Christology—an image of creation's intrinsic worth offered by Irenaeus, Augustine, and Martin Luther "on their good days."[47] His broad vision of intrinsic worth and care of creation was taken up by many who followed, some of whom even saw the degradation of Earth as a sin against God.[48]

Methodist Process Theologian John B. Cobb

In the 1970s, process theologian John B. Cobb connected Alfred North Whitehead's process of metaphysics and philosophy with Christian theology and applied this new vision of the relations among God, creation, and humanity to address justice issues such as racism, prejudice, and ecological injustice.[49] Cobb's process theology saw the world as a dynamic entity in the process of development, while God's perfection is dependent on the evolution of this world. Cobb also sees God as both present in the world and yet infinitely transcendent to the world (e.g., panentheism). His vision is a manifestation of theological Earth literacy because he offered new ways to speak of the dynamism inherent in both creation and the Creator, which caused quite a controversy in Christian circles. He argued that all created entities are intrinsically valued by God but in different ways, and each contributed to God's own developing experience and wisdom.[50] Thus, John Cobb's Earth literacy makes space for the conversation of how all living things are valuable, but they are not equally valuable. This will be taken up later by Jay McDaniel who sees different forms of subjectivity, agency, and responsibility attributed to different subjects of Earth rather than just one form of agency, namely human agency. It is also taken up by John Haught, who asserts that each of Earth's subjects affect God: "There is an aspect of God's being...by which God feels or experiences everything that occurs."[51] This allows Earth's subjects to be something other than passive cogs in a machine. It also challenges a static vision of a divine clockmaker's perfection, a topic explored in chapter 11.[52]

Essentially, Earth literacy was manifested by these pioneering theologians in a variety of ways, but it contributed to the emergence of ecotheology by offering both new literary tools (terms, images, and metaphors) and new ways to describe the relationships between God and creation. One huge catalyst that spurred the ongoing development of theological Earth literacy was a painful one: the accusation that Christianity was to blame for the ecological crisis.

ANGST AS INSPIRATION FOR CHANGE

In the twentieth century, there were those who laid the blame for the ecological crisis squarely at the feet of Christians. They accused this religion of fueling the alienation of humanity from the natural world and justifying exploitative practices as God's mandate for humanity. Early critiques were offered by Max Weber and Harvey Cox, and later by Lynn Townsend White Jr. These discordant voices forced many Christians to reflect on whether these accusations had merit. This was a painful reflection process, but it yielded much fruit; it unearthed areas of deficiency or neglect within Christian theology and stimulated a reappraisal of Christianity's doctrines in light of humanity's new understanding of creation.

One early critique was offered by Max Weber in *The Protestant Ethic and the Spirit of Capitalism* (1904).[53] He argued that when the vision of a distant, Unmoved Mover God was linked with the denouncement of the fallen material world, the exclusive sense of divine election, and the Protestant work ethic, the result was twofold: a powerful impetus to embrace capitalism and the desacralization (and abuse) of the created world. Christians were given a divine invitation to remold a fallen world in God's glory and did so via promotion of industry fueled by capitalism.[54] Weber insisted that this vocational domination was taken on with such gusto, but "to God's glory" soon became understood as "to humanity's glory."[55] Another critic was American Protestant theologian Harvey Cox.[56] He suggested that the desacralization of nature was because the biblical Creation story separated humanity from the rest of creation.

The ideas promoted by Weber and Cox did not gain much traction until the publication of American historian Lynn Townsend White Jr.'s famous article in the journal *Science* in 1967. In this publication, he argued two main points: "Christianity is the most anthropocentric religion the world has seen" (especially in its Western form);[57] and its anti-ecological influence on the development of science and technology stems from the instructions offered in Genesis for humans to subdue the earth and have dominion over "every living thing that moves upon the earth" (Gen 1:28). Instead of advocating for the dismissal of religion completely, surprisingly, White indicated that the remedy lay in remembering those in the Christian Tradition who did not adhere to these two central ideas (namely St. Francis, the "greatest spiritual revolutionary in the Western history"). He also indicated that Christians must recognize the ecological crisis as both a moral and spiritual crisis.[58] There were many who followed White's lead, including Hal Lindsey, who wrote *The Late Great Planet Earth* (1970) to argue that Evangelicals gave little to no attention to the care of Earth, as well as landscape architect Ian McHarg, who indicated that Judaism and Christianity have long been concerned with justice and compassion but "assumed nature to be a mere backdrop for the human play."[59]

These accusations did not go unheeded, and in making coherent and faithful responses to these accusations, a deeper theological Earth literacy emerged. A key respondent to Lynn White's criticism was Protestant theologian H. Paul Santmire. In his text *Brother Earth: Nature, God and Ecology in Time of Crisis* (1970),[60] he excavated and exposed those in the Christian Tradition who take a theocentric (not anthropocentric) approach to creation. Hence, he challenged White's overarching premise that Christianity embraces an anthropocentric anthropology. In his later document, "Reflections on the Alleged Ecological Bankruptcy of Western Theology" (1973), he countered White's second assumption concerning Genesis by stating that despite the "deep-seated ecological liabilities" in classic theological doctrine, it would be dangerously facile to lay the entire blame for the ecological crisis at the feet of one book of Scripture.[61] Even more provocatively, Santmire countered White by outlining the major role wealth has in our ecological crisis: "When…a rather affluent-looking ecologist goes on national television and blames the Book of Genesis for the ecological crisis, one wonders whether he is also familiar with the creation paean of Psalm 104, not to speak of the strictures of the prophet Amos and Jesus against the wealthy."[62]

Santmire's theological Earth literacy revealed itself more clearly in his next text, which offered a historical portrait of Christianity's ambiguous relationship with creation. He combed through major historical voices in Western Christian thought to demonstrate that Christianity originally had a "pronounced and pervasive ecological dimension." Its "bankruptcy" came when it "became locked in with the forces of modern science, modern philosophy, and modern industrialism."[63] Through his work, Christians can appreciate how some Christian voices distorted the good news because their understandings of God, creation, and humanity were inadequate or inaccurate. Believers need not abandon Christianity entirely, nor should they naïvely ignore its culpability in the ecological crisis. Instead, they can appreciate the important role religion can play in correcting distorted ideas and promoting new behaviors.

SUMMARY

Cultivating theological Earth literacy enabled the emergence of the distinct academic discipline of ecotheology in the 1980s. This would have been impossible were it not for the many contributions of the aforementioned pioneers who appreciated the intrinsic worth of creation, who offered the linguistic tools to describe, poetically and mystically, the intertwining of the numinous and cosmic, who understood our evolving world in provocative ways, who realized the ethical imperative for developing a reimagining of humanity's place in creation, and who saw how religion played an important role in causing—and addressing—the ecological crisis. The next chapter offers a portrait of the birth of ecotheology within six vital theological areas. Each of these domains demonstrates how a robust Earth literacy can supply the substrate and desire for constructing an ecological theological anthropology (ETA)—the central task of the second part of this book. It is this new relational framework that will enable Christians to engage the mystery of human suffering in new ways.

4

THE BIRTH OF ECOTHEOLOGY

Despite the blossoming of a new planetary consciousness in the imaginations of believers, by the mid-twentieth century the idea of Earth literacy had yet to make significant inroads into the academic domains of theology. Consequently, the doctrines of the Christian faith had yet to incorporate the new appreciation of Earth, and Earth literacy had still to be manifested in the daily lives and religious rituals being celebrated. The new scientific appreciation of humanity's much larger family history, the intrinsic worth of all of creation's web of life, and the dynamism inherent to our world needed a more thorough articulation. This began in earnest within numerous domains of theology in the latter half of the twentieth century and culminated in the birth of ecotheology in the 1980s.

Since theology itself is a complex tapestry of interwoven ideas, and ecotheology is interdisciplinary, a description of its birth can only be described by weaving together its many threads—six threads, or domains, of theological reflection to be exact. Each thread offers a vital hue to the portrait of ecotheology and helps readers understand the depth and breadth of how Earth literacy has affected theology. The six threads are titled *Cosmology*, *Systematics*, *Ontology*, *Justice*, *Natural Theology*, and *Spirituality-Praxis*. Within each domain, there are several voices, or midwives, whose work has helped to birth this new theological discipline.[1] This is neither an exhaustive overview nor a systematic dissection of ecotheological ideas; rather, it is a descriptive portrait of ecotheology's emergence so that readers can understand the foundations for the distinctly ecological theological anthropology offered in this text.

COSMOLOGY

Thomas Berry: A Cosmic Storyteller

Passionist priest and cultural historian Thomas Berry (1914–2009) was a pioneering figure who, at the cusp of the 1980s, narrated a new, more accurate story of how our universe came to be, how it is developing, and where it may be going. He offered theology a more functional cosmology—or our universe story. He was also a scholar of Teilhard de Chardin and is open about the influence he had:

> I have learned from [Teilhard] three things of special import. The universe has a psychic-spiritual dimension as well as a physical-material dimension from the beginning; the universe story and the human story are two aspects of a single story; and there is need to move from an excessive concern for redemptive processes to a new concern for creation processes.[2]

These and other insights cultivated Berry's Earth literacy in his theology, which ultimately became manifest in the following assertions: the biospiritual nature of the cosmos, the connectivity and dynamism of the universe, the ancient and irreversible quality of our cosmos, the unique role humans have in the unfolding universe process, and the situation of Earth as the primary referent for all human endeavors. These are all essential aspects of the universe story, or cosmology, offered by Berry. Berry gradually refined this narrative in the late 1970s,[3] and nearly a decade later, it was published in a special edition of *Cross Currents* (1987).[4] His formulation of the sacred universe story rose to more public prominence when Berry crafted "Twelve Principles for Reflecting on the Universe" in (1987)[5] and included it as the tenth chapter of his popular text *Dream of the Earth* (1988). His level of Earth literacy enabled him to diagnose the sickness afflicting modern Western consciousness as the embrace of a dysfunctional "origin story." His work offered an alternative cosmology to captivate the human imagination and feed a deep spiritual longing.

The seeds of this cosmology were first planted during Berry's childhood in rural Greensboro, North Carolina, where a local meadow across the creek from where he lived helped shape his theological imagination; he saw how the existence of the meadow was a medium for divine revelation; thus, Earth became, for him, a primary referent for determining right and wrong actions.[6] This wisdom incubated during his youth and adolescence and began to germinate during his seminary training as well as after his ordination in 1942. His vocation as a teacher, storyteller, historian, and writer was where his cosmological vision eventually materialized, especially during his tenure at Fordham when he founded the Riverdale Center for Religious Research (1970–95). This creative milieu is where Thomas Berry wove the wisdom from science, history, anthropology, and world religions into a coherent and evocative narrative that articulated the story of the cosmos, the role of the human in this developing cosmos, and our way forward in what he called "a new Ecozoic era." This new geobiological age promises mutually enhancing relations among humans and the "larger community of life."[7] Hence, by the 1990s, Berry's sacred universe story was inspiring believers to recognize and revere the sacredness of Earth as a communion of subjects and not as a collection of objects to be exploited, commodified, and exterminated.

SYSTEMATICS: DEFENDER, ARCHITECTS, AND ADVOCATE

John Haught: Defender

John Haught (b. 1942) is an American theologian who criticized other theologians who espoused a purely otherworldly spirituality in theology, as well as scientists who understood nature as radically impersonal, barren, and impermeable to divine influence. He thought the prevailing way of envisioning nature precluded any way of incorporating divine purpose (i.e., teleology) and he set out to change this.[8]

Through his philosophical writings, Haught offered a more coherent way to understand our evolutionary world faithfully. At the dawn of the 1980s, Haught's work consisted of defending the congruity between religious "myths of meaning" and "the fabric of nature disclosed by modern science and consistent cosmological theory."[9] He facilitated a dialogue between religion and science by connecting the process philosophy of Alfred North Whitehead with other great thinkers in philosophy, theology, and science (e.g., Michael Polanyi, Paul Tillich, and Karl Rahner). He addressed the "academic suspicion of cosmic teleology"[10] and wrestled with how we can faithfully describe the relationship between God's purposefulness and creation, an area of theology he felt is often neglected due to embarrassment.[11] He also investigated how human appreciation of this divine cosmic purpose (and hence the worth inherent to the cosmos) intensifies how we care for our human neighbors. As such, Haught contributed much to ecotheology; he defended Christian beliefs concerning God, creation, and the world, and he constructed better ways for understanding them in light of evolution. His meticulous and systematic approach to defending essential aspects of faith enabled him to articulate a deep relationship between *ecos* (ecology) and *theos* (God). This became the sorely needed philosophical undergirding for the alternative worldview that sustains ecotheology.

Jürgen Moltmann and Gordon Kaufman: Architects

Two other theologians who worked within systematic theology to change the way doctrines of faith are articulated and lived out were German theologian Jürgen Moltmann and American theologian Gordon Kaufman.

In 1985, Jürgen Moltmann articulated how the environmental crisis was "nothing less than a crisis in human beings themselves,"[12] and thus, he sought to construct an ecological doctrine of creation to correspond to the relational, social doctrine of the Trinity he had outlined in *The Trinity and the Kingdom of God* in 1981. He argued that if we see God as a Trinitarian community, then we will not see "his [*sic*] relationship to the world he has created as a one-sided relationship of domination."[13] It is a relational understanding of God that will help humanity to reimagine our relations within Earth's many webs of life and develop a "non-hierarchical, decentralized, confederate theology."[14] He saw that a theological doctrine of creation must be guided by the desire to "find a way into the community of creation, to reawaken the awareness of that community and to restore it."[15] However, to construct this new doctrine of creation and to understand its implications, theologians had to cross both religious and scientific boundaries. Moltmann did both; he listened attentively to rich sources in Judaism (e.g., Hebrew Bible, the Sabbath, and Kabbalistic traditions such as *zimsum* and divine *Shekinah*) as well as to scientific and secular contributions (e.g., "sciences, technologies, and economies that impact the relations between human beings, machines, and nature").[16] He "absorbed" them all into his systematic vision of Christian theology. Moltmann also realized how the mindscapes of theologians and scientists have changed: "We no longer desire to know in order to dominate or analyse and reduce in order to reconstruct. Our purpose is now to perceive in order to participate, and to enter into the mutual relationships of the living thing."[17] Consequently, in his groundbreaking text *God in Creation* (1984), he succeeded in expanding the "Christological concentration" in Protestant theology and reconnected systematic theology with the larger "inhabited globe"[18]—both of which became formative aspects of ecotheology.

Gordon Kaufman was also an important midwife of ecotheology in two ways: he reimagined the nature and function of theology and helped to direct the reconstruction of our understanding of God and Christ (two primary religious symbols of Christian faith) in light of our ability to cause a nuclear holocaust. In *Theology for a Nuclear Age* (1985), he described how humanity's capability to inflict suffering was not new; rather, what was unique was our ability to obliterate the future for all of creation. As a result, this unprecedented historical and religious situation demands a creative response from theologians that goes beyond merely repetition of traditional precepts. He asserted that since humanity has become aware of our emergence from the cosmos, and we have been graced "with the power to take some measure of direct responsibility for the further unfolding of that very creativity,"[19] then theologians need to speak of God and Christ in "ecological terms." This means that how we imagine God and Christ must engage our contemporary biological and historical-cultural origins and processes.[20] Our new context, the nuclear age, has also made humanity urgently aware that if human life is to continue, *all* factors (e.g., physical, biological, and historico-cultural) must be authentically appreciated and engaged, not destroyed, poisoned, exploited, or oppressed.

He argued that this novel situation is the ultimate test for theology and its symbols, "if 'God' is to continue to be a viable symbol for orienting human life."[21]

Kaufman offered his own descriptions of God for an evolutionary world: God as the primordial, mysterious, "hidden creativity,"[22] tendency, power, or "ecological reality"[23] behind, within, and working through biological processes as well as human history and cultures. Kaufman also advised against highly personal and politically motivated symbols of Christ;[24] instead, he symbolized Christ as the spirit of "creativity and liberation, and healing, of reconciliation and reconstruction" at work in the world.[25] It is the narrative of Jesus's life, ministry, and death on the cross that brings humanity back to the roots of our being: interdependent and self-giving. This, he claimed, is "the very structure or activity which Christians call God."[26] Thus, Kaufman saw aspects of systematic theology as the work of the human imagination to create a coherent framework of meaning that will provide an overall orientation for human life.[27] His work has become a guide for many ecotheologians who have followed.

Sallie McFague: Advocate

Acutely aware of the historical and cultural context in which she was writing, American feminist theologian Sallie McFague became a strong advocate for Earth in two ways: by developing a metaphorical theology, one that bridged literature and theology, and by offering a provocative understanding of the world as God's body.[28] Like Kaufman, her motivation was her membership in the first generation of humans able to harness nuclear power and cause the destruction of all life on Earth. Equipped with many theological tools,[29] McFague constructed a new model for understanding the relationship of God and the universe that spoke to the urgency of her historical moment:

> We belong, from the cells of our bodies to the finest creations of our minds, to the intricate, ever changing cosmos. We both depend on the web of life for our own continued existence and in a special way we are responsible for it, for we alone know that life is interrelated and we alone know how to destroy it. It is an awesome and unsettling thought.[30]

Her writing in the 1980s advocated for new symbols, language, and imagery to depict God's presence and power within the created world and the relationship God has with the created world, including humanity. She argued that in an ecological, evolutionary, and nuclear age, the most appropriate ecological models for God include Mother, Lover, and Friend. The most coherent way of imagining the relationship between God and the world, then, was by using the organic metaphor of the world as God's body. This model proposed a way for understanding the Creator of the universe as intimately immanent, as life or "being" itself, and challenged the image of an utterly transcendent clockmaker God. Consequently, the world, in her vision, becomes "a sacrament of the invisible God."[31] Thus, our vocation is to care for this sacred body of God. However, one controversial aspect of this model is that God is vulnerable; Earth, as the body of God, can be hurt; therefore, God risks injury and requires humanity's care.[32] This challenges the classic vision of an invulnerable, immutable God. Nevertheless, McFague's way of imagining God as well as her strong moral imperative to tend, guide, and befriend the world carefully (because it is both an expression of God and necessary for life),[33] bequeathed much to ecotheology and inspired this discipline to be concerned with both the spiritual and physical life of believers.[34]

ONTOLOGY OF COMMUNION

Douglas John Hall: Ontology as Being-With

Canadian United Church minister Douglas John Hall indicated that Christian thinkers commonly attribute a static understanding of the "image of God" to humans only. They also believe that any highly valued cultural qualities (e.g., rationality, power, maleness) best describe what this image entails.[35] Hence, this narrowly defined image of God can sanction the devaluing and exploitation of anyone, or anything, that falls outside culturally accepted social, political, racial, class, gender, or species boundaries.[36] Hall recognized that cultural norms have a great impact on how this symbol is understood (and used); hence, he asserted that the image of God must be used in "jarring" ways to unearth distortions embedded in our cultural consciousness. Only when we are roused into seeing these distortions can we reimagine how we understand God, creation, and humanity and more faithfully appreciate what being made in the "image of God" means in an evolutionary world in crisis.[37]

Hall suggested that the root cause of our ecological problems is our ontology: how humanity understands who we are, that is, human "being," and how this understanding is used to guide how human society operates. If "humanness" is defined by radically autonomous individuality, pure rationality, self-sufficiency, and self-reflective capabilities, and if these qualities reflect vital characteristics of God (because we are made in the image of God), then this ontological vision sanctions the ruling, controlling, and exploitation of those who are dependent on others and have less than "fully" developed capacities for rationality and self-reflection. If this autonomous, independent Enlightenment "man," as defined above, is the measure of who is made in the image of God, then all organisms outside the human family—and many within the human species, such as women and people with disabilities—do not meet this standard of "being." Because they are less than human (e.g., they are objects lacking intrinsic worth), they do not deserve the same rights as human subjects and can be exploited.[38] Hall concludes that the exploitation of Earth has more to do with who we think we are rather than with our activities.[39]

To remedy this, Hall suggested Western theology should cultivate a more authentic understanding of personhood. This is where a scientific Earth literacy helps; science has illustrated very concretely that our true ontology is one of communion, that is, "Being-With," rather than the static, independent notion of "Being." For Hall, this communion is not an absorption of one into another and a loss of particularity, much like a raspberry does when blended into a smoothie; rather, it understands "being" as a dialectical, mutually empowering relationship with that which is not one's own "being" (i.e., an "other").[40] In 1965, Martin Luther King Jr. beautifully described this concept of communion in his commencement address for Oberlin College:

> All I'm saying is simply this: that all mankind [*sic*] is tied together; all life is interrelated, and we are all caught in an inescapable network of mutuality, tied in a single garment of destiny. Whatever affects one directly, affects all indirectly. For some strange reason I can never be what I ought to be until you are what you ought to be. And you

> can never be what you ought to be until I am what I ought to be—this is the interrelated structure of reality.[41]

Hall also espoused this ontology of interconnectivity (Being-With) and offered three irreducible distinctions within his ontology of communion: a "being-with" that is oriented toward God who is the Ground and Source of all being;[42] an interpersonal "being-with," for example, relations among our human neighbors; and a "being-with" that involves the "inarticulate but not silent" physical universe.[43] Once a person exists, all three loci are irreducible, inseparable, coequal, and are dimensions of our total relatedness. This relational understanding of being will broaden our understanding of the "image of God," which, in turn, will allow others to possess intrinsic worth.

Another key facet of Hall's ontology is how relatedness is not static or predetermined. Instead, "being-with" requires a continual, personal choice. One can choose to initiate a relationship and decide whether or not to respond to another. Thus, we can turn away from our nature as relational beings; our current crises illustrate that we have done so.[44] Hall's great gift to ecotheology is his radical reorientation of human ontology toward "being-with" the world, each other, and God, and the broadening of human understanding of being made in the "image of God."

Raimon (Raimundo) Panikkar: Cosmotheandric Intuition

Raimundo Panikkar (1918–2010) lived a diverse life; his mother was an affluent, well-educated Spanish Roman Catholic, and his father was a Hindu from an affluent family in South India. Hence, he enjoyed a dual sense of belonging along with a simultaneous alienation within both cultural and religious realms. He was a Jesuit scholar with doctorates in philosophy, chemistry, and theology, and he dedicated his life to the "mutual understanding and cooperation among religious traditions."[45] His greatest contribution to the birth of ecotheology in the 1980s was how he brought his unique experiences of diversity to theology by constructing an integrative cosmotheandric vision of the relations among God, the world, and humanity.[46]

In his article "The Cosmotheandric Intuition" (1984), Panikkar had a hopeful, holistic, mystical attitude toward creation, and he critiqued the tendency in theology to disembody and dematerialize God and diminish the worth of matter.[47] Panikkar realized that this disembodiment of God prompted humanity to do the same: "Haunted by the need to preserve his 'dignity,' [humanity] stripped himself of his animality, then his body and senses, and soon enough he put aside his feelings until he became a 'thinking rod,' a *res cogitans*, and a speaking machine."[48]

The alienation of humanity from our materiality caused many like Panikkar, to search for ways to understand why our rootedness in creation is so important to ontology.[49] Panikkar saw the metaphysical (transcendent), noetic (conscious thinking), and empirical (material) as the three irreducible, coextensive dimensions of reality.[50] Hence, he named his understanding of being "cosmo-the-andric" to reflect his commitment to all three dimensions. His elegantly crafted description of the relations among these three dimensions allowed him to maintain the crucial distinction between the finite and infinite while still affirming a unity in diversity.[51]

Panikkar's gift to ecotheology was offering a way of articulating a cosmotheandric ontology that (1) affirms interconnectivity, intimacy, and dynamism; (2) retrieves humanity's "ecological sensitivity"[52] in our embrace of our mystical yearning for the transcendent; and (3) celebrates the divine urge for "time, space, and [humanity]."[53] Panikkar's groundbreaking work bequeathed to ecotheology a "positive (and not merely dialectical) middle way between the paranoia of monism and the schizophrenia of dualism."[54]

JUSTICE MOVEMENTS

Thanks to the monumental efforts of social activism from the 1950s onwards, it became clear in the 1980s that "just human" relations were predicated on "just Earth" relations. However, the ecological dimension of human civil rights movements was underappreciated until more recently. For example, Drew Dellinger has argued that Martin Luther King Jr.'s overarching vision of justice for African Americans was deeply rooted in a cosmic vision of justice. In a 1967 television interview, King is clear that "it would be foolhardy for me to work for integrated schools or integrated lunch counters and not be concerned about the survival of the world in which to be integrated."[55] By the 1980s, this sentiment was at the forefront of social justice movements. For example, the World Council of Churches' General Assembly in Vancouver in 1983 affirmed peace, justice, and the integrity of creation as the three central Christian values.[56] The following four midwives show how justice movements were imperative to induce the birth of ecotheology.

Rosemary Radford Ruether: Women and Earth

Rosemary Radford Ruether (b. 1936) is arguably one of the most prominent among feminist voices of the 1970s. In the 1980s, she brought to the world's attention the intertwining oppression of women and nature in a coherent and persuasive narrative of liberation. In her book *To Change the World* (1981), she directly connected the fate of Earth and women.[57] Two years later, she spoke of the need to rethink the hierarchical and androcentric (male-centered) classic chain of being within Western creation theology to liberate both women and Earth.[58] She asserts that for women who struggle daily to survive and care for their families, the poisoning and deterioration of the natural environment both reflects and exacerbates their own experiences of injustice. Thanks to her training as a historian of Christianity, Ruether was able to articulate the complexity of the oppression women experience and identifies distorted power structures or relations (e.g., militarism, sexism, anti-Semitism, colonialism, racism, class conflict, and ecological despoliation) as the bitter roots of social injustice. Often, these are understood as divinely ordained, thus sanctifying the oppression of Earth and women, who are closely aligned with Earth due to their procreative capacities.[59] This is why many know Earth as "Mother Nature." Understanding that this coupling of women and Earth called for justice for both was a part of Ruether's writing even prior to the 1980s. In *New Woman/New Earth* (1975), she writes,

> Women must see that there can be no liberation for them and no solution to the ecological crisis within a society whose fundamental model of relationship continues to be one of domination. They must unite the demands of the women's movement with those of the ecological movement

to envision a radical reshaping of the basic socio-economic relations and the underlying values of this society.[60]

Ruether continued to build on this foundation through the 1980s until it became part of the broader vision of justice that guides eco-theology and ecofeminists today; in the 1990s, Ruether warned privileged North American ecofeminists that their experiences of creation will only be "recreational self-indulgence" if not enmeshed in an equally strong commitment to transform unjust social, economic, and political structures that oppress and kill.[61] Her powerful witness to the shared oppression of women and creation was—and is—invaluable.

Sean McDonagh: Indigenous Peoples and Earth

Sean McDonagh was a Columbian missionary and priest, who advocated for both the forests and peoples of the Philippines. Just as Ruether connected the oppression of woman and Earth, McDonagh connected the cry of the Earth and the suffering of indigenous peoples. In *To Care for the Earth* (1986), he asserted that "very little reflection on this damaging relationship between human beings and the earth has emerged from Christian thinkers,"[62] and thus, he dedicated his book to exposing the ideas gifted by the Christian Tradition that can help cultivate social and ecological justice. The lens that helped him understand Scripture, creation theology, and the biblical call to social justice was the context of suffering, poverty, and ecological destruction in Negros, Philippines. It was the suffering of the indigenous T'Boli tribe that motivated him to construct a beautiful and faithful understanding of God, Christ, nature, Scripture, stewardship, sacramental life, moral theology, spirituality, mission, and Christian witness.

His scientific Earth literacy helped him to critique many elements of the Christian Tradition that were too human-centered as well as to speak to the immediate causes of cultural and ecological degradation. Consequently, McDonagh offered a justice orientation and cosmic foundation for doing theology: "Unless the environment is preserved, social justice for all human beings, not to mention other creatures, will simply be a dream."[63] Theologians, he asserted, should have a critical and a creative response to our current crisis rather than a romantic fixation on the past. This way, we may respond creatively and with great faith to our current problems just as "Jesus and Mohammed" did in their time.[64]

Dorothee Sölle: Laborers and Earth

Just as Ruether and McDonagh appreciated how intertwined the destinies of the Earth, women, and indigenous peoples are, Dorothee Sölle brought our attention to how laborers are caught up in Earth's destiny as well. In 1984, Dorothee Sölle wrote *To Work and to Love: A Theology of Creation*, where she integrated her feminist and liberation theologies with her growing awareness of the sacredness of Earth. In the first chapter, she admited that "ten years ago I was not so conscious of the sacredness of the earth. It is when we are confronted with the utter threat to that which we love that we rediscover the wellsprings of our love and realize our interdependency anew."[65]

The threat she spoke of came from the real threat of a nuclear holocaust during her life and her unique experience as a German adolescent living with the painful knowledge of both the atrocities committed by the Nazi's and the entrancement of many of her fellow German citizens with elitist propaganda. As a result, Sölle committed herself to finding truth and living justly, even if this entailed questioning the authority of political, economic, social, or ecclesial institutions.

For Sölle, "choosing life in the face of death" meant walking the path hewn by Jesus the revolutionary, and participating in creation through love, suffering, and work.[66] She believed that humanity is "born into the process of liberation"[67] and this is the root of our belonging to Earth.[68] Our shared, cocreative vocation as members of the Earth community means we must work to build just relations and recognize the truth of mutual dependence. She saw the violation of Earth reflected in the violence done to other marginalized groups because of distorted political and religious worldviews.[69] Thus, Sölle's vital contribution to ecotheology was her keen listening to the voices of those at the margins, especially poor laborers. As she stood in solidarity and worked alongside those thirsting for justice, their experiences informed her theology. In *To Work and to Love*, she outlines many sources of her theological ideas: a Squamish Chief who affirmed the sacredness of all life on Earth;[70] a lesbian feminist theologian Isabel Carter Heyward, who understood the yearning *eros* of

God as the source of creation's interrelatedness;[71] Sakokwenonkwas, who appreciated the spiritual essence of all matter[72] and the shared human disposition to frailty and death; Martin Buber who articulated "becoming," not being, as a vital ontological category;[73] Nicaraguan priest Ernesto Cardenal, who asserted that Earth belongs to those who work as cocreators and not to those who pay for property;[74] and St. Francis, whose affirmation of Sister Death reminded humanity of our co-suffering with all of creation.[75] Hence, Sölle grounded her theology in wisdom gained through her intimate knowledge of the suffering in human societies and the "prostitution of workers."[76] This, she affirmed, is a reflection of a deeper alienation from, and exploitation of, Earth.

Jean Vanier: People with Disabilities and Earth

Jean Vanier offered a unique and often underappreciated aspect of ecotheology: how to *actually* live in a vulnerable communion of subjects regardless of whether it is a human community or an aquatic ecosystem. Vanier is the founder of L'Arche—"the Ark" in English—communities where people with disabilities are intentionally the core members while those people who are fully abled are the assistants. The privileging of the experiences of people with disabilities in the structure and functioning of L'Arche communities demonstrates that their gifts are central to the well-being of the community; the wounded, beautiful, and ordinary human beings who are both abled and disabled struggle to love, to witness to love, and to be loved in return. This is the model for how all Earth's communities should live and love. Vanier celebrated interdependence and saw the value of vulnerability in building authentic communities. He also reaffirms the necessity of sacrifice, limitation, and vulnerability in just, loving relations:

> A community is essentially a place where we learn to live at the pace of humanity and nature. We are part of the earth and we need the heat of the sun, the water of the sea and the air we breathe. We are part of nature and its laws are written in our flesh. That doesn't mean that scientific discoveries aren't useful too. But they have to be at the

> service of life, applied to create an environment in which human beings can truly grow—whether in town or country, middle class areas or slums. A community should not be primarily a grouping of shock-troops, commandos or heroes, but a gathering of people who want to be a sign that it is possible for men to live together, love each other, celebrate and work for a better world and a fellowship of peace.[77]

Both what Vanier wrote and how he lives are testaments of how to understand and live Thomas Berry's vision of a planetary communion of subjects:

> Living with men and women with intellectual disabilities has helped me to discover what it means to live in communion with someone. To be in communion means to be with someone and to discover that we actually belong together. Communion means accepting people just as they are, with all their limits and inner pain, but also with their gifts and their beauty and their capacity to grow: to see the beauty inside of all the pain.[78]

As other midwives focused their theological attention on cultivating an awareness of God's intimate presence within *other-than-human* creation, Vanier proclaimed God's intimate presence in the pain and woundedness of the human heart: "I think we can only truly experience the presence of God, meet Jesus, receive the good news, in and through our own poverty, because the kingdom of God belongs to the poor, the poor in spirit, the poor who are crying out for love."[79] Vanier understood God's presence in the cry for friendship and communion of those deemed unworthy or less human by human society; thus, he offered L'Arche as a model of authentic *human* community. However, his connection between abundant life and finding one's spiritual or emotional place of belonging in a human community was not separate from the physical space where this happens:

> Human beings need bread if they are to grow. If they don't eat, they die. And if they are to grow spiritually, they, like plants, need sun, water, air, and soil. The soil is the

community—the place they are planted, take root, grow, give fruit and die so that others may live.[80]

This focus on Earth as the physical substrate for community life and spiritual development would later become more prominent in L'Arche communities.[81] Nevertheless, Vanier's focus on the sacred gifts lying hidden in disability and vulnerability laid the foundation for understanding God's presence and power in the joys and pains of created life and for understanding how we are being called to live in our cosmic and planetary communion.[82]

THEOLOGY OF NATURE

John Polkinghorne and Arthur Peacocke

Two British scientist-theologians who aided in the birth of ecotheology in the 1980s were John Polkinghorne and Arthur Peacocke. These men fostered a deep reverence for the Book of Creation and brought science and theology into meaningful conversation in their unique methodology: critical realism.

In the late 1980s, theoretical physicist John Polkinghorne recognized that scientists (especially in the physical sciences) were playing an increasingly significant role in establishing a fruitful dialogue between science and religion.[83] This revived a theology of nature, not natural theology, and was a precursor to ecotheology.[84] He indicated that a theology of nature was different from natural theology in that it was more modest, it spoke to the deep intelligibility of the cosmos made possible by scientific progress, and it envisioned God's Word as information as well as creative and redemptive power. Polkinghorne refused to marginalize God to only the spaces where science could not offer an explanation, that is, God of the gaps. Instead, he saw a theology of nature as asking different, more "meta" questions that pointed beyond, and yet included, science. Consequently, God was present within and beyond the world science was explicating. The Logos of God could be comprehended in the laws of nature by creatures made in the image of the Creator.[85] A key contribution Polkinghorne made was his affirmation that science was only possible because the universe is a creative effort, not an inert entity. He indicated that a theology of nature outlined more cohesively how the process of evolution, in itself, is not comprehensive enough to explain the immense fecundity and complexity in the universe. He claimed that the sheer abundance of creativity, including the degree of sophistication and complexity centered in the human, has occurred within very narrow physical parameters that are governed by precise ground rules, or "finely tuned," natural laws.[86] Thus, he gave ecotheology a way of relating science and religion that emphasized mutual dependency.

One of Arthur Peacocke's major contributions to science was his work in biochemistry that profiled the intricacies of the DNA structure. His endowment to theology was developing a way of understanding how science and religion relate.[87] He wrote extensively about models of God in an evolutionary world and articulated the biblical motif *continua creatio* in light of our modern understanding of Earth as a dynamic and interdependent world. In *Intimations of Reality: Critical Realism in Science and Religion* (1984), Peacocke argued that scientific theories yield partial, revisable but referential knowledge of the world and these theories are expressed linguistically via metaphors and models.[88] This is also true for theology; what we say about God is real but partial and always revisable. Theology expresses these truths via models and metaphors. This is the basis for meaningful theological and scientific discourses; both disciplines work in the same manner to make sense of our reality. Peacocke also had innovative ways for describing the creative potentiality of the world and God's creative action in, through, and under the creative processes of the world.[89] He saw God as a choreographer and artist, which was how he described God's activity in the world. He also appreciated the role of uncertainty and chance in evolutionary processes and incorporated it into his vision of God's activity. For example, Ian Barbour described Peacocke's vision of chance as "God's radar beam sweeping through the diverse potentialities that are invisibly present in each configuration in the world."[90] He also described the fullest realization of *human* potentiality in the life, death, and resurrection of Christ in ways that has inspired modern ecotheologians to see God's relationship with other-than-human organisms in unique ways.[91] A final contribution made by Peacocke was his use of an evolutionary paradigm to frame his theology of divine suffering. Embracing a God who suffers in, with, and under Earth's creative impetus has been fertile ground for many ecotheologians highlighted in chapter 11.

SPIRITUALITY AND PRAXIS

Matthew Fox: Creation Spirituality at the Heart of the Universe

In 1979, Matthew Fox wrote *A Spirituality Named Compassion and the Healing of the Global Village, Humpty Dumpty, and Us*—a title that reflects his eclectic approach to creation theology and spirituality.[92] This was the third in a trilogy of texts on spirituality,[93] and it explored "the wisdom of compassion as learned from religious traditions and from nature and the scientific study of nature."[94] After delineating the obstacles within human culture that keep compassion "in exile," he proposed a new understanding of the relationship among humans, nature, and God from his metaphor of a "cosmic, human and divine egg" (like Humpty Dumpty).[95]

As his ideas developed during the 1980s, Fox indicated that the human community lacks a practical understanding of our origins and purpose. To remedy this, he wove together ideas from medieval mystical spirituality (e.g., that of Meister Eckhart, St. John of the Cross, Abbess Hildegarde, Julian of Norwich, and St. Thomas Aquinas) and modern science into his creation theology. This creative synthesis enabled him to see the Eucharistic Banquet as a representation of cosmic hospitality, a vital dimension for sacramental theology today, and it fed his understanding of embodied spirituality.[96] Fox's creation spirituality in the 1980s, alongside the ecospiritual praxis of many religious groups (e.g., the Genesis Farm started by Miriam Therese MacGillis and the Dominican Sisters of Caldwell, New Jersey, in 1980, and Jesuit Farm Project started in Guelph, Ontario, by James Profit, SJ, and Louisa Blair in 1985) facilitated ecotheology's quickening and sustained its proliferation and innovation in the twenty-first century.[97]

SUMMARY

Ecotheology's birth in the 1980s would not have been possible without the contributions of multiple midwives. Scientific Earth literacy formed the biospiritual theological imaginations of these midwives so that they were able to describe the sacred universe story, reimagine doctrine, craft a new ontology of communion, develop new avenues to seek and sustain justice, propose a theology of nature, and cultivate Earth-centered spiritualties and practices. Each of these contributions still guide ecotheologians today, which has helped construct the ETA outlined in the next several chapters. Thanks largely to the gifts of these pioneers (and others that are not mentioned here), Christians are able to understand the relations among God, humanity, and other-than-human creation in new ways, which has inspired new theological conversations concerning the mystery of human suffering.

PART II

ECOLOGICAL THEOLOGICAL ANTHROPOLOGY

Our historic moment—blossoming scientific and theological Earth literacy, and our ecological crisis—demands the development of new ways of imagining the relationship among creation, God, and humanity. We need an ecological theological anthropology (ETA) that appreciates the ecosystems (*ecos*) gifted by God (*theos*) within which humans (*anthropos*) co-dwell with Earth's many subjects. The weaving together of these three concepts must be intentional: ecological anthropology without reflection upon God (theology) is untethered, like a tree without roots; theological anthropology without ecology is too narrow, like a firmly rooted tree with no leaves; ecological theology without the human lens (anthropology) is ineffectual, for we cannot overlook our humanness any more than a rooted, leafy tree can overlook the presence and importance of its trunk and branches. If any of the three parts of the tree are missing (leaves, roots, and branches), the tree dies. The same is true for Christian anthropology; without purposeful attention to creation, God, and humanity, Christian anthropology will atrophy, leading to what Pope Francis claims as "a wrong understanding of the relationship between human beings and the world" (*Laudato Si'* 116).

Embracing an ETA is challenging on many levels. First, it asks believers to cultivate a robust scientific and theological Earth literacy that allows them to be fluent in ecological principles and also helps them become more knowledgeable of theological wisdom. This will help facilitate a critical examination of our understanding of our humanness and our human activities. It also requires that we overcome our fragmented and "silo" thinking. We need "big picture" thinkers who are comfortable with branching out beyond their familiar academic silo; otherwise, we will not be able to address the multitude of causes contributing to our planet's destabilization and human suffering. Fragmented, short-sighted approaches to academia bequeathed by the Enlightenment period were important at one point in history when collection of vast amounts of data was crucial. However, now we need vibrant conversations to make sense of the immense amounts of data we can access at our fingertips—just ask Siri the right question and you will receive nearly overwhelming amounts of data. But do we have the skill sets to examine and apply this data in meaningful and critical ways? For Earth's sake and our own, we must become integrated, critical thinkers and see how wisdom from many sources needs to cross-pollinate with our own. An ETA is the relational framework that invites this.

In general, an ETA offers the foundational pillars upon which to understand human life. It is a way of understanding creation, God, and humanity within a sacred, unfolding cosmic narrative. An ETA has four pillars, but the way Christians manifest the wisdom of each pillar in their lives can be very different. A way to understand this is as follows: Every building, regardless whether it is a school, business, or church, has to be built on a solid foundation. Once you learn how to construct the substructure, creative license takes over and each building forms the shape imagined by its architect. But without sure footings, all buildings will be unstable and fall, regardless of what they look like. Thus, each pillar of an ETA reminds readers of what needs to be addressed or included in an authentic, faithful, and Earth-literate Christian anthropology. But how this wisdom manifests in the lives and writings of Christians may differ.

The first pillar of an ETA is eschatological hope. This is a hope in an ultimate end-time or heavenly existence, and reminds believers that the hope for peace, healing, and justice we have today is connected with the hope and love God offered at the beginning of time and will express at the end of time. This pillar offers readers a grand horizon of hope for wholeness and fulfillment that extends beyond the period when humans roamed Earth and includes all of creation. Hope of union with God spans back from the empty tomb on Easter Sunday to the Big Bang that took place 13.8 billion years ago, as well as forward to the ultimate moment of peace, when all created life will be in the embrace of our Creator.

The second pillar of an ETA affirms what it acclaims in its title: the intrinsic worth of creation manifest in interconnectedness, interdependence, and diversity. This is a radical form of optimism for all created life—as radical as the profession in Genesis that indeed, creation is very good (see Gen 1:31). What is novel is our awareness of how immensely interconnected, interdependent, and diverse our world is. Christians must appreciate that our world is very good and worthy of protection.

The third pillar of an ETA avows a numinous–cosmic communion. This is a reawakening to the intimate dance of the spiritual and material. In our embrace of the machine metaphor during the Enlightenment period, we lost our spiritual understanding of Earth. This must be rectified; otherwise, we will never appreciate God's revelation as fully as possible, nor will we care for our sacred common home.

The final pillar is an appreciation of the painfully creative cadence—identified in this text as the kenotic-kinetic—that animates our evolutionary world. Earth is beautiful and harsh, creative and cruciform, and believers must see themselves as part of this ancient, costly cadence in order to reexamine suffering and sacrifice inherent in our world. When we do, we can differentiate between inherent suffering and that which human sin inflicts. This is a crucial but often overlooked part of our human journey.

5

FIRST PILLAR: ESCHATOLOGICAL HOPE

Thanks to our scientific Earth literacy and the contributions of ecotheology, the relationship among creation, God, and humanity is being reimagined and aspects of Christian theology, spanning from the doctrine of creation to redemption, are being described in new ways. The first pillar of an ETA reconnects the beginning and the end of time to offer a more inclusive appreciation of hope. Eschatology is the study of what the final heavenlike phase of existence (the *eschaton*) will be like. It engages the tension between wholeness and fulfillment present in the world (the "already") and what human imaginations can envision that life ought to be (the "not yet"). The hope in the "not yet," articulated by Christianity as union with God, helps sustain our hope in our world that is good but unfinished. Our planetary consciousness and the work done by ecotheologians, such as those that will be examined in this chapter, has broadened our appreciation of how large and dynamic this horizon of hope really is; hope originates at the moment of creation and extends from this present moment until the *eschaton*. Hence, God's overflowing love has enabled all creation to participate in the realization of our final future with God, each in ways particular to their nature and capabilities. Other-than-human creation does not experience annihilation at end-time because creation is no longer thought of as merely a stage for the human–God drama. Nor is the rest of created life assimilated into the human experience of communion; all of creation will have a final dwelling place in God and experience a unique relationship with God. This means even sparrows that fall to the ground (see Matt 10:29) will experience abundant life with God in their own way.[1] Hope for eternal rest in God's loving embrace at the end-time is not just an exclusive right of humans.

This first pillar also affirms that ultimate communion with God, who is perfect love, justice, wholeness, and peace, also breaks through into the "here and now" for us to glimpse, experience, and participate in, although partially. This dual promise of abundant life (e.g., healing, ecosocial justice, wholeness, and love) both now and at the end-time is expansive enough that all of created life is included, not just human beings. Thus, eschatological hope offered by an ETA pays serious theological attention to how intertwined the destiny is for all created life. Our cosmic family shares a common origin because of God's initial overflowing goodness, but we also share a common destiny because our Creator is eternally luring the whole cosmos toward abundant life, healing, and justice in the present moment and at the *eschaton*. Accordingly, our understanding of creation as an old, sacred, unfolding universe story offers a new horizon of meaning for both eschatology and Christian hope by appreciating *both* the vertical (movement toward the divine) and the horizontal (connectivity of past, present, and ultimate future) dimensions of created life in new ways.[2] This innovative way of understanding our sacred universe story enables the reimagining of theological language, images, and metaphors, especially in its affirmation of humanity's shared, although differentiated, eschatological destiny.

For many believers, these concepts seem novel, but they are not, for the roots of these ideas run deep in the Christian Tradition. These deep roots come from St. Irenaeus's optimism in creation, St. Maximus the Confessor's attention to diversity and particularity within his vision of what he called the cosmic liturgy, and Pierre Teilhard de Chardin's christological vision of God's luring of the unfinished cosmos upward and forward toward fulfillment and peace.

First Pillar: Eschatological Hope

ANCIENT ROOTS

St. Irenaeus

St. Irenaeus (AD 130–202) refused to accept the Gnostics' description of a passive, alien, transcendent God, and their denigration of the material world. In response, he described creation as a dynamic, continually maturing, universal creation history encompassing God's first creative act until the end of days.[3] Thus, he had a radical optimism for creation, and it showed in his eschatology when he denied that all of creation will be eradicated at consummation. He asserted that "neither the substance nor the essence of the creation will be annihilated"[4] at the end-time, and this optimism is centered in his belief in the unity of all created things and the immanence of God in creation: "For even creation reveals Him who formed it, and the very work made suggests Him who made it, and the world manifests Him who ordered it."[5] Every moment, including the present moment, is connected with the beginning and end for "the material-vital-spiritual-goodness" of the end-time flows back and qualifies the present.[6] This is not a circle that emphasizes the backward momentum to the beginning and the obliteration of material life at the end-time; rather, life can be better characterized by an ever-spiraling, forward momentum toward the *eschaton* that never loses its vital interconnectedness with the beginning. The incarnation, as part of this dynamic movement toward full communion with God, overcomes the incompleteness and distortion of creation and inaugurates the final days of salvation:

> The Word, being made man, summing up all things in Himself, so that as in the super-celestial, spiritual and invisible things the Word of God is supreme, so also in things visible and corporeal He might possess supremacy, and...He might draw all things to Himself at the proper time.[7]

The "not yet" fully realized present moment is always being nourished, critiqued, and renewed by both the fullness of God's self-realized at the end-time and the vitality of God at the moment of creation's birth.

St. Maximus the Confessor

This eschatological optimism is expanded upon by St. Maximus the Confessor (AD 580–662) as described by Hans Urs von Balthasar.[8] Balthasar offers Maximus the Confessor as a guide for contemporary spiritual world sojourners, especially for those who share his optimism for the created world's participation in the bridging of the great chasm between God and the world.[9]

The essential question for Maximus was how finite, created beings could be in an intimate relationship with an infinite, noncreated Being both now and at the *eschaton*. Maximus's response lies in his understanding of the Cosmic Christ, the beating heart of the cosmic liturgy; his Christocentric vision of creation's worth precludes a pessimistic destruction of the fallen created world at the *eschaton*.[10] It is precisely his commitment to polarity, inherent to the unconfused Christ of Chalcedon (e.g., Christ as fully human *and* fully divine), that allows Maximus to highlight an important facet of the incarnation's saving work: the sustaining and preservation of creation in all its diversity. Maximus never had enough praise for all the different syntheses in the created universe that are realized through Christ. It is Christ who "unites man and woman,...unites the earth by abolishing the division between the earthly paradise and the rest of the inhabited globe,...unites earth and heaven,...unites sensible and intelligible things,...and ultimately—in an ineffable way—unites created and uncreated nature."[11] His synthetic Christology embraces and celebrates the perfect union of the two natures of Christ as well as the unified multiplicity characterizing the universe. This helps to replace a "human only" understanding of eschatological hope with one that celebrates the abundant life (e.g., already and not yet) of creation via its diversity of parts. Maximus's attention to both the particularity of the individual and to the unity of the cosmic whole allows him to recognize that an individual being cannot realize his or her fullest particular selfhood in isolation from the whole cosmic community of which he or she is a member. It is only in and through the dialectic of being receptive to an "other"[12] that a person's true self is revealed and he or she participates in the Divine Source of all life—both now and at the end-time. For Maximus, the perfect model of this dialectic was the love of God made visible through Christ's authentic relationship with the world, which enabled his true divine self to be revealed.

Maximus's eschatology led him to imagine God's transcendence ("not of this world") in a way that does not mean it is "not of nature," or otherworldly.

Maximus is clear that when one is fully receptive to the unifying, christological heart of the universe, there and only there, can one find one's true, unique, personal, and natural self and *telos*.[13] This christological heart of the universe is described by Maximus as the inner, eternal origin and as the goal that orients and orders the world, making it intelligible. Hence, Maximus respects both the horizontal (historical development of the world) and vertical (movement of the world toward the divine) dimensions of reality, and this is why humanity can discover the "seeds of truth planted by the Creator" in the cosmos.[14] Balthasar indicates that Maximus keeps separate but in "perfect balance" the spiritual and material as well as the transcendent and immanent, and consequently, affirms a holistic vision of reality.[15] However, what is missing in Maximus's work is the appropriate language and imagery to capture the evolutionary dynamism of the world. This was the gift given by Pierre Teilhard de Chardin.

Pierre Teilhard de Chardin

Pierre Teilhard de Chardin (1881–1955) helped to lay the linguistic and theological foundations for a contemporary, ecocentric eschatology that appreciates our 13.8-billion-year history. Teilhard de Chardin, both a scientist and priest, proclaimed,

> The joy and strength of my life will have lain in the realization that when the two ingredients, God and the world, were brought together they set up an endless mutual reaction, producing a sudden blaze of such intense brilliance that all the depths of the world were lit up for me.[16]

Teilhard's optimism toward created life, his enthusiasm for understanding the physicality of matter, and his hope for the future converged via his primary metaphor that grounded his work and spirituality: the sacred heart of Jesus beating at the core of an evolving, unfinished universe.[17] His devotion to Christ's sacred heart allowed him to imagine the fire of love as an apt descriptor for God's action in the world. Divine love for and in the material world that was modeled perfectly by Christ inspired Teilhard: "So, my God, I prostrate myself before your presence in the universe which has now become living flame."[18] With this inspiration, Teilhard formulated what he called an Omega Point as the future point of convergence of all human progress and evolutionary history. This Omega Point was the risen Christ: "If we say 'God of the Above' + 'God of the ahead,' what does this new equation, fundamental to all Religion in the future, give us if not an ultimate whose dimensions are 'theocosmic,' that is christic? In a system of Creative Union, it is not only the Universe but God himself who is necessarily 'Christified' in Omega, at the upper limits of Cosmogenesis."[19] Teilhard moved theological discourse away from *only* understanding God as a static, apathetic, first mover, and from understanding redemption as a purely otherworldly end (although he did envision the end as purely spiritual and not material). Instead, he offered an understanding of God as active in our evolutionary world, yet eternally up ahead, drawing all of creation toward divinization. God cannot be merely a fixed end point; He was both the Prime Mover preceding the process of evolution and the "Gatherer and Consolidator, ahead of us,"[20] who connected the entire evolutionary process as one unified, eternal, sacred story of becoming. This hopeful eschatological vision allowed Teilhard to imagine new metaphors to describe God, including God as the "cosmic eddy"[21] of animating force behind every event from the energies inherent to an atom, to evolution, and to our vast mountain ranges. This, he claimed, is the intangible at the heart of the universe.[22] Teilhard's optimism and evocatively dynamic language inspired his readers to bathe themselves "in the ocean of matter"[23] so they can connect with the sacred heart of the risen Christ present in the world.

This pillar of an ETA requires grounding in three commitments: a radical optimism for all created life, the affirmation of unity in diversity, and the recognition of the movement of our unfinished cosmos toward completion in the risen Christ. There are many modern expressions of these truths and much is promised; therefore, when this pillar is embraced fully, a believer can fall deeply in love with "that endlessly rotting and renewing riot of life of which we are a clever and troublesome bit"[24] and be inspired to work tirelessly for peace, justice, and abundant life for all of creation—both now and at the end of time.

MODERN FRUITS

Modern voices in ecotheology express the three classic commitments, namely a radical optimism for the cosmos, an awareness of unity in diversity, and recognition of the world as a dynamic and unfinished adventure moving toward fulfillment in God.

Radical Optimism

Jürgen Moltmann has said that "everywhere people feel deceived, abused, dispirited, exploited, and estranged so that they no longer trust the inbuilt goals and hopes of our progressive societies, universities, churches, and sciences. They refuse to live goal-oriented and future-conscious, since they refuse to freeze that future in its present image."[25] Ecotheologian Arthur Peacocke concurs: "Hope has become one of the lost virtues of our age and its loss infects every aspect of our cultural and social life. 'Where there is no vision, the people perish' (Proverbs 29:18) applies as ever."[26] A robust vision of hope is needed to address humanity's vertigo caused by the false feeling of power over the world and our insatiable hunger to control every aspect of Earth, including the very evolutionary processes from which we emerged.[27] Thus, the vision of hope offered by the first pillar of an ETA is vital for reminding humanity of the source of all our proximate hopes: God's bottomless and overflowing love for creation.

Affirming Earth's worth by placing it within our visions of eschatological hope is important because human-centered visions of the end-time that exclude Earth's participation are diminishing our abilities to discern divine revelation in creation today and exacerbating our planet's rapidly destabilizing life systems. If there is no room for sparrows, or anyone that lives on the margins of human society in heaven, then why do we need to care for them now? Traditionally, believers have been entranced by the story of nature's fallenness from a state of static perfection and humanity's redemption as otherworldly (e.g., a spiritual and non-material "heaven"). Accordingly, at the end of time, all of creation, except for some humans (e.g., fully abled, dominant, civilized, male), will be destroyed. What this has cultivated is "a gospel of annihilation" and, as ecotheologian Catherine Keller states, this has promoted despair.[28] The vision of a fallen, chaotic creation, in turn, sanctions the destruction of the wilderness of Earth, and all those associated with Earth such as women or the core members of L'Arche, and places all hope in an otherworldly, disembodied existence.

In classic Christian eschatology, the *tehom* is often described as an evil wasteland or chaotic abyss; therefore, it must be controlled and ultimately vanquished at consummation or the end-time. Catherine Keller calls this demonizing of the primordial waters "tehomophobia," which is a dislike and fear of the chaotic aquatic wilderness at the beginning of creation. The reason humanity fears this watery chaos is because the wild always resists human exploitation and self-immortalization. This fear was translated into Christian doctrine as an unease and aversion to all things "mortal, fleshy, feminized, unpredictable and complex" and sanctioned the "indifference and even vengefulness of church and culture toward creation."[29] For example, "if the seas had been primordially identified as a churning waste, a watery wilderness, we have correspondingly treated them as the ultimate sewer."[30] Thus, the way to control the wilderness is to demand its final annihilation at the end-time; chaos will only be tamed by an ultimate form of order, namely a divinely sanctioned eradication. However, if we lose this phobia, then the vivid imagery of Revelation that announces that "the sea was no more" (Rev 21:1) can be understood as an astute ecological critique of the unjust imperial marketplace economy (facilitated by maritime trade). Once this critique is made, then the *eschaton* can be understood to proclaim the end of unjust economic paradigms carried out by those "whose trade is on the sea" (Rev 18:17) rather than the promotion of the vanquishing of the sea itself. Consequently, losing our tehomophobia will allows us to read Scripture with new eyes and discern new wisdom concerning eschatological hope.

Unity in Diversity

Developments in ecotheology have highlighted our universe's radical interconnectivity, which is the content of the next pillar and will be thoroughly investigated there. However, this interconnectivity impacts how Christians envision eschatological hope; every part of our diverse world contributes to the whole, and hence needs attention in any doctrine concerning hope.

Robert J. Russell explains that there is a unity in diversity, even in our empirical world. He asserts,

> A compelling case can be made that quantum systems are "non-local": when two particles that had been in a bound state are widely separated, their individual properties remain correlated in ways that defy a classical explanation. These correlations may indicate that the particles...remain part of a single, "non-separable" system.[31]

Thus, even at such small scales, individual parts of creation remain related to the whole, and the whole is dependent on each particular part. This empirical truth reminds believers that we are inextricably intertwined with the rest of creation; we all have a common origin and we all will have a shared destiny. This vision of unity, however, does not mean that we all have to have the same experience of the end-time. Unity in diversity is not a process of homogenization where those who are most powerful determine what the experience of God's embrace will be at the end of time. This is a human impulse that Rosemary Radford Ruether identifies as "imperial colonization": a process that eliminates all others for the propagation of one dominant religious idea, one dominant culture, economy, race, or gender.[32] Thus, the diversity of our world requires that serious theological attention be paid to the exclusivity or narrowness of Christian understandings of the end-time.

Our Unfinished Adventure Going Somewhere

Twentieth- and twenty-first-century artisans of science began to articulate the truth offered much earlier by wordsmiths, such as nature writer Richard Jefferies (1848–87), who articulated how divine chaos has "limitless hope and possibilities."[33] Modern ecotheologians have embraced this in their vision of hope that our universe is moving toward abundant life at the *eschaton* and that God is present and active—directing, sustaining, and empowering—at the chaotic edges of space and time. These grace-filled places and moments are brimming with potential for creativity and newness.[34] Interestingly, Catherine Keller indicates that the Greek meaning of *eschaton* is "edge," like a spatial or temporal rim, and only secondarily does it mean "end." Therefore, we can understand *eschaton* as the "edge" of chaos where a final new creation is achieved, not merely as a static end-time when chaos is defeated by order and material life is replaced by a better spiritual existence.[35]

Thanks to modern scientific explorations of chaos theory and other areas, the stranglehold of mechanical determinism and reductionism that emerged over the last four centuries has begun to diminish, leaving room in our imaginations for new understandings of time and space, uncertainty and order, matter and spirit, as well as a deeper appreciation of Earth's inherent transformational power. Humanity has awakened to the universe's infinitely open, creative *telos* or trajectory as well as our own emergence from Earth's creative impetus. We are part of, and contributors to, the complexity of our planet's life systems. For example, our scientific appreciation of Earth's hydrosphere, our growing knowledge of evolutionary transformations taking place on land, and the nature of ambiguity and uncertainty within indeterminate systems (e.g., tornados, tides, gas particles, and cloud formations) aid theological conversations regarding uncertainty, ambiguity, and God's providential care.

More recently, physicists and theoretical scientists such as Werner Heisenberg, David Bohm, and Stuart Kauffman have eloquently described the indeterminacy within quantum and atomic levels of life and the complexity in behavior systems (i.e., cells, neural networks, ecosystems, and economic systems) as cosmic *potentiality* lying hidden in disorder or chaos.[36] At a larger level, we can appreciate the great expanses of intertidal habitats as places of great creativity.[37] Some examples of creativity quite literally at the water's edge are the mudskipper fish, which use their pectoral fins to move and perch on mangrove roots, or the marine horseshoe crab, which scuttles over sandy beaches at night to spawn at the water's edge. Aquatic life transfigured within interfluent areas into terrestrial tetrapods, which then began to ramble across terra firma during the Devonian Period over 360 million years ago and diversified into every imaginable creature. Our whales are now appreciated as adventurous mammals that have returned to the hydrosphere but still retain the remnants of their former hip bones.

This new scientific appreciation of indeterminacy, ambiguity, and interconnectivity has allowed for the emergence of a new, "non-interventionist" and organic understanding of divine activity in the world.[38] Hence, planetary experiences of chaos, uncertainty, and the emergence of novelty do not have to be places of fear, desolation, and the absence of God; instead, they can remind us of how chaos, transformation, and cruciformity are built into the very fabric of the universe story. Having emerged from Earth, human existence must also include ambiguity and painful transformations. It all needs to be part of theological conversations concerning how we appreciate God's presence, power, and care. Hence, contemporary ecotheologians with a well-formed scientific Earth literacy have been able to describe the universe as evolving to the edge of chaos as it is drawn into the open horizon of the future by the risen Christ who is known as both the promise of new life and the cosmic Attractor, or Divine Magnetism, that directs and sustains Earth's own creative capabilities.[39] They have contributed to the renewal of a teleological understanding of how God is a personal deity who animates *theosis*, the luring of all creation toward the fullness of life. This new vision promises hope to sufferers who are experiencing alienation, futility, and loneliness in their chaos brought on in part by the vision of a purely mechanical and atomistic world and a distant, apathetic Creator of this "clock-like" world.[40]

The alternative being offered by ecotheology affirms that some randomness, indeterminacy, and chaos need not be something to fear, and God's providential care does not have to be limited to special moments of divine intervention. Appreciating Earth's potentiality and creativity present at the water's edge can inform our understanding of the term *Emmanuel*—God with us—and reveal God's presence and not absence during moments of great transformation. It can also speak to God's self-limitation and labor to bring forth new life from death. Thus, scientific Earth literacy of our universe story can offer new depth to how Christians understand hope, especially when one's suffering seems meaningless, when transformation seems impossible, and when great courage is needed to face that which thwarts individual and global well-being today.

SUMMARY

Via the new language and imagery, the many contributors to this pillar—old and new—describe a hope for the future that lives at the creative edges of vulnerability, uncertainty, and chaos. It is here where our continuously creative and loving God waits, eternally luring the cosmos toward abundant life, healing, and justice in the present moment and at the *eschaton*.

In light of planetary destabilization and widespread injustice, theology needs a new, prophetic horizon of hope, nourished by an appreciation of cosmogenesis. Theological conversations concerning eschatological hope cannot be blissfully ignorant of atrocities such as the Holocaust, the Rwandan genocide, or slavery. Nor should Christians believe these moments of sin and pure destruction are justified as a byproduct of natural selection or a warped belief that the more horrific the atrocities, the closer to the end (and perfection) humanity will be. Ultimate answers to how God reconciles, heals, and transforms these wounds of the past will always transcend human intellectual capacities, but modern Earth-literate eschatological visions of peace and justice at the *eschaton* can better equip people of faith to experience wholeness and healing in their lives, companion those who are suffering more compassionately, and labor diligently to address injustice in our world today.

6

SECOND PILLAR: THE INTRINSIC WORTH OF CREATION

Our sacred universe story affirms the intrinsic worth of each creature because each one is a unique realization of divine love and a contributor to the great unfolding cosmic story. This second pillar helps articulate how human dignity, worth, belonging, and purpose are derived from a much larger context of meaning, namely, the intrinsic worth of all other interconnected, interdependent, and diverse expressions of created life.

The pillar also affirms that our creaturely brothers and sisters are unique, material subjects in the universe story who are inspirited, or animated, by the Spirit, or *rūah* (life breath of God). One only has to look at the recent Catholic encyclical *Laudato Si'*, which states, "There is a divine manifestation in the blaze of the sun and the fall of night" (no. 85). In the incarnation, the Divine Word made flesh, God chose to take part in the material world in the fullest sense by embracing the biological tissue comprising all creatures over 13.8 billion years and the evolutionary processes out of which all life emerged. This vision of the incarnation expands beyond the historical time period of Jesus and is often called "deep" incarnation. Readers can find this stream of thought in the imaginations of ecotheologians such as Denis Edwards and Ilia Delio, who use ideas of deep incarnation to ascribe intrinsic worth to all of creation and not just human creatures.[1] Thus, much of modern ecotheological thought is centered on this second pillar.

This chapter illustrates that the intrinsic value of our sacred, evolving universe is characterized by interconnectivity, interdependence, and diversity. Like the first pillar, the vision of creation's intrinsic worth has deep roots in the Christian Tradition, but our modern scientific Earth literacy has allowed new nuances to emerge. Hence, this section will begin by exploring three ancient Christian sources: St. Maximus the Confessor's affirmation of interconnectivity, St. Francis of Assisi's vision of the interdependency and kinship, and St. Thomas Aquinas's radical affirmation of diversity. Subsequently, modern ecotheological visions of intrinsic worth will also be explored.

ANCIENT ROOTS

St. Maximus the Confessor

The writings of Maximus the Confessor (d. 662), as revealed by Hans Urs von Balthasar, demonstrate that Scripture and the cosmos narrate the same story of God's revelation but with different language and syntax. God's one sacred narrative speaks via two mediums, but the message is coherent in both: the created world possesses intrinsic value that is manifest in diversity and polarity. Although Maximus was not privy to modern scientific findings that reveal the deep interconnectedness of all created life, he still understood our world's profound interconnectedness with God. Maximus best describes his vision of connectivity in and through his understanding of Christ as Logos (Divine Wisdom that formed the universe).[2] For Maximus, the diverse created world is where the "incarnational mission is playing itself out to full completion,"[3] and he makes use of Irenaeus's term "recapitulation" to demonstrate both the union of the divine with the material world and the participation in God by all created things:

> This same Logos, whose goodness is revealed and multiplied in all the things that have their origin in him, with the degree of beauty appropriate to each being, recapitulates all things in himself (Eph 1:10). Through this Logos there came to be both being and continuing to be, for from

> him the things that were made came to be in a certain way and for a certain reason, and by continuing to be and by moving, they participate in God. For all things, in that they came to be from God, participate proportionally in God, whether by intelligence, by reason, by sense-perception, by vital motion, or by some habitual fitness.[4]

The interconnection of the cosmic Christ (Logos) with the architectural components, the *logoi* of the universe, is the source of the intrinsic worth of creation. This is best illustrated in the two natures of Christ. Maximus describes the intimate kinship between the divine and human natures of Christ via the phrase "theandric" (the coupling of the terms God [*theos*] and man [*andros*]), much like his predecessor Cyril of Alexandria (376–444) had done.[5] Maximus would not compromise his vision of a perfect union of the divine and of humanity in the person of Christ, nor his praise of "all the different syntheses between diverse creatures that are realized through Christ."[6] Ultimately, his commitments cost him his life; he refused to cave to political pressure to emphasize one nature of Christ over another and was exiled, where he succumbed thanks to the hardships he endured.

Maximus's dual commitment to the interconnectivity and worth of Christ's human and divine nature is a key component of modern ecotheological position, asserting that all creatures possess intrinsic worth. The *logoi* are intimately connected due to the singular source of their intrinsic value, the Logos. Consequently, all created life must be respected and honored, each in its own way. Hence, all of life's forms give glory to the Creator and prove that "heavenly and earthly beings join in a single festive dance, as they receive the gifts that come from God."[7] When this grounding of creation's intrinsic worth in the Divine Logos is coupled with Francis's vision of kinship, more nuance is added to our understanding of the intrinsic worth of creation.

St. Francis of Assisi

St. Francis of Assisi (1182–1226) did not write many texts, but his life lived in community and his beautiful canticle clearly resonate his beliefs as well as any book. One of his primary beliefs was that all of creation bore both intrinsic and instrumental worth thanks to the gift of the Spirit in the Pentecost event. For example, an earthworm is valuable not only because God made it, but also because this earthworm possesses instrumental worth and can be used as a source of food for a robin, which also possesses intrinsic worth. This resonates in Francis's Canticle of the Sun; sister moon and stars are "precious and beautiful" because God made them in the heavens (intrinsic worth), and it is by way of Brother Wind and precious Sister Water that God is praised and God's creatures are sustained (instrumental worth). Thus, intrinsic worth does not preclude a concurrent instrumental worth. However, intrinsic worth is never absent.

The second feature of Francis's primary belief focused on how the Holy Spirit connects all of creation in a deep fraternal kinship. It is the third Person of the Trinity offered concretely at Pentecost who is the "magnetic force," or familial bonds of love, bonding the three persons of the Trinity, and it is this same force that bonds and sustains all life.[8] In Francis's mind, the Holy Spirit affirms, preserves, and nourishes all creation, including "married women," "youths," "sick," "children," "all peoples everywhere on earth who are and will be,"[9] and all elements of the created world.[10]

Francis's affirmation of the diversity of our created world is quite provocative, both in his historical moment and ours. His belief was that the ascent to God (divinization) is actually achieved by a descent deep into the world. He saw Christ as a model for this; Christ descended into the world as the suffering servant, and hence, to become more intimate with God and Christlike, one must embrace the world as he did. To become more like God, one must immerse oneself into the material world and recognize that we are dependent on the rest of created life in our spiritual journey to God. We cannot find union with God when we are alienated from Earth. Francis believed that the ascent to God (a destiny we share with creation) is accomplished via a descent into the world and thus, is not just reserved for more ethereal creatures such as humans (or birds). Rather, all parts of creation work together to journey to God. This vision of interdependence is the basis for Francis's kinship model.[11] St. Francis modeled this deep kinship as he lived and loved within an interconnected and interdependent world as did Christ the Suffering Servant.

St. Thomas Aquinas

St. Thomas Aquinas (1225–74), in *Summa Contra Gentiles*, revealed how the created world affirms God, the Triune Creator, through its myriad forms: "God would not make the whole universe to be the best of its kind if he made all the parts the same, because many levels of goodness would be missing in such a universe."[12]

Similarly, in his *Summa Theologica*, Aquinas proclaimed, "For goodness which in God is simple and uniform, in creatures is manifold and divided; and hence the whole universe together participates in the divine goodness more perfectly, and represents it better than any single creature whatever."[13] Consequently, diversity reveals Godself better than singularity, so the diminishment of Earth's diversity via mass extinction events and the promotion of monocultures has serious theological ramifications: humanity will lose the ability to fully understand God's goodness. This truth makes saving Earth's bountiful creativity a spiritual endeavor.

Unfortunately, this facet of Aquinas's (and other subsequent theologians') work was missed or underemphasized due to the anthropocentric and hierarchical understanding of the world (e.g., the great chain of being) that saturated Aquinas's mindscape. Aquinas was not the only one to endure this fate; Augustine, Bonaventure, John Calvin, and Johannes Kepler all affirmed some degree of intrinsic worth of creation, but their human-centered bias prevented their full exposure.[14] Modern ecotheology has recovered this gem from Aquinas to emphasize the necessity of Earth's diversity to reveal God more fully and retrieved St. Thomas's love of all that is created without the accompanying hierarchy of worth.

Many modern ecotheological fruit have germinated from Maximus's exploration of cosmic and sacred polarities inherent to the Christ of Chalcedon, Francis's passionate kinship model, and Aquinas's systematic reverence of the range of God's creativity. From this firm root system, coupled with scientific Earth literacy, the intrinsic worth of creation can be appreciated in the interconnectedness, interdependence, and diversity that characterize creation. As a result, this second pillar of an ETA challenges a disembodied Christianity, radical individualism, and the systematic destruction of biological and cultural diversity that is currently putting all futurity into question.

MODERN FRUIT

Earth's Prolific Creativity

To begin, Earth's immense creative urge will be explored. Maximus, Aquinas, and Francis, living in the sixth and thirteenth centuries, could not have even begun to imagine the scale of Earth's interconnectivity, interdependency, and diversity; even the seventeenth-century mindscape thought that the upper limit of Earth's creative ability was only about ten thousand species of invertebrates.[15] Today, we know that in a small amount of soil there could be upwards of ten trillion bacteria (representing as many as ten thousand species), that the class Arachnida (spiders) manifests in more than thirty-eight thousand species, but it is the viruses that outnumber all other life forms—over ten million varieties exist in the virosphere that pervades every ecosystem on Earth.[16] Biologist Colin Tudge affirms Earth's prolific urge to create that will continue to elude perfect scientific tally:

> We don't even know how many kinds of creatures there are—how diverse biodiversity really is. So far biologists have listed around two million different species. But about 30 years ago an American scientist counted all the beetles in one fairly ordinary tree in Panama and found 1100 species of them, many of which were new to science; and beetles are only one group among many—what about the mites and worms and fungi and goodness knows what else. From all this he concluded that in the world as a whole there could be 30 million different species—but that's not counting microbes, of which there could be hundreds of millions of kinds. Now most biologists feel that he may have got carried away, and there are probably (only!) between five and eight million. But we don't know.[17]

Earth's creativity will continue to astound human imaginations, but it is clear that our knowledge of Earth's prolific creativity is vastly different from our theological predecessors and affects how the Creator of this world, and creation itself, is appreciated by believers. However, there are other scientific discoveries that have impacted the way ecotheologians envision the intrinsic worth of our universe as well. Some of these include the common origin of the universe and the physical consanguinity of our 13.8-billion-year family history. Robert J. Russell writes that "the discovery that all things had a common origin at t = 0 can inspire a spirituality of connectedness through a cosmological common origin to all creatures."[18] This new spirituality has been inspired by the modern telling of our sacred universe story that highlights a common birth and physical connectivity spanning immense amounts of time. When connected with St. Francis's premodern kinship models of solidarity, believers have a powerful way of imagining the intrinsic worth of creation.

God's Prolific Creativity

Reflection on Earth's fertility and creative tendencies has also allowed ecotheologians to connect a key component of Christianity's doctrine of Creation, God's continuing activity in the world (*creatio continua*) with Earth's own creative impulses (*concursus*). This recognition of biodiversity as the fruits of God's continuing creative endeavors that began at the moment life began (*creatio originalis*) and God's ultimate creation of new life at the eschaton (*creatio nova*) speaks to the intrinsic worth of creation in new ways. Other core theological constructs have been reimagined by theologians possessing a robust Earth literacy, resulting in new paths of investigation concerning intrinsic worth of creation. These include a focus on the unity of diversity that is the Trinity, the incarnation as a manifestation of evolutionary emergence, and the Creator Spirit as the green face of God.[19]

One clear example of how scientific Earth literacy has changed the way modern believers articulate the intrinsic worth of creation is the work of Sean McDonagh, one of the ecological midwives discussed in chapter 4. McDonagh indicates that Earth's creativity is an attribute of God and can be understood as an outpouring of the Divine creative urge: "The principle of expressive Being which we identify with the Father is the urge to create. This outpouring surge of energy manifests itself in our highly differentiated universe…all finely tuned into one living community."[20] Thus, Earth's intrinsic worth is connected to divine creativity and is characterized by diversity rather than homogeneity. McDonagh also allows his understanding of biodiversity and cosmogenesis to impact how he connects the intrinsic worth of creation with the incarnation:

> Each reality in the universe has its own inner radiance, which points to and reflects the ultimate mystery of God.... If, for example, flowering trees and shrubs had not appeared 300 million years ago, then mammalian life would not have followed. Without that concentration of nutrients no human being, including Christ, would ever have walked on Earth. So that particular memory and every other memory of the emergent process is carried within the Christ reality. In him all things are united.[21]

Hence, like those who preceded, ecotheologians affirm that the intrinsic worth of the cosmos is because of God's presence and activity within the world. However, this truth has come alive in new ways thanks to their scientific knowledge of Earth's tendency toward creativity that is beautifully manifested in the biodiversity of Earth's many webs of life.

Humanity's Prolific Creativity

Scientific Earth literacy has allowed a more nuanced understanding of intrinsic worth in the imaginations of believers, and this has had several results. First, it has allowed humanity to imagine the term *respect* as a potent verb that can elicit a response to difference or alterity, which counteracts today's fear (and rejection) of the unfamiliar, including Earth's communities from which we have become estranged. This verb is more profound than merely tolerating, acquiescing, or homogenizing difference (e.g., the "melting pot" metaphor) because each "other" can reflect something of God and should be embraced for who they are and what they bring to creation (e.g., the "salad" metaphor).

Another result of our scientific discoveries is an awareness that humans are always participants in life rather than mere observers; there are no disengaged believers, only participants and subjects who uniquely contribute to (and/or frustrate) the realization of Earth's creative potential. This challenges us to name who we see as intrinsically worthy or authentic dialogue partners in theological conversations.

A third result of a deeper appreciation of the intrinsic worth of our interconnected, interdependent, and diverse universe is the ability to critique radical forms of individuality and distorted understandings of autonomy prevalent in human societies today. The "I am an island" mentality is empirically mistaken; the iron in our blood, the calcium in our bones, the carbon used in photosynthesis, the nickel buried in the mountains, the helium we inhale from balloons (to change the tenor of our voices at birthday parties), tell us that we are not radically separate beings who can extract ourselves from our dependency on the cosmos for abundant life. All the elements of our bodies were forged as early as three minutes after the Big Bang and in the cores of stars that died long ago. They are telling us our family history, for we are literally stardust of long dead stars.[22] Consequently, the radical individualism we cherish as the basis for the modern socioeconomic belief in personal accumulation of wealth is inaccurate; however, this new knowledge ought to inspire humanity to embrace interdependency and solidarity as the foundations of human society.

Invigorating Our Care of Creation

A final fruit of a more nuanced theological appreciation of intrinsic worth is the realization that we are destroying Earth; the rate of habitat loss, mega-extinctions, ecosystem disruptions, and the immense loss of biodiversity and cultural diversity are significant features of our current ecological and human crisis. This loss of diversity is a death knell for Earth and all its creatures, as international activist and scientist Dr. Vandana Shiva attests.[23] This reality must impact, and be impacted by, theological constructs. Thankfully our new context is resonating in Christian theology. For example, Sean McDonagh has written regarding the threat GMOs pose to our world, including human populations.[24] He allows his Earth-centered understanding of the Spirit and the incarnation to help him respond to this crisis:

> The Spirit leads us to a deep respect for the beauty of the world and the balance in nature. He also leads us to a deep appreciation for the dignity and excellence of people. Violence to the ecological balance in nature and violence to the rights of people are a contradiction to the Gospel.[25]

The reality of planetary destruction must be countered by passionate, scientifically Earth-literate believers who have a broad appreciation of the intrinsic worth of creation. Only a vision of intrinsic worth characterized by interconnectivity, interdependence, and diversity will inspire more adequate and just ethical practices that protect our planetary home. For example, readers saw earlier that St. Thomas spoke of the need for diversity in creation to manifest God's self-revelation,[26] but this Earth-centered affirmation did not inform his vision of theological virtues, which remained human-centered. Contemporary ecotheologian James Nash, on the other hand, is aware of our current mass extinction event (the sixth in Earth's history) caused by human activities. He indicates that "the destruction of habitat—which may be a single type or size of tree or grass—will mean the extinction or numerical decline of a species. And if the species is a "keystone," on which many other species are dependent in the intricate bridgework of nature, whole ecosystems may decline or disintegrate."[27] Nash's new knowledge about our world does impact his vision of theological virtues; to achieve abundant life, happiness, and moral excellence, he offers nine ecological virtues that Aquinas could not have even imagined. These include sustainability, adaptability, relationality, frugality, equity, solidarity, biodiversity, sufficiency, and humility.[28]

Another contemporary theologian who calls believers to care more vigorously for creation is Jay McDaniel. He is very aware of our ecocrisis and has let this inform his understanding of moral virtues. He claims that to overcome the anthropocentrism of the past and to adopt a biocentric (Earth-centered) ethic of care requires the embrace of three "moral virtues": (1) a reverence for life articulated as an "inward disposition that is respectful of, and caring for, other animals, plants, and the Earth" and that refuses to "draw a sharp dichotomy between human life and other forms of life"; (2) a commitment to noninjury or nonviolence articulated as the refraining (as much as is possible) "from the violation of other creatures' interests"; and (3) an exercise of active goodwill understood as "the active fostering of opportunities for an animal to realize its interests."[29] Thus, for modern theological imaginations, biodiversity is both an empirical fact and a moral value, and the appreciation of how connected, interdependent, and diverse our world is has very real moral dimensions to which theology must attend.

This attention can take many forms. For example, if other-than-human species, such as indigenous Amazon flora, obscure oceanic invertebrates, or nocturnal cave dwellers, are intrinsically worthy as our kin, then we must keep in balance their instrumental worth to humans (e.g., food, medicine, and so on) with their intrinsic worth. Another example is fishing: the sacrifice of the lives of fish to sustain human lives. This activity can be affirmed as good when the appropriate reverence is demonstrated (i.e., an appreciation of fish as a manifestation of divine revelation) and the ecosystems that fish belong to are not harmed (and perhaps are enhanced by human interactions). Christians who are equipped with a broader understanding of Earth's biospiritual nature and intrinsic worth can join other prophetic voices condemning unjust ethical practices, such as trawling for fish with nets the size of football fields to accumulate profit for corporations located far from the impacts of their activities. These activities can be called sinful because they endanger ecosystemic biodiversity by not respecting the sacredness of Earth in all its myriad forms. Humanity's infringement on and destruction of habitats, regardless of whether it is by the paving and concretizing of massive swaths of the lithosphere, by poisoning the hydrosphere, or by the constant bombardment of the atmosphere with pollution and artificial light, does not recognize the intrinsic worth of those deemed "other."

Furthermore, we know with frightening clarity that the diminishment of Earth's biodiversity mirrors the loss of diversity in human communities. Ecofeminists have illustrated how the adoption of rigid dualisms of worth that render certain groups (women, nature/animals, nondominant ethnicities, the poor, the disabled) inferior to and always at the service of their more "superior" opposite (men, humans, white people, the wealthy, the fully-abled) has diminished diversity and promoted stagnant and nonsustainable monocultures.[30] Adopting a worldview that promotes interconnectedness, interdependence, and diversity helps to uncover and deconstruct these dualisms. It is this second pillar of an ETA that allows individuals to speak prophetically of the worth of those within our human family who fall outside of constructed cultural norms, whose "otherness" manifests physically, mentally, economically, socially, or ethnically, and causes them to be marginalized and exploited by the powerful. The wellspring of love for our human sisters and brothers is far deeper when it is God's overflowing love of our entire sacred universe rather than just God's love of humans. The latter's vision of God's love is too shortsighted. Not only does this pillar help us to love our human brethren better, it will also expose the "hemorrhaging of biological diversity today"[31] that is destroying our planetary home.

SUMMARY

In conclusion, the second pillar of an ETA affirms the intrinsic value of creation in all its diverse, interconnected, and interdependent manifestations. This is a vital component of any relational framework that strives to inform how humanity ought to live, love, and suffer as members of our planetary community. We need to embrace the truth that "each creature lives in God's presence, and has its own relationship with God, to whom it is all valuable and intimately known. Only after that realization may questions of human ethical conduct arise."[32]

The sacred cosmic story is a wondrous, divinely inspired kaleidoscope of creativity that tells an intimate account of kinship within a cosmic web of life and with the Creator of such a world. It is this new awareness that must inform human pursuits, including theology. Modern visions of intrinsic worth informed by our encounters with the evolutionary cosmos will allow for more fruitful theological conversations of some of the more painful parts of the universe story, such as physical limitation, extinction, predation, and suffering.

7

THIRD PILLAR: OUR SACRED COSMIC COMMUNION

Following Pope Francis's groundbreaking "green" encyclical, *Laudato Si'*, many around the world are publically reclaiming the sacredness of our planetary home.[1] But why are we *re*claiming this? When did we lose the ability to appreciate Earth as sacred? As was seen in earlier chapters, with the entrancement of theological imaginations using the machine metaphor, there was little tolerance for understanding Earth as alive and even less for speaking of an imminent, animating Spirit in creation. When this metaphor was coupled with the rising anthropocentrism, believers' ability to understand the closeness of God, the working of God in and through creation, and the sacredness of our world shriveled. Thus, as Carolyn Merchant aptly expressed in the title of her book, the eighteenth century marked the "death of nature" and a desacralizing of our universe. But as was also noted earlier, not everyone was enamored with the machine metaphor.

Before looking at more contemporary dissenting voices, let us look at a few nineteenth-century voices working outside science. A good example is Lord Byron (1788–1824). He was an English poet and prominent figure in the Romantic Movement who rebelled against the highly ordered and materialistic scientific worldview to offer an alternative way of encountering the world. Between 1812 and 1818,

Lord Byron published a protracted poem, *Childe Harold's Pilgrimage*, and this narrative described a journey of conversion to a deeper more authentic experience of the created world. One example is the canto below:

> There is a pleasure in the pathless woods,
> There is a rapture on the lonely shore.
> There is society where none intrudes,
> By the deep Sea, and music in its roar:
> I love not Man the less but Nature more,
> From these our interviews in which to steal
> From all I may be, or have been before,
> To mingle with the Universe, and feel
> What I can ne'er express, yet cannot all conceal.[2]

Another prominent poet of the Victorian era who was inspired by Lord Byron's worldview was Elizabeth Barrett Browning (1806–61). In her poem *Aurora Leigh*, she begins with the firm affirmation that "truth, so far, in my book / the truth which draws through all things upwards, / that a twofold world must go to a perfect cosmos. Natural things And spiritual, / who separates those two in art, in morals, or the social drift tears up the bond of nature and brings death."[3] Hence, our encounter with the physical world, especially its wild places and lonely shores, is much more than merely a material encounter with the parts of a machine. It is also an encounter with the divine.

Modern voices are also articulating this truth but in ways that differ from the aforementioned poets thanks to their scientific and theological Earth literacy. For example, in *Dream of the Earth*, Thomas Berry envisions Earth as a biospiritual planet and our primary referent for encountering the numinous.[4] Pope Francis articulates these sentiments quite poetically:

> The universe unfolds in God, who fills it completely. Hence, there is a mystical meaning to be found in a leaf, in a mountain trail, in a dewdrop, in a poor person's face. The ideal is not only to pass from the exterior to the interior to discover the action of God in the soul, but also to discover God in all things. (*Laudato Si'* 233)

Thus, Byron, Browning, Berry, and Pope Francis's intuitive coupling of the sacred and cosmic inspires the third pillar of an ETA and instructs believers to immerse themselves in the ocean of the divine present in and beyond our world. But to move beyond the machine metaphor and achieve this immersion, we need to explore the deep Christian roots of this pillar.

Abbess St. Hildegard of Bingen and Jesuit Pierre Teilhard de Chardin offer the deep roots of this third pillar. Both are theologians and artisans of science, but with the latter privy to knowledge of evolutionary mechanisms and the former, not. The commonality among nineteenth-century poets, a German twelfth-century mystic, and a French Jesuit paleontologist is their ability to articulate their encounter with the ineffable lying at the heart of the cosmos. And just as the Earth's landscape is solid but never still, Hildegard's understanding of *viriditas*—inspirited, embodied fecundity—and Teilhard de Chardin's dual commitment to the cosmic and numinous, give this third pillar both a solid footing within the Christian Tradition as well as the space and sustenance to develop new creative expressions of this synthesis.

ANCIENT ROOTS

St. Hildegard of Bingen

St. Hildegard of Bingen (1098–1179) was astutely conscious of the sacred balance, dynamism, and order of the universe. This perception of the world offers much to a contemporary ETA. Her articulation of God's overflowing, powerful, vivifying, redeeming, and sustaining love as *viriditas*, defined as "an inspired and embodied fecundity"—the "greening freshness of life"—is a vital aspect of her legacy.[5] This is seen vividly in her hymn *Item De Virginibus*, where she used *viriditas* to describe God's overflowing goodness: "O most noble Greenness, rooted in the sun, shining forth in streaming splendor upon the wheel of Earth."[6] Later, in her hymn *De Sancta Maria*, she described Mary, the mother of God, as the "greenest, most fertile branch."[7] Also, in the hymn *De Sancto Disibodo*, she celebrated St. Disibode as the "life-giving greenness of God's hand."[8] Therefore, Hildegard used *viriditas* to describe God and God's grace working in and through the created world, including the saints. However, Hildegard's primary use of this vitality was to describe the main activity of the Word, Christ, whom she indicated "has kindled every spark of life" and has "awaken[ed] everything to life."[9] Matthew Fox, in *Illuminations of Hildegard of Bingen*, explains how this term *viriditas* celebrates the "exquisite greening of trees and grasses" as well as the bringing of "lush greenness to shriveled and wilted people."[10] Renate Craine, a student of Hildegarde, affirmed Fox's perspective, indicating that *viriditas* is a "Christic dynamic, or the symbol of dying and rising in everyday life."[11] Consequently, Earth's "greening power" is an evocative metaphor in Hildegard's writings and is a multivalent symbol that affirms the coupling of the cosmic and numinous.[12]

This way of encountering the world effectively dismantles the prevailing dualistic view of matter and spirit inherent to classic theological anthropologies. It also articulates her radically immanent understanding of God's Otherness and creative power within the universe. Her analogy of greening power to describe an important attribute of the divine nature is more helpful for describing God's relation with our evolutionary world than that of the potter or craftsman (as described in Isa 64:8; 2 Cor 4:7; Rom 9:20, 21), for the latter evokes purely human-oriented understandings of God (the potter is a human vocation), and the product of God's creative efforts is a complete, static object (a pot). Hildegard's metaphor of *viriditas* allows the product of God's creativity to have room to grow, and greening power is a vocation more affiliated with Earth than humans. Hildegard's appreciation of *viriditas* as immanent Otherness (i.e., cosmic-numinous) penetrates, animates, and transforms the very depths of the material world. As such, it is a vital contribution to modern attempts to understand God and God's activity in an evolving universe.

Another key facet of her anthropology is the belief that creation is birthed within God, out of God's very spiritual essence, rather than God withdrawing Godself to allow space for creation. In her art, hymns, and writings, she drew upon the imagery of pregnancy and interconnected concentric circles to illustrate this profound intimacy of the divine Spirit of God and the material world. Marsha Newman outlines this aspect of Hildegard's worldview:

> Hildegard's was a very visual and visceral experience of the spirit, prompting her to create an intricate symbolic expression of nature and the universe. What some have thought to

> be the feminine aspects of Hildegard's art emerge in images of womb-like enclosures, and images of fertility, like the world egg and the mandala; and of pregnancy, with the child fully depicted within its mother's translucent womb. She sees evidence of the spirit in the life-giving universe: the begetting of children, the blossoming of plants. These are for her symbols of the pregnancy of matter with spirit, and therefore of the holiness of the material universe.[13]

Hildegard also did not shy away from a corporal earthiness within her descriptions of the divine incarnation:

> You see that that fire has a flame in it the color of the sky, which burns ardently with a gentle breath, and which is as inseparably within the blazing fire as the viscera are within a human being;...But after he assumed flesh, the Word also remained inseparably in the Father; for as a person does not exist without the vital movements within his viscera. So the only Word of the Father could in no way be separate from Him.[14]

The communion of spirit and matter is elegantly articulated as a spiritual ambience from within matter not unlike the internal quickening during pregnancy. This prohibits a sharp separation of spirit and matter, which occurs when the Spirit of God is seen as an external force being imposed by God from a distance. Barbara Newman recognizes this in Hildegard's writing: "Hildegard's keen sense of divine immanence led her to envisage the creative power not as a force propelling the world from without but as an ambiance enfolding it and quickening it from within."[15] Hildegard's synthesis of the numinous and cosmic, based on her understanding of *viriditas* and *ariditas*, was not an abstract exercise but guided her medical, moral, sacramental, and ecclesial practices.[16]

Pierre Teilhard de Chardin

Although he had access to twentieth-century scientific discoveries including the theory of evolution, Pierre Teilhard de Chardin's work also embraced the deep intimacy of the sacred and the cosmic that

Hildegard professed. He stated that "a different view now prevails: in a universe whose evolutive structure has finally been appreciated, matter and spirit are not seen as two terms mutually integrated in the unity of one and the same movement (spirit emerging experientially in the world only upon progressively more fully synthesized matter)."[17] Teilhard believed in a personal God who was eternally laboring in the world to divinize and redeem it: "God is at work within life. He helps it, raises it up, gives it the impulse that drives it along, the appetite that attracts it, the growth that transforms it. I can feel God, touch him, 'live' him in the deep biological current that runs through my soul and carries it with it."[18] His dual commitment to the divine and to the world, encountered through science and theology, is how he articulated the communion of the cosmic and numinous. Teilhard named the numinous or sacred dimension of the created world as "Christic Density," and he claimed that this was deeply interconnected with the "cosmic Density" he discovered in his studies of evolution.[19] In one of his many letters, Teilhard exclaims,

> My views, as you know, hardly change, but they simplify themselves and interlock with such an increase of intensity—in the interplay (so wonderfully contrived) of what I call the two lines of curvature (or convergence)—the cosmic ('natural') and the Christic ('supernatural').[20]

Teilhard's cosmic-Christic synthesis is what this pillar calls the numinous-cosmic communion and Teilhard was introducing this to reawaken humanity to the presence of the sacred in the world during a time when Western scientific minds promoted an alienation from Earth as machine. Teilhard was able to develop Hildegard's Christic understanding of *viriditas* by understanding the incarnation in light of evolution. He also developed new language to describe how God dwells at the heart of the cosmos and animates the evolutionary processes toward the Omega point—the sacred heart of the risen Christ.

Thus, both Teilhard and Hildegard searched for and found the numinous at the heart of created life in all its grandeur and limitations, but their journeys never ended with this discovery. For these great minds, this numinous-cosmic communion was not a noun but a verb, inspiring their actions in the world. This great legacy has been passed to ecotheologians who allow modern scientific discoveries about our world to draw them closer to the numinous heart of our world.

MODERN FRUIT

The third pillar of ETA affirms that Earth is a biospiritual planet. As a result, humanity becomes one of many unique, interconnected manifestations of this creative communion of matter and spirit, rather than the solitary bearer of a static image of the Creator. Earth literacy, humans, and all of Earth's constitutive parts have been repositioned within a much larger galactic context that speaks poignantly of the biospiritual (numinous-cosmic) nature of the cosmos, Earth, and the human person. Consequently, this deep unity of the sacred and the cosmic needs to be incorporated into an authentic Christian anthropology. If we believe that our world is a sacred communion of cosmic subjects and we (alongside Earth's many other subjects) are participating in the communication of divine revelation, then humanity will be liberated from the distorted view that we are the only subjects and beneficiaries of the doctrine of creation and redemption. The Earth will also be liberated from being a spiritually bereft, static machine. Both emancipations are necessary to understand further God's self-communication in the Book of Scripture and the Book of Nature. Rediscovering both sources of divine revelation will also add new content to theological investigations of the mystery of suffering.

So what are some ways in which the cosmos speaks of the interconnectivity of matter and spirit? Since spirituality is beyond the purview of science but matter is not, let us begin first with the creation of matter. NASA has given believers a scientific portrait of our universe's birth:

> According to the theories of physics, if we were to look at the Universe one second after the Big Bang, what we would see is a 10-billion degree sea of neutrons, protons, electrons, anti-electrons (positrons), photons, and neutrinos. Then, as time went on, we would see the Universe cool, the neutrons either decaying into protons and electrons or combining with protons to make deuterium (an

> isotope of hydrogen). As it continued to cool, it would eventually reach the temperature where electrons combined with nuclei to form neutral atoms.[21]

In a modern rendition of Carl Sagan's cosmic clock,[22] Neil DeGrasse Tyson offers a gorgeous recreation of NASA's above depiction at the beginning of most episodes on his TV show *Cosmos*. Tyson choses to use a calendar rather than a clock to show viewers just how long our universe story is and how January 1, the birth of all matter and energy, began with quite a bang![23] Viewers are shown how inextricably intertwined matter and energy were at the beginning of time. It is Earth literate theologians who address the spiritual implications of this creation narrative; this moment the universe burst forth was the great creative birthing of abundant life within God from a primordial singularity of unadulterated and undifferentiated energy. God was the source of the "celestial furnace" out of which all matter and energy emerged, and our Milky Way galaxy is just one of billions of galaxies within this ever-expanding universe.[24]

A scientific meditation upon the remarkably dynamic and radically interconnected state of matter and energy at the origin of the universe can help believers understand the dance of the biological and spiritual that began at the Great Flaring forth and continues today. God is the source of all energy whether it is Hildegarde's greening power or the divine energy carried by the biological currents through Teilhard's soul.

The intimacy of matter and energy at the beginning of time (and now) offers a way of understanding the intimacy of the numinous and the material world. This is impossible with the static machine metaphor. Believers can understand how all matter, derived from the originating movement of God making space in Godself for the cosmos, reflects a primordial communion of the numinous and cosmic in God. In addition, the ongoing process of differentiation of matter and energy in our unfolding universe can be a more dynamic model to help believers describe how the Spirit can continue to be present and active in the world without being trapped in matter.

The machine metaphor is also incompatible with other new scientific findings that suggest the whole is more than the sum of its parts; intimate scientific encounters with our cosmos are telling believers that there is something ineffable in the world. For example, chaos theories in mathematics, such as the butterfly effect, point to an elegant unpredictability inherent in our material world that transcends purely mechanistic natural laws that govern life and physical structures.[25] The field of epigenetics grapples with the mystery of how external lifestyle changes act at a genetic level by the turning off of detrimental genes (e.g., those promoting heart disease, inflammation, or oncogenes) and the turning on of disease-preventing genes.[26]

Another example of our planet's inherent unpredictability and grace, beyond what machines are capable of, is demonstrated by monarch butterflies, spawning salmon, or migrating geese; zoology has recognized that each creature is beautifully adapted and equipped with diverse gifts of perception (e.g., electromagnetic sensory perception) to encounter creation uniquely within their own niche, and this occurs in ways humanity may never fully understand. Neurobiology also wrestles with the elusive and complex nature of consciousness that defies a purely physiological explanation. Likewise, recent explorations into the "Dark Universe" in astrophysics has turned upside down our perception of the cosmos; dark matter and dark energy, whose existence and properties can only be inferred, constitute approximately 96 percent of the universe, whereas ordinary physical matter (e.g., planets, stars, and so on) makes up just marginally more than 4 percent.[27]

These findings, coupled with the celebrated discovery of the Higgs boson particle in March 2013—an entity that is neither force nor matter and yet fills the universe—offers a radical departure from classical notions of Earth as a machine. These few examples uncover the inadequacy of the machine metaphor, and consequently, believers are free to encounter creation differently. If we open ourselves to new possibilities afforded by the unpredictable creativity inherent in our material world, we will discover new things about God, including our participation in a numinous-cosmic communion.

As the earlier nineteenth-century poets, twelfth-century mystic, and nineteenth-century Jesuit attest, science alone cannot ground this third pillar. Modern scientific discoveries have, however, fed the imaginations of many theologians and helped in the retrieval of the Holy Spirit as an ecological hermeneutic for understanding our biospiritual planetary communion. For example, Mark Wallace (and others), describe the third Person of the Trinity as the "Earth God of the Bible" who infuses all things with her sensuous presence, transformative vitality, and the essence for constructing a sustainable spirituality responsive to our evolutionary reality and planetary crisis.[28]

Matthew Fox also highlights that Wisdom literature offers a sensual description of the numinous Spirit to such a degree that it is "almost voluptuous."[29] This sensuality is only viable in the minds of believers if it is intimately connected to matter (human bodies). Other ecotheologians, such as Elizabeth Johnson, also explore the synthesis of the mystical, numinous, and spiritual in material existence and offer a dynamic vision of this. For example, Johnson offers ways of describing the immanent Creator Spirit as the one "who pervades the world in the dance of life."[30] Thus, as scientific and theological Earth literacy intertwined more purposefully after the 1980s, it has become clear that life can be characterized by two dimensions held together in a creative synthesis: the material and spiritual. Accordingly, this third pillar plays a vital role in reinvigorating Christian anthropology.

SUMMARY

Ecotheologians are encountering reality very differently from some classical theologians formed by a mechanical worldview or peers who still embrace the machine metaphor. Hence, an ETA can recover and discover deeper, more ancestral perceptions of biospirituality atrophied by the ideas of Descartes and others. It awakens us to how our intellectual bias toward mechanistic processes and purely material origins are diminishing our abilities to perceive the divine in our midst. When people of faith cultivate a rich scientific and theological Earth literacy and appreciate the numinous-cosmic communion, humanity will encounter the sacred in long-forgotten relationships with our other-than-human brothers and sisters, and truly appreciate the intrinsic worth of our planetary communion of subjects.

The worldview offered by this pillar enhances our appreciation of what many have known intuitively for centuries: the cry of the wild pierces us to the heart of our being, awakening our cosmic memories "more familiar to us than our mother's voice."[31] The presence of the numinous at the birth and unfolding of our universe is the source of these memories of a deep ontological kinship. They are held in the very genetic coding of the human body and in the sacred spaces where we dwell. Therefore, this awakening to the numinous-cosmic communion allows "the experience of the trees and flowers, birds and wind and stars, rocks and the sight and sound of the rivers and the sea" to once more satisfy our deepest psychological and spiritual needs because they rekindle in us "memories" of an even deeper childhood.[32] Botanist and theologian John Feehan also indicates that this is not just experienced by humans; when every creature fulfills the role and purpose in creation that it is bequeathed, it is not only an ecological fact, but also, it is a manifestation of the numinous.[33]

John Muir knew this. His lyrical account of the sooty gray bird called the American dipper describes the coupling of the numinous and cosmic. Muir explains that in its genes, proteins, morphology, and behavior, this aquatic insectivore is so attuned to its environment, belonging so intimately and joyfully to its dwelling place, that it resonates and emanates the spirit of the stream or waterfall. He states, "In a general way [this bird's] music is that of the streams refined and spiritualized."[34] Thus, this pillar can reinforce humanity's intuitive awe of creation, broaden the circle of intrinsic worth to those beyond the parameters of the human species, and amplify the human antiphon to the sacred gift of creation "so that it is now more than a cry: it is a hosanna."[35] Our appreciation of the numinous-cosmic communion should also feed our horror at the destruction of Earth and the extinction of Earth's many creatures by human hands.[36]

The communion of the numinous and cosmic is that which connects, vivifies, and sustains all created life—past, present, and future—in our unfolding cosmic family history. Hildegard, Teilhard de Chardin, and contemporary ecotheologians describe this communion as a dynamic, creative synthesis that can become distorted when one of these poles—either the numinous or cosmic—is overemphasized to the detriment of the other. This is what happened during the Enlightenment when the numinous was disassociated from the cosmic. This had wide ramifications: the alienation of humans from God in creation that then made it easy to justify using this machine (Earth) to benefit the only creature endowed with access to the numinous (e.g., via a soul).

The machine metaphor, devoid of any spiritual dimension, set in motion patterns of thinking and behaviors that are threatening the survival of our planetary home. For believers, this distortion has also inhibited our ability to understand God as the one who responds in great love and lament to suffering. It was hard for believers to see how a distant, apathetic Clockmaker was endlessly toiling to redeem our unfinished and sinful world, relieve our suffering, and transform our lives. However, believers with a well-formed Earth literacy can witness to the inextricable intertwining of the numinous and cosmic in such a way that the Book of Nature can once more serve as a profound source of our experience of God. This will cultivate what Robert J. Russell calls "kataphatic spirituality," one that appreciates the "numinous encounter with the Holy in and through nature," and can help transform how we understand many human experiences, including suffering.[37] This pillar, alongside the first two, is crucial for how we perceive our world, God, and humanity. However, it is the fourth pillar that demands that serious theological attention be paid to the painful aspects of our evolutionary world. Under this intense scrutiny, a new concept—the kenotic-kinetic—will be introduced to help believers to engage better with both the joy and pain of the sacred universe story.

8

FOURTH PILLAR: KENOSIS AS THE KINETIC OF CREATION

Philosopher Holmes Rolston III wrote poignantly of the cruciformity of our evolutionary world: "Biological nature is always giving birth, regenerating, always in travail. Something is always dying and something is always living on....This whole evolutionary upslope is a calling in which renewed life comes by blasting the old. Life is gathered up in the midst of its throes, a blessed tragedy lived in grace through a besetting storm."[1] Biologist Ursula Goodenough also indicates that "death is the price paid to have trees and clams and birds and grasshoppers, and death is the price paid to have human consciousness."[2] Scientists Lynn Margulis and Dorion Sagan also affirm the dark side of nature by indicating that Alfred Tennyson's popular depiction of nature as "red in tooth and claw" might just as well have cast nature as "green in stem and leaf."[3] Theologian Niels Gregersen affirms that this cosmic sacrifice is part of the birthing woes of nature's "unstoppable creativity,"[4] while Gloria Schaab's midwifery description of God as transcendent Mother birthing "the incarnate cosmos through the immanent creativity of the cosmos itself" gives readers a way of understanding the pain inherent in our evolving world.[5]

This final pillar of an ETA pays serious theological attention to the dark side of our creative, unfolding universe and uncovers the sacrificial dialectic of receptivity inherent in the world. This painful dialectic speaks of the suffering inherent in bringing forth newness and is called the *kenotic-kinetic*. This term, which will be explored in more depth in chapter 10, has been designed to represent the unique relationship between creativity and cruciformity that can also be seen as self-actualization (or self-affirmation) and self-sacrifice (or self-emptying). It is this movement between self-actualization/creativity and self-sacrifice/cruciformity that characterizes our evolutionary world at many levels. For example, new genetic codes erupt via the disintegration of that which went prior; the fragments of hipbones in whales echo a lost terrestrial identity; the human appendix is a relic of a super-fibrous, bygone era but has been repurposed as a hotel for good bacteria. Both self-actualization (i.e., creation or new code; new modes of locomotion; repurposing) and self-emptying (i.e., disintegration of previous code; loss of ability to walk; becoming superfluous) can occur at the individual level but can also occur at the community and planetary level.

The term *kenotic* in this phrase has been chosen because it is derived from *kenosis*. *Kenosis* is derived from the Greek terms *keno* and *kenoein*, meaning "to empty." From Scripture, kenosis can be understood as two movements occurring in the life of Christ (affirming and emptying), and they are usually articulated in tandem. A main example is found in St. Paul's second letter to the Philippians (Phil 2:6–11) where there is a movement of descent, or self-emptying, (vv. 6–8) and ascent, or self-affirming (vv. 9–11). Thus, in his self-emptying, Christ affirmed his true self as the second person of the Trinity—that is, "born in human likeness" and "Lord, to the glory of God the Father." These two movements cannot be uncoupled, even though the self-emptying is often overemphasized.

Jürgen Moltmann affirms that classic thought has applied kenosis to Christ, but he also shows that it is fitting to see kenosis within the life of the Trinity. Moltmann highlights the work of Hans Urs von Balthasar to show that kenosis is not merely a self-limitation or self-renunciation on God's part; "it is the self-realization of the self-surrender of the Son to the Father in the trinitarian life of God."[6] Hence, self-sacrifice is intimately intertwined with the affirmation of the true identities and activities of God, Christ, and the Holy Spirit; "the Son by virtue of his self-surrender exists wholly in the father, the Father wholly in the Son, the Spirit wholly in the Father and Son. Kenotic self-surrender is God's trinitarian nature."[7] Other contemporary theologians, including Ian

Barbour, also indicate how traditional understandings of kenosis as only the self-emptying of Christ have broadened to appreciate also our Triune God's self-sacrifice in the creation of the world.[8] Robin Ryan, in his exploration of Elizabeth Johnson's theology, indicates that Johnson believes that "the self-emptying that is affirmed of Christ in the New Testament (Phil 2:6–11) is characteristic of God from the beginning of creation."[9]

Consequently, if kenosis characterizes the Creator of the world, then a kenotic disposition infuses what God has created. Denis Edwards adds dimension with his introduction of kenosis as receptivity. He argues that since "the universe can be understood as unfolding 'within' the Trinitarian relations of mutual love," or divine *perichoresis*, then the universe can be understood as possessing a relational, kenotic disposition that involves being receptive to the other.[10] This idea of receptivity would be undernourished if self-sacrifice were not held in tension with self-affirmation; if you are attentive to a friend without letting their experiences affect your personhood or influence your activities or character, then you are not actively receptive to the "other" (your friend) and are just passively listening as an objective, apathetic observer. Hence, kenosis involves acts of self-sacrifice as well as the active genesis or building up of a life beyond one's own.[11]

This pillar holds both poles in tension by describing kenosis as an emptying or sacrifice (disintegration or diminishment) *and* a building up (creation or genesis). Yet, due to our finite nature, humans and other-than-humans are unable to achieve kenosis, for this is reserved to describe the Triune God and Christ. Our evolutionary world, however, possesses a kenotic disposition. The incarnation and the cross are our gateways for glimpsing the self-affirming, self-sacrificial propensity of the Trinity, and this is reflected, albeit dimly, in the creative, cruciform dynamic animating our planetary communities. Each member of creation, in their own way according to their unique nature, participates in this cosmic dialectic of creativity (self-affirmation) and cruciformity (self-sacrifice). For this reason, the term *kenotic* in the phrase *kenotic-kinetic* has been chosen.

The term *kinetic* is derived from the Greek term *kinein*, meaning "to move," and it was chosen in order to be faithful to the inherent dynamism of our unfolding universe and the dynamism inherent in the Triune communion. Thus, kinetic can be understood theologically as *creatio continua* and *concursus*: God's ongoing creative activity in the history of the universe that enables, and nurtures, creation's own creative impetus. Elizabeth Johnson indicates that although God is continuously creating,

> God does not act like a bigger and better secondary cause determining chance atomic events, or initial conditions of chaotic systems, or genetic mutations. Rather, divine Love empowers the structure of creation which operates with its own integrity....God lets the world be what it will be... not intervening arbitrarily in its evolution but participating, lovingly, in its becoming.[12]

Johnson insists that the emergence of novelty in our evolutionary world can only occur "because it has been endowed by its Creator with an inner tendency, a quiet, powerfully pulsing drive, to become something more."[13] Thus, this pillar reminds believers that the pulsing creative drive toward newness necessarily includes an accompanying disintegrative aspect, namely the destruction of something prior/older/less well-adapted. Creativity and cruciformity cannot be uncoupled and interact dynamically, and consequently, the word *kinetic* was chosen to highlight this and complement the term *kenotic*.

For this pillar, the term *kenotic-kinetic* recognizes the inextricable coupling of self-emptying or self-sacrifice (manifest as loss of identity, death, diminishment, disintegration, and destruction) with genesis, innovation, and the emergence of newness. Each member of our Earth's communion participates in this cosmic dialectic due to its emergence from and participation in cosmogenesis. Hence, a kenotic disposition is inherent in all created life but is revealed in different ways: the self-giving of the first stars during a supernova offered the matter for the creation of new life forms; solitary hydrogen atoms with unique forms and functions lose their individual identities as hydrogen couples with oxygen to form an innovative new molecule—water; a carrot's disintegration and ingestion enables the transfer of energy and materials within a complex food web; a predatory bacteria sacrifices motility and independence for a new symbiotic relationship within a eukaryotic cell and enables an innovative form of life (mitochondria) to emerge; the second, "backup," pelican chick is displaced from the nest and left to die to ensure the survival of the other, stronger chick; the disintegration of a human body after death releases vital molecules and minerals back to Earth. Within Earth's life systems, only humans possess the capacity to attempt to deny our participation in this innate dynamic. This distorted belief in our ability to transcend this kenotic disposition has contributed to the current human and ecological crises. All subjects in Earth's planetary communion are participants in this universal movement of self-actualization and self-giving, and it will be shown how a human creature's kenotic disposition can be modeled on the loving movement of self-actualization and self-giving inherent in the cosmos, the Trinity, and the incarnation.

As with the other pillars, an excavation of the historical rootedness of this pillar in the Christian Tradition will be undertaken. In this instance, it will be done via an examination of St. Clare (1194–1253), the desert mothers (fourth–sixth centuries), and Hildegard of Bingen. Each offers valuable contributions that have enabled modern ecotheologians new ways of describing a kenotic-kinetic within our sacred universe story that is modeled after Christic kenosis. Their conceptions of radical poverty, the spiraling movement to abundant simplicity, and the dynamic of receptivity and interdependence helps in the construction of this pillar, which is the cornerstone for our final part of the book.

ANCIENT ROOTS

St. Clare

St. Clare, a diligent student of St. Francis, indicated that Christ, "Poor Crucified," reigns over and holds together all of created life because of his poverty and humility.[14] Since humanity was created to be "the diligent imitator of the Father of all perfection," and pride and vanity has destroyed our true nature,[15] our faith in Christ as Poor crucified calls us to radically cast aside "earthly riches" and dismiss temporal things for those realities that are eternal.[16] This does not have to be seen as a negation of the worth of Earth but rather radical material poverty is a tool that awakens humanity to Christ's indwelling in creation. Our infatuation with material things blinds us to Christ who bonds all material life. For this pillar, St. Clare's wisdom calls us to prayerful contemplation and an emptying of oneself of Earthly vanities so that we can become more Christlike.[17]

St. Clare's movement toward self-emptying, however, when uncoupled from the accompanying movement of self-affirmation or genesis, can become distorted, compounding suffering of some. For example, the overemphasis on self-emptying demanded that certain races, genders, and classes completely self-abnegate for the benefit of a powerful few. St. Clare's wisdom requires strengthening by the wisdom of "abundant simplicity" offered by the desert mothers and Hildegard's vision of receptivity and interdependence; to do otherwise risks promoting a distorted form of self-emptying that glorifies suffering and rejects creation.

The Desert Mothers or *Ammas*

The human condition is fraught with the tension of incompleteness and completeness, of immaturity and maturity, and the desert mothers engaged this with gentleness and compassion. "Just as it is impossible to be at the same moment both a plant and a seed, so it is impossible for us to be surrounded by worldly honor and at the same time to bear heavenly fruit."[18] Self-deception blocks humanity from God, each other, and creation, and spiritual stagnation stems from a denial of the movement toward fulfillment in God. The desert mothers' description of the strengthening/affirmation of one's true self by becoming more receptive to the Other (God) is paradoxical; to be more "me" or "myself," I must be receptive to "you" or "thou" by sacrificing some of what makes me, me. This paradoxical concept is found alongside another: abundant simplicity.

The *ammas* affirmed that to live with abundant simplicity entails two concurrent actions: First is an interior and exterior detachment from all that possesses the sojourner's heart or mind (e.g., materials, emotions, attitudes) and blocks an intimate relationship with God, the Source of abundance. Second, there must be a creative and active growth of one's "burning love for God" through compassion and service to the world.[19] The *ammas* never sought to exalt or denigrate themselves, nor believe the material world to be inherently evil, nor did they deny themselves material things just for the sake of the denial themselves. Instead, their lives reflect their desire to live *harmoniously* and thus, *abundantly* in creation.

In the same vein as St. Clare, who saw poverty or simplicity as the "strong arms" that take hold of that "incomparable treasure hidden in the field of the world and in the hearts of men,"[20] the desert mothers understood that their utter dependence on God, lived via simplicity and service in the world, would initiate and sustain the building up of their true selves via an interior movement into abundant life in God dwelling at the heart of the created world. For example, Laura Swan indicates that it was Amma Macrina the Younger's ascetic training that taught her the important lesson of "abundant simplicity" and when "Basil returned from his studies in Athens with a head swelled with pride," she passed along this wisdom, "cut[ting] him down to size," humbling him. It was her vision of simplicity that became an important thread in his monastic rules and allowed him to discover abundant life in service of others.[21] Amma Syncletica also spoke to this sense of simplicity and balance achieved through the ascetic life of discipline, and challenges her disciples to be constantly open in vulnerability to recognize their dependency on God's tutelage, and yet remain hopeful that they will arise and act with the "strength and courage of the desert.[22] Amma Sarah, via her words spoken about daily, small, unostentatious practices of self-discipline, speaks to the humility at the heart of the ascetic's movement to God.[23] Hence, the ascetic mothers found and accepted their true created nature as participants in a communal, cosmic body of Christ by living a balanced life of abundant simplicity.[24]

The *ammas*' articulation of the paradox of living simply to live abundantly is often misunderstood. The embrace of austere corporal disciplines and physical withdrawal from the busyness of the world through a life lived in the desert should not be seen as an overt rejection of creation. For example, Amma Matrona indicated that the physical isolation of the desert is not of utmost importance, but rather it is important to nurture the inward pursuit of God. She writes that "many people living secluded lives on the mountain have perished by living like people in the world. It is better to live in a crowd and want to live a solitary life than to live a solitary life but all the time be longing for company."[25] Amma Syncletica also emphasized that geographic isolation is only a tool to moderate one's life and it is the latter that is of utmost importance in an inner journey to God.[26] Thus, these female desert ascetics affirmed a way of life that embraces authentic balance (abundant simplicity) in order to experience God's indwelling in creation.

It is through solitude, prayer, sacrifice, and contemplation of God that believers at any point in history are able to perceive and understand

God's indwelling, and consequently, the kenotic movement inherent to the created world. It is by withdrawing from corporeal distractions through poverty/simplicity that one grows in true knowledge of oneself and of God. But this knowledge only becomes aflame when one immerses oneself in the world via giving of oneself by serving others. It is this harmony or balance between self-denial and growth, contemplation and action that helps an ascetic to recognize when poverty itself is becoming an idol. Amma Syncletica warned her followers of this: "So how are we to distinguish between the divine and royal asceticism and the demonic tyranny? Clearly through its quality of balance....In truth, lack of proportion always corrupts."[27] The desert mothers' embrace of harsh physical discipline cultivated "a spiraling movement of simplicity" toward God, and it was ever hopeful because "God has chosen humanity along with all creation as the vehicle of Divine Revelation."[28]

St. Hildegard of Bingen

Benedictine Abbess Hildegard offered even more depth of meaning to this spiraling movement of abundant simplicity to God by emphasizing receptivity and interdependence. Her understanding of the greening power of creation from the last chapter and her understanding of humanity as a microcosm of the larger macrocosm augments the ideas of St. Clare and the desert mothers.

In her *Book of Divine Work*, Hildegard's second vision, "On the Construction of the World," and third vision, "On Human Nature," present a Christlike human figure at the center of concentric circles who chooses to give of himself continuously (stretch himself outward) to balance and sustain creation. Her choice of geometric shape is intentional; circles not only symbolize the cyclical patterns of Earth's seasons but also the eternal oneness of God with creation.[29] This vision depicts all of creation enveloped within the central bodily cavity of the Godhead (depicted at the top outside of the circle). Hildegard's vision also speaks prophetically of creation's dependence on God and participation with God in bringing forth abundant life. For example, she depicted the outer levels of creation laboring to expel their vivifying breath inwardly. Thus, they work with God, symbolized as the Godhead enveloping creation and the central stabilizing human figure, to bring Earth alive with life via Earth's greening power. The inward breath of the creatures is balanced by an outward stabilizing force symbolized by the outstretched arms of Christ. The role of the central figure is different from that of the expiring creatures but both are necessary for life. This dialectic—breath inward and pressure outward—signifies an interdependent set of relations, a differentiation of roles, and opposing stabilizing forces analogous to a spoked wheel. A spoke is not the central hub, but they both labor in tandem to allow the wheel to fulfill its function. For Hildegard, the relations among creation, God, and humanity are based on reciprocity:

> God has composed the world out of its elements for the glory of God's name. God has strengthened it with the winds, bound and illuminated it with the stars and filled it with the other creatures. On this world God has surrounded and strengthened human beings with all these things and steeped them in very great power so that all creation supports the human race in all things. All nature ought to be at the service of human beings so that they can work with nature since, in fact, human beings can neither live nor survive without it.[30]

Therefore, the Christlike figure both sustains (self-emptying) and is sustained (self-affirmation) by creation, and all of creation participates in this dynamic of reciprocity initiated and completed by the second person of the Trinity.

In vision 3, "On Human Nature," Hildegard asserted that humanity is a microcosm of the macrocosmic universe and hence also participates in this dialectic of self-affirmation and self-emptying. In this vision, she explained how air and the winds are reflected in what she called "the humors" and organs of the human organism: "Thereupon, I noticed how the humors in the human organism are distributed and altered by various qualities of the winds and air, as soon as such qualities come into conflict with one another, because the humors themselves take on these same qualities."[31] Although this is not an accurate scientific understanding of the working of the human body, it validly depicts how humanity is inextricably intertwined with other-than-human creation—not the lords over creation. We suffer when Earth suffers, something our ecological crisis has painfully exposed. Hildegard saw humanity as a balancing, strengthening element in creation not unlike the center axle of a cosmic wheel. This act of self-giving to sustain others is what it means to be Christlike and affirm our identities as the image of God. From Hildegard's visions, humanity's unique gifts and obligations can be celebrated without desecrating the giftedness of other aspects of creation and exploiting them. It also teaches humanity that we are not immune to the costly cadence of cosmogenesis—no matter how much we try to deny this.

Accordingly, her understanding of humans as microcosms of the cosmic macrocosm reveals how much humanity is caught up in a web of dependency with the rest of creation. In her fourth vision, "On the Articulation of the Body," she depicts this; her mandala weds the ebb and flow of abundant life and death in Earth's many seasons with the lives of the human laborers who work upon the land. Matthew Fox indicates that "Hildegard celebrates the deep psychological healing that occurs when microcosm and macrocosm are wedded again."[32] Her integrative and dynamic vision shows how the rhythm of human creativity should be in step with the cycles of fertility inherent in Earth; the cutting of wheat, tending the soil; harvesting fruit; being birthed from the ground; returning to the soil after death; rest; celebration; and contemplation are all directed and sustained by the rhythm of Earth's ecosystems gifted by the Creator.

From her illuminations, Hildegard teaches her modern readers the worth of acknowledging and living attuned to the dynamic, cosmic ebb and flow of giving and receiving found in nature. She is telling us that we must get back to our roots and "participate in the fruitfulness of the earth by cultivating the soil and harvesting, and to enjoy its fruitfulness as well."[33] To understand the nature and purpose of humanity, we must dislodge the machine metaphor (and our technician designation) from our imaginations and retrain our minds to be attuned to the source of all that pervades creation. Only then will human activity be in harmony with the work of God. This includes acknowledging the wisdom inherent in the ebb and flow of Earth's creativity and cruciformity. Once we are attuned to God in our evolutionary world we can be the recipients of the power and vitality of Earth. Hildegard affirmed this: "God has formed humanity according to the model of the firmament and strengthened human power with the might of the elements. God has firmly adapted the powers of the world to us so that we breathe, inhale, and exhale these powers like the sun, which illuminates the Earth."[34]

Hildegard's appreciation of the dynamic of life and death, which she articulated as *viriditas* (greening power) and *ariditas* (aridness or lack of vitality), can deepen humanity's receptivity to God in and through creation: "the realm of the living which glorifies and praises God."[35] Like the desert mothers, she instructs her followers that, when we are receptive to Earth's powers, we will fulfill our unique *telos* given by our Creator, namely to serve others as Earth is at the service of humanity. This understanding of service is based on reciprocity, the dynamic of giving and receiving, and not domination and exploitation: "All nature ought to be at the service of human beings so that they can work *with* nature since, in fact, human beings can neither live nor survive without it."[36] This passage, argues Fox, is "not only talking *about* interdependence," but is also an example of true receptivity; humanity is being invited "*into* the hospitable cosmos that will befriend humankind and lend us its very great power."[37] Thus, the human may be a central figure in many of her visions, but she is not anthropocentric. She is Christocentric, and this vision of Christ at the center of the world allows her to focus on reciprocity and interdependence rather than apathy and dominance.

St. Clare, the desert mothers, and Hildegard all offer nuanced visions of mutuality, reciprocity, abundant life, and self-emptying that can be cornerstones of our understanding of the kenotic-kinetic. And as our ecological crisis intensifies, our call to recognize our participation in the cosmic kenotic-kinetic becomes more emphatic. It is Hildegard who illuminates our path forward: "Those who trust in God will also honour the stability of the world: the orbits of the Sun and the Moon, winds and air, earth and water....We have no other foothold. If we give up this world we shall be destroyed."[38]

MODERN FRUIT

Contemporary ecotheology has not yet fleshed out in great detail this pillar of an ETA. For many, focusing on Earth's creativity was a more important task. However, modern voices in theology are beginning to pay more attention to the shadowy side of Earth's creative impulses. The number of theological voices speaking on the costly cadence animating our evolutionary world and the depth of their engagement are growing. Initial engagements such as those by Arthur Peacocke, Thomas Berry, and Jay McDaniel have informed more nuanced descriptions made by Christopher Southgate, Gloria Schaab, and Elizabeth Johnson. What they speak of is clear—cosmic destruction, disintegration, self-giving, and limitation that are inextricably intertwined with cosmic creativity, innovation, self-affirmation, and growth. This is the promise of the green lying hidden in the dark corners of our sacred cosmic story and is the focus of the final part of the book.

SUMMARY

This pillar affirms that Earth's evolutionary processes provocatively and tragically narrate how new life emerges from death and disintegration. Earth's spirited creativity often emerges from profound destruction. It is from the ashes of one life that another emerges transformed. Thanks to a more robust Earth literacy, believers are more aware of the many manifestations of Earth's kenotic-kinetic and these depictions can aid, not hinder, how they understand the Trinity, the Holy Spirit, the incarnation, and the cross. The tension and interplay between violence and creativity, sacrifice and surprise, growth and extinction, ambiguity and stability, visualized in our evolutionary world requires a place in an ETA. If this kenotic-kinetic does not become a more established concept within theological dialogue, humanity may have a skewed vision of the cosmos; for example, we will either possess a romanticized vision of a cosmos devoid of suffering or a truncated and cynical belief that creation is only ruled by death. Both will negatively affect how we understand God and humanity.

The challenge for theology today is to find a way to speak coherently and faithfully of our loving Creator's involvement with, and providential care of, creation and humanity in light of evolution, predator-prey relations, extinction, the Holocaust, the sacrifice of the first generation stars, and every sparrow that falls to the ground (see Matt 10:29; Luke 12:6). All of these are unique manifestations of a cosmic kenotic-kinetic, and a theological appreciation of this will broaden our understanding of human suffering so that we can adopt more fruitful and faithful responses to some forms of suffering.

This pillar and its theological interpretations outlined in the subsequent chapters may also help to critique modern Western cultural trends claiming that every frustration, limitation, pain, or inconvenience is intolerable and must be controlled; that death should be an instantaneous passing from life to nonlife; and a high and attainable goal to aim for is a life free from suffering. This pillar also hopes to cultivate more discerning believers who can delineate between necessary suffering inherent to the kenotic-kinetic and unjust suffering inflicted on the most vulnerable that must be eradicated. Often inflicted suffering is concealed and tolerated within social structures and prevailing cultural mindsets because people mistakenly think that it is "natural" (e.g., slavery) or divinely sanctioned because it is just the way creation works (e.g., eugenics as a model of survival of the fittest). We need discerning believers who can tell the difference between inherent and inflicted suffering.

Consequently, this fourth pillar celebrates the kenotic-kinetic animating cosmogenesis and reveals anew the immensely transformative power hidden in the sacrifice, self-giving, and receptivity at the heart of the cosmic creative effort. Not only is the dialectic of destruction and creation, self-nourishment and sacrifice interwoven into the very fabric of the unfolding universe, this sacred narrative also endlessly illustrates that the cosmos *responds* to unavoidable disintegration and suffering through genesis and innovation. As part of this 13.8-billion-year family history, humanity can resonate with this transformative principle in response to our own suffering and respond in unimaginable ways to God's invitation to greater intimacy in the darkness before the dawn. The root of this ancient kenotic-kinetic is within the triune family and in the moment God made space in Godself for the emergence of the universe 13.8 billion years ago. This costly cadence manifested again uniquely by pre-sentient beings (through disintegration/reintegration), and yet again by sentient beings (through suffering/emergence of novelty). When the *Homo sapiens sapiens* emerged, this kenotic-kinetic manifested and was described quite distinctively, but it was two thousand years ago when it was manifested even more uniquely in Christ.

The kenotic-kinetic is continuously present and is the driving force luring creation toward divinization and final fulfillment in the risen Christ. It connects all created life and enables us to know the relations among God Creator, the incarnation, and the Holy Spirit. This pillar reminds humanity that, as participants in and contributors to our unfinished universe groaning in the pains of childbirth, our journey will be unavoidably costly but it can also be deeply creative and transformative. Hence, the kenotic-kinetic within an ETA speaks vibrantly and in radically new ways to how new life emerges out of suffering and death.

PART III

ENGAGING THE MYSTERY OF SUFFERING

9

HOW SUFFERING IS UNDERSTOOD

All roads may lead to Rome but, in this case, all the paths offered thus far to cultivate Earth literacy and embrace an ETA have led to a theological engagement with the mystery of suffering. Suffering, derived from the Greek term, *paschein*, meaning "to suffer, endure, or undergo," is a complex, interpretive, personal yet universal experience that differs in kind and cause with each individual sufferer. Suffering for an individual ultimately draws its significance and magnitude from the way the sufferer sees the world and their place within it. This is why two individuals can both suffer from cancer, but after receiving the same treatment, one can be utterly destroyed (mentally, socially, spiritually), while the other is transformed—even if both die as a result of their ailment.

Our experiences in our families, schools, and in society in general as well as the culture within which we dwell inform how we describe and respond to suffering. Robert Faricy asserts that theological descriptions and interpretations of suffering and redemption were affected by the cultures within which Christianity was being practiced: "At different times in the history of Christian thought, different models—conditioned by the cultures they existed in—were used to express and to explain the mystery of the redemption."[1] For example, early Christianity used slavery as a model for understanding suffering and redemption, and then in the early Middle Ages, Roman law was the prevalent lens for understanding these theological terms.

Thus, it is important to pay serious theological consideration to how our twenty-first-century evolutionary worldview affects theological descriptions and interpretations of suffering. But to understand the path ahead, one must see whence we came and appreciate the theological legacy that already shaped the theological imaginations of sufferers today.

This chapter explores prominent theological descriptions and interpretations of suffering offered in Scripture as well as those offered by the patristic writers of the early church. Then, space is given for the suffering voices from the margins, as witnessed by liberative writers, as well as post-Shoah voices who speak of radical suffering. Each of these three categories will offer a vision of suffering that is available for us today.[2] This is a modest landscape, encompassing only three overarching categories that span from the classical to the modern industrial eras. Readers are reminded that these categories do not exhaust the myriad ways suffering is interpreted; rather, they paint in broad strokes to reveal some of the portraits of suffering that still influence theological imaginations today.

CLASSIC SOURCES

Scripture

There are many descriptions and interpretations of suffering in Scripture as well as those voiced in the early church by patristic writers and ascetics. These can be organized within the following eight thematic subcategories: suffering as punishment (retribution–expiation), messianic suffering, divine discipline (apostolic suffering), a call to intimacy with God, witness and purification, lament, mystery, and cosmic travail. By isolating and outlining these different, yet often overlapping, dimensions of suffering, contemporary sufferers will be better able to recognize aspects that impact their understanding of suffering. This approach can also address the concepts that are inadequate or incoherent in light of cosmogenesis, and rediscover lost or ignored aspects lying hidden in the annals of Christian Tradition.

Suffering as Punishment (Retribution–Expiation)

Early Christian communities developed their descriptions and interpretations of suffering from their acute experiences of persecution and their cultural conditioning, especially with regard to the phenomenon of slavery. During this period of Christian thought, suffering was brutal, fiercely resisted, and yet one of the accepted actualities of finite life. There was no insulation from the elements, an infected toe could kill, and infant and maternal mortality rates were significantly higher than today. Hence, for Christians, the problem with suffering was not its existence—that was a given—but its distribution.[3] This demanded the full attention of a newly emerging Christian theology that claimed God was all powerful and infinitely good. This wrestling with how suffering is distributed by God is reflected in many ways in Scripture.

One common and potent way of understanding suffering in Hebrew Scripture was that suffering was "a punishment and just requital of wickedness."[4] This simplistic but perhaps instinctual "cause and effect" explanation of suffering has deep roots.[5] It emerged most notably in the narrative of Genesis (see 3:17–18) when Adam's fall from grace was understood as a loss of primordial perfection, a sin of rebellion, or a despoiling of cosmic bliss in the Garden of Eden. As a result of this fall, suffering and death were used as the primary methods of atonement. Another provocative use of this cause-and-effect explanation is in the Deuteronomic writings (see 6:1–3; 30:15–18) where it is used to help the people of Israel understand their covenantal relationship with God.[6] In Deuteronomy 30, Moses promises Israel that if they keep the commandments, they will become numerous and prosper. He also warns that if they fail to keep this covenant, they will perish. Joshua indicated that Achan's sin of taking what was properly God's brought God's anger on the whole people of Israel (Josh 7). Later Joshua elaborates:

> But just as all the good things that the LORD your God promised concerning you have been fulfilled for you, so the LORD will bring upon you all the bad things, until he has destroyed you from this good land that the LORD your God has given you. If you transgress the covenant of the LORD your God, which he enjoined on you, and go and serve other gods and bow down to them, then the anger

> of the Lord will be kindled against you, and you shall perish quickly from the good land that he has given to you. (23:15–16).

The Book of Judges works to temper Joshua's vision of a vengeful God who punishes for wrongdoing, rebellion, and infidelity. It does so by emphasizing that, despite what God says (as outlined by Joshua and other prophets), God is free to act differently and does so by showing infinite mercy and forgiveness. The prophets Isaiah (see Isa 49) and Jeremiah (see Jer 15) describe suffering in history as the result of the sins of the people, but they also promise better times ahead if they mend their ways. Thus, the covenantal relationship promised much when God's laws were observed but grave peril when they were broken: "Tell the innocent how fortunate they are, / for they shall eat the fruit of their labors. / Woe to the guilty! How unfortunate they are, / for what their hands have done shall be done to them" (Isa 3:10–11). A final statement comes in the last book of the New Testament, where it is suggested that Christ's suffering and death is atonement for human sin (see Rev 16:1–2; 4–6; 10–11; 17–19). On the one hand, suffering is understood as retribution or just punishment for human wrong doing, disobedience, and rebellion. On the other hand, salvation entails a return to an Edenic state of cosmic perfection that is only made possible through Christ's suffering and death (see Isa 52:13—53:12; Rom 3:23–26; 2 Cor 5:21; Gal 3:10, 13; John 3:16; 1 Pet 2:24; 3:18).[7]

Suffering as retribution and compensation for sin is how Scripture writers attempted to reconcile God with the immense suffering in the world. The more profound the prophets' understanding of God became, the more acute became the problem of how suffering was distributed: How can God who is all powerful and all loving cause or allow some to suffer and not others? Consequently, suffering as punishment for sin dominated the imaginations of Scripture writers, notwithstanding Job, as well as many generations of Christians who followed.

There are, however, side effects of embracing the "punishment for sin" description of suffering. First, suffering as divine retribution for sin interprets human suffering (individual, corporate, and cross-generational) as the cost that must be paid to satisfy divine justice.[8] The prevalence of this interpretation has overemphasized divine wrath to the detriment of other traits, such as God's mercy and love. Accordingly, God becomes a tyrannical dictator who is radically "Other" and impassable, which seems incompatible with God who is present and compassionate. This interpretation of suffering also effects how some suffering is approached; if suffering is understood as being caused by disobedience or rebellion to the will of the Father (or any dominant figure in society), then it could be seen as something to endure passively and not question or transform.

Messianic Suffering

This subcategory explores how the suffering undergone by Christ was used by the gospel writers as a "rich resource for the followers of Christ."[9] In John's Gospel, Christ is described as the light of the world, and suffering and death will never quench the light of Christ: "What has come into being in him was life, and the life was the light of all people. The light shines in the darkness, and the darkness did not overcome it" (1:3–5). Thus, Christ was the suffering Savior of Hebrew Scripture who emptied himself to participate in human suffering (see Zech 9:9; Isa 53; Acts 8:32–35), and the conquering King-redeemer whose victory over suffering and death revealed the power Christ possessed (see 1 Tim 1:15–17; 1 Cor 15:53–58; Rom 3:25–26; 8:3, 31–39; John 16:31–33). These two dimensions of messianic suffering were accentuated in the New Testament. For example, the apocalyptic methodology in Revelation is used to imaginatively convey the totality and certainty of Christ's victory over suffering (see 1:5; 7:13–17; 19:11–21).

The Synoptic Gospels offered Christ as the ultimate example of their confidence in God's ability to defeat "even the furthest extremes of suffering and death"[10] as well as God's ability to compassionately respond to suffering in the present (see Luke 10:30–37). The Gospel of Mark emphasizes that Christ was the Messiah (see 1:1; 8:27–30), but also instructs us what this messianic identity entails, namely, the suffering of many things (see 8:31). The Gospel of John articulates how even the worst consequences of suffering are met and overcome (see 8:31–36; 4:13–14; 6:30–36) in the presence of the light of the world. Paul, in his famous hymn concerning Christ's self-emptying (see Phil 2:6–11), also demonstrates this paradoxical pairing of suffering and victory inherent to messianic suffering. First, verses 6–8 describe "the career of the Messiah Jesus as 'downward mobility' from divine supremacy to the depths of solidarity with human suffering" as a slave.[11] Then verses 9–11 balance this downward orientation with a divine ascent or exaltation to remind readers of how "the name of Jesus now exalted evokes universal worship of him as LORD."[12] Hence, Jesus Christ portrayed in the New Testament illustrates the following dimensions of messianic suffering: Christ's authority over suffering and death (see Mark 5:35–42); his suffering as atonement for human sin (see Mark 2:1–12; Rom 3:23–25); his gentle, practical compassion for those who suffer, even for one's enemy (see Mark 6:34; Luke 13:34; Matt 5:43–48; Luke 6:35–36); his active combat with natural, social, and supernatural forces that give rise to suffering (see Col 3:1–5; Matt 4); his refusal to adopt a simplistic cause-and-effect understanding of suffering while still retaining a sense of suffering as an ultimate punishment (see Luke 13:1–5); Jesus's unwavering dependence and trust in God as "the source of his activity" (see John 14:18–20; 16:20–22).[13]

Divine Discipline (Apostolic Suffering)

This subcategory allows followers of Christ to identify with his experiences of suffering (public humiliation, vilification, shaming, and rejection alongside the physical pain of crucifixion) and death (see Phil 3:7–11) as well as share in his Messianic suffering. The suffering that is a result of being disciples enables Christ's followers to participate in the exaltation of being conformed to the risen Christ (see 2 Cor 4:7–11; 2 Cor 11:30). Thus, suffering, understood as a share in the suffering of Christ (see 1 Pet 4:12–14; 1 Pet 2:19–25), can be used as a sacrificial catalyst for transformation. This description of suffering as divine discipline or sacrifice for communal transformation—"they die on behalf of the community to give it life by their death, and to inspire it by their example"[14]—is also described in Proverbs 3:11–12, Sirach 2:1–18, 2 Maccabees 7, Isaiah 28:23–29, James 5:7–12, Philippians 2:12–18, and Hebrews 12:1–13.

In the New Testament, suffering is the mark of a true disciple of Christ and the consequence of a Christian life (see Eph 3:7–13; Matt 10:38; Acts 14:22; Col 1:24; 2 Tim 3:10–12; Rev 1:9) and hence, suffering that is "taking up one's cross" (Mark 8:32; Matt 16:24; Luke 9:23) is the byproduct of following Jesus into a world hostile to his message. Scripture writers are clear that enduring suffering as a divine discipline must also evoke the compassionate activity of relieving other people's suffering; "a disciple's response to suffering is practical and active because it is laid in the pattern of Christ."[15] Consequently, through suffering, disciples become alive in love (see Eph 4:32—5:2).

Therefore, "taking up one's cross" as an obedient disciple of Christ allows sufferers to interpret their suffering as a gift to God and a way to establish communion with God. It can also be a way of atoning for human sin. However, when this interpretation is uncritically applied, it can be perilous to marginalized individuals and groups (as is witnessed by liberative writers later in this chapter). Hence, when carefully employed, the interpretation of suffering as divine discipline or sacrifice can empower transformation in human sufferers like that of Christ the Suffering Servant of Scripture whose sacrifice alone accomplished human salvation.[16]

Call to Greater Intimacy with God

Rabbinic Judaism speaks of suffering as a blessing that God bestowed on humanity to create an opportunity to draw closer to God.[17] The psalmists and the Prophet Isaiah also saw suffering as an opportunity for closeness with God (see Ps 63:1–11; Isa 55:1–6) and in the New Testament, the narrative of Christ's life, death, and resurrection brought humanity a new depth of intimacy with God (see Phil 3:7–8; John 3:16; Rev 21:4). This subcategory also reveals the unfathomable depth of God's merciful, unconditional, and compassionate love despite human sin and unfaithfulness (see Hos 2:10; Isa 43:4; 54:10). Again, it takes great discernment to ensure that this way of envisioning suffering does not justify and compound the suffering of the most vulnerable.

Witnessing as Test of Faith and Purification

Once more, in rabbinic Judaism and in Hebrew Scripture (see Jer 12:1; Eccl 8:10–14; 9:2–3, 11–12) there are writers who object to the classic description of suffering as a result of wrongdoing and instead, they present suffering as a test to which all were subjected.[18] The psalmists warn that humans should not become preoccupied with the punishment (or lack thereof) of the wicked but focus instead on the more positive aspects of suffering such as a test of faith, witnessing of faith, or purification.[19] Thus, their personal experiences of unjust persecution and the incomprehensibility of the distribution of suffering motivated a description of some forms of suffering as a test, which cleans a believer's faith or a trial by which it becomes authentic and mature (see John 12:24; Gen 22; Luke 9:23). The narrative of Abraham's willingness to sacrifice his only son provides a classic formulation of this idea of testing or witnessing (see Gen 22:1–19), as does the story of Joseph (see Gen 37–50). Other examples are found in the wisdom of Proverbs (see 3:11) and Ecclesiastes (see 3:18). In Paul's experience, discipleship involves suffering as a test of one's stamina and faith (see 1 Thess 1:6; 2 Thess 1:4).

Consequently, suffering is not punishment for wrongdoing but it is a form of pedagogy: a way of teaching what is right. However, prudence is needed with its application. A corollary of this idea is that suffering becomes an opportunity to witness to God's desire, power, and compassion to overcome all evil and suffering.[20]

Lament

This subcategory explores the darkest realms of suffering and illuminates how some anguished cries to God during this time are not a failure of loyalty to God but a witnessing of deep faith. In the individual psalms of lament (Pss 3; 16; 22; 73; 88; 116) and the Book of Job, suffering manifests socially, psychologically, and physically, and threatens every dimension of human existence. As a result, people in this state are described as groaning, crushed, and dried up, and manifest symptoms of dissolution that are often depicted with words such as *pour out*, *melted*, or *empty*. In these scriptural texts, people enduring this severe form of suffering experience abandonment and chastisement and are mocked by friends, neighbors, and intimates. People who cry out in lament are often depicted as imprisoned or caged in pain, cut off from the experience of personal or corporate salvation, and entangled in the cords of death's grasp. There is also a very practical corollary of this subcategory of suffering: the prophetic practice of naming unjust suffering and exposing those responsible for inflicting unjust suffering (see 2 Sam 12:7; Mic 3:9–12) inspires individuals (and communities who hear the cries of lament) to contest unjust suffering and to work to relieve it, whenever possible.

Mystery

The writer of Ecclesiastes delves deeply into the abyss of mystery that is suffering (see 3:1–2, 9–14; 8:10–14; 9:2–3; 11–12). For example, Ecclesiastes states, "What do workers gain from their toil? I have seen the burden God has laid on the human race. He has made everything beautiful in its time. He has also set eternity in the human heart; yet no one can fathom what God has done from beginning to end" (3:9–12 NIV). The Apostle Paul also explores the "foolishness" of those who follow Christ to the foot of the cross (1 Cor 4:10) because this path taken by Christ mystifies and defies human expectations (See 1 Cor 1:18–31; 2 Cor 13:4).

It is the Book of Job, however, that offers the most sustained engagement with the mystery that is suffering. This text transects many of the categories of description offered in this chapter and presents the clearest refutation of the classical description of suffering as punishment; Job's absolute innocence means his suffering could not be interpreted as retribution. Daniel Harrington indicates that this text "examines how one can hold together the three propositions that God is omnipotent, that God is just, and that innocent persons like Job can and do suffer."[21] Hence, Job does not solve the problem of innocent suffering nor take refuge in a more pleasant vision of life after death. Rather, Job proffers a realistic assessment of human suffering and death as a mystery as old as the universe. In doing so, Job illuminates the inadequacies of embracing wholeheartedly the description of suffering as retribution for wrongdoing.[22] Job also offers other aspects to this subcategory: the promotion of a respectful "silence" when one faces the great dark abyss of suffering; the articulation of suffering as an opportunity that tests one's faithfulness; the affirmation of the possibility that suffering can be made redemptive or restorative via accepting suffering faithfully and prayerfully;[23] and the appreciation of God's revelation in creation, even in interpretations of suffering.

So, in light of cosmogenesis, Job's appreciation of mystery reverberates in new ways, and sufferers today can appreciate several things: that they are a minuscule part of the complex, ambiguous cosmos (see 38:4–5); they are an accumulation of ashes and dust (see 42:6); and despite our scientific and technological advances, humanity will never comprehend the entirety of God's designs, intentions, and power.

Cosmic Travail

Paul said that the whole of creation was groaning in travail. It was subject to frustration and limitation (see Rom 8:20), and suffered the pain of childbirth (see Rom 8:22). As will be noted later, this subcategory is an important precedent for descriptions offered by those formed by Earth literacy. However, Paul's description of creation in travail was colored by his anthropocentric understanding of mortality being the wages (punishment) for sin (see Rom 6:23). Nevertheless, he still offers two vital dimensions to this subcategory of cosmic travail. First, he admits that creation is still undergoing travail, still groaning: "The whole creation has been groaning as in the pains of childbirth right up to the present time" (Rom 8:22 NIV). Second, he situated human suffering within this larger horizon of labor: "Not only so, but we ourselves, who have the first fruits of the Spirit, groan inwardly as we wait eagerly for our adoption to sonship [*sic*], the redemption of our bodies" (Rom 8:23 NIV).

Early Church

The writers during the patristic period (AD 100–450) inherited many concepts and metaphors from Judaism as well as from Scripture to help make sense of suffering. However, these descriptions and interpretations were not unanimous; during the patristic period there were antithetical descriptions of humanity and thus, different ideas about the cause of suffering. For example, some saw Adam as a perfect being who destroyed humanity's state of perfection by his disobedience and pride, and brought suffering upon himself and all his descendants (e.g., Augustine).[24] Others understood that human beings begin as imperfect and immature creatures who undergo a process of gradual development until they find their ultimate completion in God (e.g., Irenaeus) and that juxtaposes the idea of Adam's perfection.[25] However, there were seven predominant ways to describe suffering in the patristic period: punishment and divine wrath; testing and purifying; schooling in the ways of Divine Wisdom; medicinal suffering; aesthetic theme of harmony; steadfast witness; and mystery.

Punishment and Divine Wrath

Many patristic writers reaffirm and rearticulate the Scriptural descriptions of suffering as a result of humanity's prideful rebellion and transgression against God. For example, St. Cyprian makes use of Psalm 89:31–33 in his description of suffering as retribution for human sin: "If they violate my statutes and do not keep my commandments, then I will punish their transgression with the rod and their iniquity with scourges."[26] Desert mother Amma Syncletica, (fourth century) commented that "in the world, if we commit an offense, even an involuntary one, we are thrown into prison; let us likewise cast ourselves into prison because of our sins, so that voluntary remembrance may anticipate the punishment that is to come."[27] Augustine strongly emphasizes this interpretation of suffering; namely, suffering and evils of the human condition as righteous punishment for sin:

> Man's nature, indeed, was created faultless and without any sin; but that nature of man in which everyone is born from Adam, now wants the Physician, because it is not sound. All good qualities, no doubt, which it still possesses in its make, life, senses, intellect, it has of the Most High God, its Creator and Maker. But the flaw, which darkens and weakens all those natural goods, so that it has need of illumination and healing, it has not contracted from its blameless Creator—but from that original sin, which it committed by free will. Accordingly, criminal nature has its part in most righteous punishment.[28]

William Harmless indicates that Augustine introduced the term "original sin" into the theological conversation concerning suffering as punishment for sin in a two-volume treatise countering Caelestius's assertion that infants do not inherit Adam's sin. Hence, "original sin" would forever be "linked with his name"[29] and influence his followers, especially St. Thomas Aquinas. Since Aquinas saw evil as a privation or an absence of the good that ought to be present,[30] and this privation is either a natural evil suffered (*malum poena*) or a moral evil done (*malum culpae*),[31] then Aquinas interpreted Augustine's vision of the fall as the following: Adam and Eve lived in a state of "original justice," or blissful goodness, in a harmony made possible by God's grace. When they were disobedient, they were punished via suffering. This state of suffering, whether natural or moral, was not part of the original harmony and, after the fall, infected each subsequent generation of human beings.[32] From this vision, St. Thomas interpreted original sin as a loss, a privation, or a disordered disposition that grows from the dissolution of the harmony humanity originally possessed in the Garden of Eden.[33]

The Council of Trent (1545–63) formalized the understanding of original sin emanating from Augustine's and Aquinas's understanding of the fall, and this became a cornerstone of the faith.[34] Thus, the rebellion and disobedience of Adam at the beginning of human history has sickened all human persons and only God can heal this malady.[35] This interpretation of suffering still dominates Christian imaginations and needs reevaluation in light of the cruciformity inherent in our evolutionary world.

Testing and Purifying

Another influential description of suffering offered by the patristics is how suffering involves God's desire for "his household [to] be tested."[36] Similar to Scripture, this description allows suffering to be understood as a test of one's virtue, and when applied astutely, can allow for a more positive meaning to the experience of human suffering.

Christian ascetical practices and martyrdom during the third and fourth centuries were molded by earlier biblical understandings grounded in this vision of suffering as a test from God or as a purifying fire to be endured to attain a higher intimacy with God. John Chryssavgis affirms that this motivated many ascetics: "[The] dry desert, from the third century until around the end of the fourth century, became the laboratory for exploring hidden truths about Heaven and earth....The hermits who lived in that desert tested and studied what it means to be human."[37] For example, Amma Sarah illustrates how Christ is her strength in her painful journey of detachment and growth that will purify her and join her more intimately with the Beloved.[38] This dimension of suffering was often coupled with other positive elements of suffering, namely schooling in the ways of Divine Wisdom and steadfast witness.

Schooling in the Ways of Divine Wisdom

In many instances, patristic writers described human suffering as a tool for educating or advancing human beings who are ignorant in the ways of Divine Wisdom. This is equivalent to suffering as pedagogy seen in Scripture. This concept helped them to interpret their personal and communal experiences of suffering in ways that made sense to them and helped them to respond positively to their suffering. For example, the work of St. Irenaeus in the second century asserted that evil and suffering are necessary for "soul making" for this is how we learned or developed our capacities for charity, compassion, cooperation, courage, self-control, and forgiveness.[39] Another example is Bishop Titus of Bostra (fourth century) whose work indicated that suffering and evil seems "to school us better than good towards virtue."[40]

Medicinal Suffering

Patristic writers also described suffering as medicinal for the wounds made by sin. This enables a believer to interpret their experience of suffering in a way that allows for a constructive, transformative response to suffering when given the right divinely graced medicine. For example, St. Basil of Caesarea asserts that "just as a beneficent physician may inflict sufferings and pain on a body as he grapples with the sickness and not the patient, so the good God dispenses salvation for the whole by punishment of the parts."[41] For many sufferers, they imagine that their suffering is the sickening of their body as a result of their sins. For them, God is the only physician capable of healing them, for the root of their suffering is spiritual and not physical.

Aesthetic Theme of Harmony

If suffering was one face of a two-sided coin, then beauty and joy can be understood as the other face. Many writers in the patristic period understood this and indicated that another dimension of suffering is how it acts aesthetically to augment our appreciation of creation's beauty and harmony. Paintings are made more beautiful when the artist orders both the light and the shadows in ways that are aesthetically pleasing. St. Augustine wrote, "For as the beauty of a picture is increased by well-managed shadows, so too the eye has skill to discern it, the universe is beautified even by sinners, though considered by themselves, their deformity is a sad blemish."[42] Consequently, suffering was interpreted positively, namely as something that qualifies and amplifies one's understanding of beauty and joy.

Steadfast Witness

Another dimension of suffering is how it offers the opportunity for both an individual and a community to be credible witnesses to Christ. Cyprian of Carthage embraces this understanding of suffering: "Your present witness is more splendid and brings you greater honor because it became more assured in suffering."[43] Those suffering unjustly can take refuge in this description for as "water, light, air are shared by all, so the just must endure the evils of the unjust."[44] Thus, those who suffer innocently can use their experiences as authentic witnessing to Christ, and by their steadfast witness, they can guide others to conversion.

Mystery

From Scripture, the patristic writers were bequeathed many descriptions and affirmations of suffering as a divine and cosmic mystery. Like their forerunners, the early church fathers and mothers were acutely aware of the immensity of pain and suffering being suffered in their communities as well as the limitations and inadequacy of the theological tools to interpret this suffering. Hence, they relied on Paul's affirmation that God's ways and judgments are incomprehensible to us (see Rom 11:33). Our human intellect cannot penetrate this mystery that is suffering.

In his *Confessions*, St. Augustine indicated that in the midst of the sorrow of life, which is a "land of death," one may not find happiness or understand the dark abyss that is human suffering. Nevertheless, one can be confident that in light of this mystery, a Christian response to suffering is the acceptance of the life, death, and resurrection of Jesus and, in ways beyond our understanding, this acceptance will transform our suffering.[45]

The desert mothers also appreciate the limitation of human comprehension of God's saving activity. Amma Syncletica writes, "We sail on in darkness. The Psalmist calls our life a sea and the sea is either full of rocks, or very rough, or else it is calm....We always set our course by the sun of justice, but it can often happen that the secular is saved in tempest and darkness."[46] Accordingly, embracing Christ does not offer a life devoid of suffering to his followers; rather, it is a reminder that suffering and death never have the final word.

Today, the theological imaginations of many sufferers are still entranced by these classic descriptions and interpretations. Believers need to hear the voices of those who suffer on the margins of society, as witnessed by liberative writers and those who experienced the Holocaust, in order to challenge some of the aspects assumed by these classical visions as well as some of the uncritical applications of these ideas concerning suffering. When one does listen attentively to these new voices, readers can understand these classic categories better and expand their horizons to begin to engage divine, ecosystemic, and human suffering in new ways.

MODERN SOURCES

This section outlines two more categories of descriptions of suffering offered by more contemporary sources: the witness made by sufferers living on the margins of society and that of the voices from the Holocaust.

Witness of Liberative Writers

Contemporary society is very different from the world of antiquity. We have immediate access—daily and even hourly—to the massive suffering occurring worldwide, and yet at the same time, we deceive ourselves by believing in the possibility of living a life devoid of suffering via "a life of hyper-consumerism and the entertainment of spectacle."[47] Scientists Lynn Margulis and Dorion Sagan indicate that this deception is unique to our species: "Among the dazzling array of reasons implying our superiority over the rest of creation, one scientific argument stands out to us in curious contrast to the rest: humans are the only beings capable of wholesale self-deception."[48] Our world is also highly stratified; our technocratic, industrial, and capitalist global world is comprised of a small center of producers and possessors (20 percent), while the rest constitutes a great periphery of the marginalized (80 percent) where the majority of people live, is exploited, and suffers.[49]

Contemporary contextual theologies critique anthropocentric (human-centered), androcentric (male-centered), and Eurocentric (European-centered) ideas concerning suffering, especially those that focus solely on the Divine–human relationship. The problem comes when so many in our communities (e.g., women, oppressed people living in poverty, those suffering from mental illness, indigenous peoples, those living with disabilities, and the aged) are deemed "other" or less-than-human and hence, do not qualify to be in a relationship with God.

Douglas John Hall indicates that to correct this myopia, theology must make its starting point the experience of suffering of those living at the margins.[50] This orientation will expose how uncritical descriptions of suffering such as taking up one's cross can be inappropriate and often exploitative if the "other" is seen as disordered or "sinful." Ideas included in this broad description of suffering are the bearing of punishment for disobedience and rebellion, or the taking on self-abnegating sacrifice, or the enduring of suffering to appease the wrath of a powerful (and white, male, fully abled) God. Thus, the suffering that these "others" experience is often justified or glorified by those in positions of power in society. After this exposition, two other descriptions of suffering will be offered: the breakdown of relationality and the resistance to unnecessary violence against well-being. Those that live on the margins of modern society add these experiences of suffering to what has been offered by Scripture and the early church.

An Authentic Taking Up of One's Cross

One theological description of suffering that has been used to oppress many at the margins is the uncritical externalization of the self-sacrifice and obedience modeled by Christ the Suffering Servant (see Isa 53) onto marginalized groups. For example, in many cultures, it has become the moral expectation that a woman deny her selfhood for the sake of fathers, brothers, spouses, the state, employers, children, or any male in a position of power. If Christ's unquestioning obedience to God and his ultimate sacrifice of his life is not seen alongside God who liberates captives from unjust oppression, then the suffering of women becomes acceptable (or encouraged) because they are being Christlike in their self-sacrifice. This places women in untenable positions; they must silently accept unjust suffering as God's will or speak out and be alienated by their church, family, employer, and so on. Carol J. Adams states,

> Gender-based notions of proper religious behavior, in which women are to be self-less and self-abnegating, contribute to a woman's confusion about putting her safety first....The suffering servant model very likely keeps victims from establishing safety concerns as their first priority.... The religious meaning of sacrifice is thus layered on top of the social view of women as sacrificial.[51]

When Christ as Suffering Servant is coupled with an understanding of God as a vengeful Father, then the oppression, suffering, and death of women (and other vulnerable people or nonbelievers) often become justified and even glorified. Joanne Carlson Brown and Rebecca Parker ask that, in light of a historical tendency in theology to glorify suffering, "is it any wonder that there is so much abuse in modern society when the prominent image or theology of the culture is of 'divine child abuse,'—God the Father demanding and carrying out the suffering and death of his own son?"[52]

Feminist and liberation theologians as well as the "victims of slavery, racism, unjust wages, torture, human trafficking, and political oppression"[53] challenge these exploitative interpretations of suffering as an uncritical taking up of one's cross. They are offering more authentic descriptions of suffering that pay theological attention to the collapse of mutually empowering relations, the distortion of social structures and patterns of thinking, and the corporate and personal acts of violence toward the "other."[54] By taking the lived experiences of those forced to the margins of society as the starting point for theological engagement with suffering, two additional ways of describing suffering have been exposed: the breakdown of relationality and the resistance to unnecessary violence against well-being.

The Breakdown of Relationality

Suffering can be described as a neglect or breakdown of relationship, regardless of whether the context is between sexes (sexism), races (racism), women (patriarchy), economic levels (classism), people of different abilities (ableism), or species (speciesism). Thanks to the work of many contextual theologians, the disintegration of mutually empowering relations with God, self, and our many neighbors has become understood as "sin." For example, ecofeminist theologian

Rosemary Radford Ruether indicates that sin is social, historical, and personal, and that a denial of the more communal forms of sin is a major way people evade dealing with the ramifications of social sin:

> Sin has a personal as well as a systemic side. But it is never just "individual": there is no evil that is not relational. Sin exists precisely in the distortion of relationality, including relation to oneself. Although there are sins that are committed primarily as personal self-violation or violation of another individual—abuse of one's body by intoxicants, rape, assault, or murder of another—even these very personal acts take place in a systemic, historical, and cultural context.[55]

Another example comes from liberation theologian Gustavo Gutiérrez. He asserts that many classical descriptions and interpretations of sin as retribution (and suffering "caused" by this sin) fail to account for the sociopolitical and economic dimensions of sin. The doctrine of retribution is "a convenient and soothing doctrine for those who have great worldly possessions, and it promotes resignation and a sense of guilt in those who lack possessions."[56] Uncovering these new dimensions of suffering allows the narrative of the passion to speak more clearly of the suffering caused by the breakdown of relationships:

> It is the story of a man whose goal is shattered. But this despair over his own cause would be incomplete—and below the level of other human suffering—without the physical and social experience the story describes. Without torture, it would remain on a purely spiritual level. And the disintegration of his company of followers is part of this experience of suffering, for Jesus is denied, betrayed, and abandoned by his friends.[57]

Privatizing sin to only personal, individual acts of pride or disobedience against God, who is radically other, fails to take the corporate or social dimension of sin into account. When this is ignored, the concept of sin can be a powerful tool to oppress those deemed "other" in society; interpreting suffering as the punishment of rebellious individuals or groups deemed sinful because they challenge unjust social norms is a formidable tool wielded by the powerful to blame and silence those on the margins. It also allows the powerful to justify, romanticize, and glorify the suffering of the "other" while negating their own responsibility in causing the suffering of the "other." Dorothee Sölle explains this misuse:

> The concept of sin is a key to helping us understand human suffering in the light of human responsibility. It is misused, though, when seen as punishment for those who suffer.... Blaming the victim is the easiest and most superficial way to explain suffering; on the contrary, compassion and cosuffering characterize the way of Christ.[58]

Gustavo Gutiérrez also critiques how the poor have been "idealized" by the affluent and caricatured as simple people who are content with "their lot" and "close to God."[59] This only serves to insulate the economically advantaged from any responsibility for unjust social constructions and patterns of thinking that cause poverty. Christ invites all his disciples to pray as he did—"with bold speech"[60]—and hence, the violation or breakdown of mutually empowering relationships speaks boldly to the social and historical dimensions of sin and to simplistic understandings of suffering as punishment for wrongdoing. This is a vital dimension for any theological engagement with suffering in a globalized, evolutionary, and industrialized world.

The Resistance to Unnecessary Violence against Well-Being

Suffering is a component of embodied life, but voices from the margins remind believers that some suffering can be described and interpreted as the *unnecessary* violence to their well-being.[61] Some unavoidable and necessary suffering comes because we are finite creatures in an unfinished world. However, the immense suffering experienced today is not just unavoidable suffering; some unnecessary, inflicted suffering—done via social, political, and economic institutional structures or norms—violates the well-being of the "other" while guarding the well-being of those with privilege.[62] Classic visions of suffering (punishment for sin, divine test, divine schooling), when coupled with the social/religious expectations of women and other vulnerable groups, promotes a passive and silent acceptance of suffering that leaves little room for understanding how these sufferers are the beloved children of God, what a faithful resistance to injustice entails, and how they can actively participate in self-care and healing.

A source for this description of suffering as resistance to the violence against well-being comes from Scripture; in the Gospel of Mark, the story of the hemorrhagic woman witnesses to how one can faithfully describe and respond to that which is doing violence to one's well-being.[63] In this story, there are two reactions made to the woman's suffering: the woman's and that of Jesus. This woman endured multiple forms of privation that incurred violence to her well-being (physical, economic, and social). She resisted each one tenaciously and upon hearing about Jesus, acts yet again to relieve her suffering and establish well-being and wholeness (see Mark 5:27–29). Thus, her healing occurs at her own initiative sustained by the grace of God for "she reaches out, yet again, in hope of relief to the one she believes can heal her." In this way she is a model of faithful "self-care."[64] Jesus inquires, "Who touched my clothes?" (Mark 5:30)—a personal response to her act of faith. This acknowledgment opens a dialogue where the woman's voice, muted by pain, sorrow, shame, and social isolation, can be heard. Jesus restores her physical, social, and spiritual well-being and by addressing her directly, bears witness to her status as a beloved child of God *and* a woman of great faith.

This Scripture event also draws theological attention to the need to recognize the many forms of violence against well-being and respond to the spiritual, social, *and* physical needs of sufferers whenever possible. The "power" to heal lay in this suffering woman's unwavering confidence that the ultimate source of healing power resided in Jesus and the trust she had that God wills abundant life and healing for her: "Daughter, your faith has made you well" (Mark 5:34).[65] It is through a personal encounter with God that we are healed, nourished, and empowered to resist suffering, protest grave injustices, and stand in solidarity with other co-sufferers, changing "the 'I' into 'we,' enabling one to say, 'we poor,' 'we oppressed,' 'we exploited....' This...is the fruit of the dark night."[66] Jesus's power is active in the community of co-sufferers as a shared spiritual and physical power. This vision of suffering as resistance evokes a different response from merely passively bearing one's cross in silence.

Voices from the margins bear witness to scriptural and patristic understandings of suffering, such as lament, mystery, trial, discipline, and a call to intimacy; but they also offer critique and qualify simplistic and purely retributive understandings of suffering. The experience of suffering by women, those living in poverty, or others at the margins of society does not glorify, valorize, or eternalize suffering; instead, it pays close attention to social, cultural, political, and historical dimensions of suffering (social sin) as well as personal acts that cause suffering (personal sin).

The voices at the periphery invite a redefinition of sin and suffering as distorted or broken relationships, rather than purely prideful acts undertaken by individuals. An investigation of the broken relationship between God and humanity can also lead to explorations of other distorted relations among humans and between humanity and Earth. These three interpretations of suffering at the margins allow sufferers to: (1) regain choice and agency, (2) work to alleviate suffering when possible, (3) bear suffering when necessary, (4) transform suffering when feasible, and (5) stand in solidarity with other sufferers.[67] Thus, theological conversations are shifted from focusing on what a good and just God allows, gives, or denies toward a theology of activity and participation in suffering with God who is compassionately present and eternally encouraging.[68] The twofold emphasis—that is, God's affective and responsive relationship with creation and a person's authentic "taking on" or active acceptance of suffering—is the catalytic dynamism that can help alleviate suffering.

Voices from the Holocaust

While some suffering can be categorized and thereby help sufferers make sense of this experience, some suffering seems so meaningless that it defies placement in any category. Those who experienced the Shoah, another name for the Holocaust, remind readers that the horrific, undeserved, dehumanizing cruelty that describes radical suffering defies all attempts to make sense of it. This truth reacquaints theology with its limits. Hence, theologians and believers need great humility and compassion while describing and interpreting suffering in our world. To do this, radical suffering must never be forgotten. This is the gift offered by the writers from the post-Shoah period, the focus of this subsection.

Radical suffering was touched on in the previous categories of lament, mystery, and the breakdown of relationality, but it deserves to be examined on its own. This category crosses the precipice between meaningful and meaningless suffering. It represents an attack on human personhood and an "incurable wound of despair that annihilates the future, severs relationships, and withholds from suffering any possible meaning."[69] Radical suffering has the power to dehumanize and degrade human persons, inhibit spiritual transformation, and utterly destroy the sufferer. It is not the intensity of the suffering that makes it radical but its power over a sufferer, whether physical, emotional, or spiritual. It is important to note that radical, destructive suffering, where there is no transformative impetus or response, is often hard to delineate from transformative or redemptive suffering due to the interpretative nature of suffering and the complexity of human existence and growth. In the same situation, some individuals transfigure under extreme suffering whereas others are destroyed.

When radical suffering is experienced, the self-image of a sufferer is crippled due to self-loathing and despair, and all of his/her experiences are absorbed into their present experience of suffering. This sufferer has no recourse to memories of the past or to hope in a future; he/she is trapped in the meaningless misery of the present.[70] If radical suffering is prolonged, then it "can create a soul incapable of self-defense because the spark of self-respect or dignity has been snuffed out by humiliation and pain."[71]

This category of suffering is connected to other categories, but it is also significantly different. First, in this category, suffering cannot be traced to punishment for an action or *wrongdoing*; instead, it arises out of a sense that something is wrong with the very way one's life is conditioned or structured. Second, it describes a radical contingency and vulnerability for the sufferer, despite his or her best actions, placing them at the mercy of something or someone that seeks to destroy life and all that is good. Third, this suffering is always concrete and contextual, namely, a part of a particular culture, economy, society, and personal circumstance. It destroys human personhood and dignity by diminishing one's capacity to exercise freedom, feel affection or hope, and love God. Finally, it is described as undeserved and unjust—without meaning and purpose.[72]

Kristine Rankka describes this radical suffering as involving undeserved, inflicted suffering, and evoking pity and horror. It also causes those outside of this experience of suffering to become paralyzed due to its perceived meaninglessness.[73] Dorothee Sölle indicates that extreme, or "mute," suffering, which reduces sufferers to "a silence in which no discourse is possible," is the most radical stage of human suffering.[74] This radical "night of pain" is a form of suffering that turns a person inward to such a degree that he or she is unable to communicate and others cannot reach them, though one should never stop trying.[75] This muteness causes the sufferer to cease reacting as a human agent, and thus, the alienating speechlessness of the "dark night" is like a form of death.[76]

However, to stop attempting to try to reach these sufferers is not a viable option for any theology. Consequently, Sölle envisions radical suffering as qualifying all interpretations of suffering and offers her readers a potential path to reach these sufferers; in *Suffering,* she outlines the potential movement of a sufferer engulfed by radical suffering from isolation and muteness (phase 1), through communication and lament (phase 2), to solidarity and change (phase 3). Hence, when you companion those experiencing radical suffering and open your mouth "for those who cannot speak" (Prov 31:8), then these sufferers can gain access once more to the language of lament, pain, and self-expression that names, accepts, and resists the situation of suffering. Sölle and others' work after the Holocaust calls attention to how classic Christian interpretations of suffering (e.g., retribution, expiation, test, and discipline) cannot be applied universally and need qualification by radical suffering.

Recognizing radical suffering reminds believers that some sufferers "no longer have any possibility of determining a course of action, of learning from their experience, or of taking measures that would change anything."[77] Hence, people of faith are constantly called to companion those engulfed in the darkness—even if they cannot be reached—and tirelessly remind them of how the silent, stark darkness of the tomb on Holy Saturday was followed by the divine radiance of Easter morning.

10

SUFFERING IN AN EVOLUTIONARY WORLD

Identifying, describing, and interpreting the suffering inherent in evolution can be problematic when one is equipped with only the categories constructed from within a human-centered or mechanical worldview; for example, theological frameworks that understand suffering as punishment for sin are inadequate to explain suffering prior to the emergence of humanity. John Haught agrees: "Any serious encounter with evolutionary reality/science would be to relativize and perhaps even demolishes…the expiatory interpretation of suffering for it realizes that the great proportion of suffering in an evolutionary world is tragic and innocent."[1] There are, however, many sources for Christians to draw on to understand suffering in an evolutionary world.

ANCIENT SOURCES

In previous chapters, we have noted how humanity acquired knowledge of our cosmic birth and dynamically evolving world circa the eighteenth century, and in the subsequent centuries, scientists and theologians have begun to describe in great detail the emergence of humans from Earth's costly creative processes. Thus, it would be unfair to demand that ancient sources reveal these exact truths. They did not (and could not) possess an evolutionary consciousness, for it took the contributions of Wallace, Darwin, and many others to uncover the evolutionary mechanisms animating our sacred universe story. But ancient sources were important precursors to modern ecotheology. For example, Hildegard's mandala "Cultivating the Cosmic Tree"[2] entwines Earth's sacred seasons with human activity and development, and modern science has illuminated in fascinating detail how right she really was.

Thus, ancient theological foundations coupled with a robust planetary consciousness have allowed modern voices to articulate theological truths in new ways. For example, ecotheologian Thomas Berry and astrophysicist Brian Swimme describe our world as a sacred communion of many differentiated subjects, from the microorganisms in the soil to the birds of the air to the mammals cavorting on Earth's surfaces.[3] They and others narrate how the emergence of *Homo sapiens sapiens*, like all eruptions of newness in the cosmos, reveals the complexity, irreversibility, dynamism, and cruciformity that characterize the universe story. Human nature models the tensions between violence and creativity, growth and extinction, ambiguity and stability that is inherent to the cosmos.

Since humanity now comprehends the scale and scope of violence, destruction, and creaturely loss inherent within the cosmos's 13.8-billion-year history and our own more recent emergence from the cruciform Earth, theological descriptions of human suffering must extend beyond purely anthropocentric visions of suffering as punishment for human sin and attend to human suffering that is a unique manifestation of the cruciformity inherent in the evolving cosmos. This new perspective is offered by a fourth category of theological descriptions of suffering.

MODERN SOURCES

Post-Newtonian Witness

Science tells the story of how, thanks to natural selection, billions of interesting genetic combinations have survived while billions of others have been destroyed or eliminated. Modern investigations of fossil records have shown that loss at an immense scale is an integral part of our cosmic family history and the emergence of newness. For example, in the Permian mass extinction that took place over 248 million years ago, more than 90 percent of the planet's species and many other living organisms were destroyed.[4]

However, this great eradication of biota afforded new opportunities for new forms of life. The Permian loss allowed the extensive diversification of terrestrial life forms such as insects, amphibians, and reptiles because their main predators were killed off. Another great extinction event, the Cretaceous–Paleogene extinction nearly 65 million years ago, saw more than half of the Earth's species, including the dinosaurs, eliminated. Again, this death event made space for the smaller mammals, and eventually *Homo sapiens sapiens*. Currently, approximately 98 percent of species that have ever existed are now extinct.[5]

Today, there is an added sense of urgency; we are currently experiencing an "extinction spasm at levels not seen since the transition from the Cretaceous to Tertiary Period some 60 million years ago—and it has reached those levels almost entirely as a result of human activity."[6]

Humanity has also begun to realize that, as more complex organisms with neurologically based pleasure/pain systems evolved (e.g., central nervous systems, larger brains, pain receptors, and complex forms of intelligence and sentience), these complexified organisms had an advantage over those with simple chemical or mechanical systems. But the cost of this innovation was the emergence of imaginative, barbarous, and extremely effective hunting, feeding, and reproductive strategies. For many complex organisms, eating already formed proteins (e.g., meat) rather than taking in simpler ones and then building them interiorly gave them an advantage.

This sounds harmless but this requires the death of the organisms possessing these preformed proteins—something that has implications for any theology promoting a Creator of this world who is infinitely good. For example, the fluke worm (a parasitic flatworm), secures its survival by boring into the blood vessels of their unwitting host and feeding on their tissues. This behavior is similar to that of the ichneumon wasp, who lays eggs into an organism, so that the larvae can feed on the living flesh of the host, ultimately killing the host when the larvae are mature. John Haught indicates that upon realizing the cruel and destructive lifestyle of the ichneumon wasp, Darwin rejected divine design, for he could find no holy message in this story in the Book of

Nature.[7] The appearance of these brutal but effective strategies enabled some organisms to flourish by way of eating another organism, thus causing the prey to experience pain, suffering, and death. Complex feeding relationships stimulated the emergence of new psychological pain, namely, a fear of death and "nervous vigilance."[8]

Examinations of sexual reproduction also reveal the shadow side of cosmic creativity. For example, sexual reproduction brought with it an intense competition for limited resources (e.g., reproductive partners, food, habitats), as well as the painful emotions that became associated with sex and parenting (e.g., dominance, jealousy, grief). With the emergence of *Homo sapiens sapiens*, even more complex psychological and physical pains emerged with respect to this form of reproduction, especially with the increased amount of parenting our vulnerable offspring requires.

Now that we have awakened to the evolutionary mechanisms inherent in our ancient, unfinished world, it becomes clear that we require a reevaluation of some of our theological descriptions and interpretations of suffering, especially the primacy given to the interpretation of suffering as divine pedagogy or punishment and expiation for sin.

Our new awareness of the way our world works brings to the forefront of our theological imaginations the inherent and necessary suffering manifesting as diminishment, disintegration, and death. These are only a few of the many manifestations of the kenotic-kinetic that are deeply woven into the tapestry of creation. The kenotic-kinetic and suffering in sentient beings existed long before the appearance of humans (and sin) in the evolutionary story. Consequently, a fourth category is required to help describe and interpret human suffering in an evolutionary world. This fourth category is a witness from the "post-Newtonian" historical period, because scientific discoveries beyond the mechanical vision of forces offered by Newton are informing descriptions offered here. Those in this period *witness to the suffering inherent within our evolutionary universe* and articulate three thematic subcategories: the cruciformity of creation, sacrifice and labor to bring forth newness, and the costly creative kenotic-kinetic.

Cruciformity of Creation

Holmes Rolston III identifies a "cruciform naturalism" as inherent in our evolutionary reality. He highlights how there is a tension in our world that couples and checks "prolific and pathetic" cosmic tendencies.[9] Suffering, claims Rolston, is "the shadow side of sentience," and yet it is also "all the excitement of subjectivity waking up so inexplicably from mere objectivity. Rocks do not suffer, but the stuff of rocks has organized itself into animals who experience pains and pleasures."[10] John Haught also appreciates the cruciform and creative aspects of our evolutionary world and incorporates this into his description and understanding of God:

> If God is essentially compassionate love, however, we must also assume once again that all of the sufferings, struggles, and achievements of the evolving world do not take place outside of God's own empathetic care. A vulnerable God, as the Trinitarian nature of Christian theism requires, could not fail to feel intimately and to "remember" everlastingly all of the sufferings, struggles, and achievements in the *entire* story of cosmic and biological evolution. By holding these and all cosmic occurrences in the heart of divine compassion, God redeems them from all loss and gives eternal meaning to everything, though in a hidden way that for us humans only faith can affirm.[11]

We see a similar appreciation for the vital role of cruciformity in theological interpretations of human suffering in the words of ecotheologian Denis Edwards:

> First, [the term cruciform as a descriptor of creation] acknowledges honestly the pain and cost of evolving creation. Second, it leads to the thought that, in the cross, God embraces not just suffering humanity but the whole of creation in its travail. Third, it can be taken as raising the question of whether all creatures are in some way to be redeemed in Christ.[12]

Hence, modern ecotheologians are paying serious attention to the cruciformity inherent in our dynamic universe and, as a result, are offering new substance to theological conversations concerning suffering.

There is, however, another aspect worth exploring: the role of sacrifice in our evolutionary world.

Sacrifice and Labor to Bring Forth Newness

This subcategory recognizes the sacrifice and labor involved in the emergence of newness in the universe and connects this with descriptions of human suffering. The sacrifice and labor characterizing cosmogenesis enable the classic descriptions of sacrifice, witnessing, cosmic travail, testing, and schooling to be articulated in new ways. This may help some sufferers today. Thomas Berry suggests that all great transformations involve moments of great sacrifice that can be understood via the imagery of midwifery and the process of new birth.[13]

These embodied metaphors of human reproduction, alongside biblical agrarian references (e.g., the process of grains of wheat falling to the ground and dying to produce the harvest in John 12:24), can be reconfigured to help describe the idea of cosmic sacrifice.[14] Gloria Schaab iterates this: "The procreative model of cosmic creation with its emphasis on natural processes and structures and its stance of interdependency parallels the model of human procreative process facilitated through the practice of midwifery."[15]

Earth literacy and an ETA enable the terms *sacrifice* and *labor* to describe human suffering in new ways and sufferers can pour new meaning into these literary vessels. Perhaps by reimagining suffering, sacrifice, death, and new life through an evolutionary lens, alternative responses to suffering can be imagined; if sufferers feel a deep kinship for the grain of wheat, then as their lives diminish through age or sickness (inherent sacrifice and suffering associated with finite life), hope for new abundant harvests can spark different, more life-giving ways of living, loving, and dying. It can also help believers to see the difference between necessary and inherent suffering and that which is inflicted and unnecessary, and in need of redress.

Thus, this subcategory emphasizes how the universe is caught up in the laborious process of bringing forth newness from the sacrifice of another. This practical way of describing and understanding kenotic-kinetic events will deepen theological conversations concerning suffering beyond what is offered by the machine metaphor and vision of a distant, apathetic God.

Costly Creative Kenotic-Kinetic

The kenotic-kinetic animating our evolutionary world was outlined earlier as the final pillar of an ETA. This novel nomenclature stands as a reminder that the creative tendencies of our cosmos that actualize potentialities are very costly. It also describes God's presence and activity in the laborious process that is cosmogenesis. God's initial creative act (*creatio originalis* or *creation ex nihilo*) has to be seen alongside God's continuing creative impulses (*creatio continua*) that animate and nourish Earth's own creativity (*concursus*) and always held in tension with God's final creative act at the end-time (*creatio nova*). The interconnectivity of these dimensions needs to inform our descriptions of suffering.

Robert J. Russell indicates that contemporary theologians such as Ian Barbour, John Haught, and John Polkinghorne have used kenotic theology to facilitate descriptions of God's response to the cruciformity in creation and they "extend it to include the whole sweep of life on earth."[16] They use the kenosis of Christ as a model for describing (albeit partially) human suffering. What they offer is a reminder that all creation is animated by the same kenotic-kinetic, and thus, human suffering can be informed by both the incarnation and by the experience of other-than-human suffering, regardless of whether the subject is a star that must "die" so that heavy elements can form in its supernova, or a rabbit sacrificed within its complex relationship with its predator, the fox. These are all distinct modalities of our cosmos's inherent kenotic disposition. Each is a unique and painful transformative moment of grace, and together they animate the sacred and cruciform universe story.

Humans have more complex information processing, pattern recognition, and information storing systems, and concomitantly we have an intensified awareness and experience of the kenotic-kinetic animating the universe. Accordingly, any consideration of human suffering must be situated within a larger creative horizon or "arc" that is animated by the kenotic-kinetic.[17] This is a gift of a robust Earth literacy; we have a new appreciation of the experiences of all the concomitant "victims" or "casualties" of cosmogenesis,[18] and this allows believers to understand that as both creators and sufferers dwelling in an evolutionary world, they are never alone or abandoned in their suffering. They are part of a planetary communion of compassionate subjects. The root of the term *compassion* is the Latin term, *compati*, meaning "to suffer with." Our understanding of compassion is filled with new meaning in light of our awareness of the kenotic-kinetic because we can now understand the vast myriad of subjects who "suffer with" another within our 13.8-billion-year family history. Thus, other-than-human subjects (e.g., more familiar cousins such as elephants and less familiar family members such as rocks) are compassionate in that they endure loss, deterioration, and disintegration as all created life does, including humans (e.g., as humans age they undergo biological and psychological deterioration). However, the distinct expression of compassion that humans exhibit toward each other[19] is similar to that which elephants express but not at all the same as what rocks exhibit; rocks participate without inhibitions in the cosmic processes of disintegration (e.g., entropic experiences). Nor is compassion manifested in the same way for all created life. Compassion, when robustly imagined, can encompass the many diverse expressions that Earth's many subjects convey without biasing any one experience or demanding that they all be the same.

SUMMARY

This fourth category, which is the witness of suffering inherent in our evolutionary, post-Newtonian universe, enables theological discourse to envision and employ new literary tools (e.g., cruciformity, sacrifice, labor, midwifery, and the kenotic-kinetic) to more adequately help sufferers to articulate their experiences today. Theological interpretations of human suffering in the twenty-first century are achieved through a comprehensive Earth literacy guided by an ETA. Consequently, modern theological engagement with the mystery of suffering requires an integrative trifold approach: an exploration of ecosystemic suffering, divine suffering, and human suffering. From this approach, nine dimensions of promise can be offered to those who suffer in an evolutionary world.

As noted earlier, the final section of this text is committed to being *on* the ground and *of* the ground, as well as being *rooted* in the heart of God. The last three chapters are organized by three metaphors designed to contextualize the perspectives offered by each commitment: to be *rooted in* the heart of God, we will look to the Creator for a "map" of our encounter with suffering; to be *on* the ground, we will look out the "window" at the suffering within creation; to be *of* the ground, we will look in the "mirror" at human suffering as a reflection (albeit partial) of the suffering experienced by God and creation.[20]

11

DIVINE SUFFERING: A MAP

If our theological investigation of the mystery of suffering is *on* and *of* the ground (ecosystemic and human suffering), we need a reliable map to help us navigate. Divine suffering is part of the topography, alongside other divine characteristics such as love, power, and faithfulness. It will assist us because all suffering is *rooted in* the compassionate heart of God.

Today, our knowledge of the magnitude and diversity of experiences of suffering calls into question classic ways of describing God as apathetic, all powerful, and good (e.g., divine impassibility, immutability, omnipotence, benevolence). Also, as Hans Jonas frankly admits, "We should not say anything about God that we would not be willing to repeat in the presence of the children of Auschwitz."[1] So the question remains, are classic understandings of God adequate in light of the inherent suffering characterizing our evolutionary world, and would we be willing to repeat these understandings in the presence of those who endure radical suffering? This chapter attempts to answer this question. What it does not do is offer a systematic argument concerning whether or not God can suffer, for many writers have already written about this.[2] Rather, this chapter embraces the wisdom of Dietrich Bonhoeffer that "only a suffering God helps" and explores new ways to interpret suffering in an evolutionary world.[3]

Similar to the last chapter, an opening narrative will help orient readers to the context of this exploration of divine suffering and what is at stake. It is offered by Elie Wiesel and François Mauriac. The former is a man who lived through the Auschwitz concentration camp. When a child was hanged in the camp, Wiesel writes, "Behind me, I heard...: 'For God's sake, where is God?' And from within me, I heard a voice answer: 'Where He is? This is where—hanging here from this gallows.'"[4] Intuitively, the only description of God that made sense to Wiesel was that God suffered as this innocent child did. He rejects the idol of a distant, impassive God, and in this rejection, he is empowered to resist and overcome the suffering he experienced. Wiesel recounted his experiences to François Mauriac, a Catholic novelist, and the latter's receptivity to this experience of radical suffering affected his understanding of God:

> And I, who believe that God is love, what answer was there to give my young interlocutor whose dark eyes still held the reflection of the angelic sadness that had appeared one day on the face of a hanged child? What did I say to him? Did I speak to him of that other Jew, this crucified brother who perhaps resembled him and whose cross conquered the world? Did I explain to him that what had been a stumbling block for his faith had become a cornerstone of mine? And that the connection between the cross and human suffering remains, in my view, the key to the unfathomable mystery in which the faith of his childhood was lost? And yet, Zion has risen up again out of the crematoria and the slaughterhouses. The Jewish nation has been resurrected from among its thousands of dead. It is they who have given it new life. We do not know the worth of one single drop of blood, one single tear. All is grace. If the Almighty is the Almighty, the last word for each of us belongs to Him. That is what I should have said to the Jewish child. But all I could do was embrace him and weep.[5]

Mauriac's words show readers that we can companion those who suffer and understand their suffering despite not directly experiencing the suffering. This solidarity is based on faithfulness to being in relationship even during hard times and a mutual accountability for the suffering of our neighbors. This form of solidarity is achieved via a deep receptivity to suffering; receptivity awakened in these believers the insufficiency of a vision of a distant, apathetic God. God is compassion and hence, *suffers with* all of creation. To be compassionate, God must be affected by and receptive to all forms of suffering. This is not weakness or less than perfection, but a unique manifestation of perfection: choosing to suffer. Since we are made in the image of God, who is Love and the source of all compassion, we too can be receptive to and affected by the suffering in our world. Consequently, divine suffering as compassion is our map for interpreting suffering encountered in our cosmic communion of suffering subjects.

DIVINE SUFFERING

We begin with a brief exploration of modern interpretations of God who suffers. Then, we will discuss three expressions of divine suffering—the creative suffering of a Triune God, incarnation as emergent compassion, and the cosmic cross as a symbol of unconditional compassionate love—as we explore compassion.[6]

God Who Suffers

Explorations of God have always stretched theological imaginations and the capacities of human language. Today, our emerging Earth literacy and ETA offer new avenues for these investigations. God is being reimagined since we now know our world is ancient, unfinished, and dynamic, and humans have emerged from Earth's creativity. However, for all discussions of divine suffering, two aspects must be remembered. First, in the midst of divine suffering, "God remains God" and does not sacrifice transcendence to foster this intimate communion with creation.[7] Second, God's suffering "belongs to the real order" of creation (it is not theoretical or metaphorical), but it is always shrouded in mystery beyond our capacity to understand. Thus, divine suffering is not what creatures suffer but is still intimately connected to it.[8] Despite these two criteria, this God who suffers is the same God who has ultimate power over death. God is not mired in suffering, but exhibits powerfulness via compassion; in and through the vulnerability and suffering of Christ on the cross, God demonstrates God's power to save and empowers others to participate in this transformation. This God who suffers may seem "very peculiar and very ungodlike" but speaks prophetically to divine power as mutual em*power*ment expressed in and through compassion.[9]

In Scripture

One source for understanding divine suffering is Scripture. The God described in Scripture is dynamic, passionate, involved in the world, and as a result, God suffers. These characteristics were obscured when Christian thinkers embraced ancient Greek philosophy that emphasized God's transcendence and immutability.[10] Scripture scholars have shown that within the Bible, God is a God who suffers so that humanity can know how near God is and the depths to which God loves creation.[11] God shares the pain and suffering of humanity like a suffering "comrade,"[12] not a sympathetic and powerless bystander: God's pain "is never the wailing sympathy of an uninvolved onlooker, but the genuine pain of one who is directly affected, the suffering of a comrade, who takes upon himself a part of the burden."[13] In Scripture, divine suffering takes on three forms: God suffers *because* of humanity's rebellion; God suffers *with* people who are suffering; and God suffers *for* the people. Thus, in Scripture, divine suffering is not a deficiency but an essential aspect of God's nature.

In Human Experiences

Feminist theologies also contribute to our understanding of divine suffering. For example, Elizabeth Johnson indicates that using the experiences of women as new lenses to comprehend divine suffering highlights several underappreciated dimensions of divine suffering in Scripture: (1) God suffers the pains of childbirth to bring new life into the world (see Isa 42:14); (2) God suffers the travail of bringing forth justice (see Judg 2:18; Exod 3:7–8; Wis 10:15–19; Prov 1:23–27); (3) God grieves due to injustice and violence like women do when they lose a loved one (see Isa 16:9; Jer 48:31, 36); and (4) the degradation and abuse experienced by women around the world is analogous to the suffering of Christ on the cross.[14] Hence, the suffering experienced by women helps believers understand how God can suffer.

In Cosmic Experiences

Modern ecotheological scholarship has also made unique contributions to the dialogue concerning divine suffering. When describing God, many ecotheologians emphasize divine connectedness, not distance; companionship, not separation; empathy, not apathy; intimacy, not absence. These accentuations challenge classical understandings of God as immutable, changeless, and wholly "Other." For example, Jay McDaniel offers the following intimate portrait of God's immanence that stems from his Earth literacy:

> God is aware of, and empathetically identified with, each and every event in the divine body: be it a pulsation of energy in the depths of a star, a moment of sentience in the life of a bacterium, a moment of pleasure in the life of a deer, or an occasion of joy in an exchange between friends....Indeed, the world is immanent within, and present to, God, even as God is immanent within, and present to, the world.[15]

If God "empathetically identifies" with the energies and joys of this world as McDaniel suggests, then God would also suffer and grieve its sorrows. John Haught indicates that the real reason believers are afraid of connecting evolution and God is because of "the scandalous image of God's humility latent in the Christian sources themselves."[16]

Within our evolutionary world, one can discern "a momentous story" of God's self-sacrificing, compassionate love and "divine self-giving to the universe."[17] This vulnerability contradicts a popular idea that God's power is "power over" creation and demands that theology incorporate vulnerability and the "infinite depths of divine compassion" in how God is understood.[18] Ecotheologian and Franciscan sister Ilia Delio develops an exquisite portrait of a divine suffering God as abundant Love in her text *The Humility of God*. God is not unmoved or radically separate from the cruciformity of creation; instead, God is present to this suffering out of an abundant love for creation. Delio's vision of God reminds believers that "we are called to let go and enter into the storm, to love as passionately, extravagantly and wastefully as God has loved us."[19] Her description of divine suffering is molded by the wisdom of St. Francis who "experienced…a God of such compassionate love that He bends low to press us to his cheek."[20] God, whom St. Francis loved, was not the immutable God of intellectuals formed by Greek philosophy, but a God that the birds worshipped in their morning songs. St. Francis's God is so involved with creation that it is impossible to understand the suffering God apart from the suffering of God's creatures.[21] Thus, the God of evolution suffers due to an excess of compassionate love rather than a privation or deficiency, and is powerful in powerlessness, bending low in "foolish nearness" to love a world that is free to respond to Love with love—or not.[22] This general overview however, requires more detail, which is offered in the next sections that explore three important expressions of divine suffering as compassion.

Compassion: The Creative Suffering of a Triune God

Gloria Schaab's work, *The Creative Suffering of the Triune God*, demonstrates how a shift toward Earth literacy and the embrace of an ETA can help minister to those who suffer. Schaab argues that Christ's cry of dereliction on the cross can be described as an expression of the suffering of a Triune God who is laboring in creation to bring new life from suffering and death. Here Schaab integrates a trinitarian understanding of God with Arthur Peacocke's panentheistic model of God's relationship with creation and his use of the terms *in*, *with*, and *under* to describe this relationship.[23] She also uses three female images for God drawn from theological, mystical, and biblical traditions of Judaism and Christianity to help us understand divine suffering as well as a procreative model of divine travail.[24] As a result, Schaab envisions God's presence in the world and experience of the world (including pain, suffering, and death) in a provocative manner not unlike Hildegard: "Like a mother with the child of her womb, God in this model envelops, enfleshes, and permeates the very being of the cosmos."[25] Schaab's ecofeminist, panentheistic, procreative, triune model of the creative suffering of God allows her to delineate a differentiated model of divine suffering:[26] transcendent sympathy (suffering *with* the cosmos); incarnate empathy (suffering *in* the cosmos); and immanent protopathy (suffering *under* the kenotic-kinetic of the cosmos).[27] It is important to note that the prepositions *in*, *with*, and *under* can be used interchangeably because the Triune God is a unity of diversity and one in relationship to the cosmos. Accordingly, the distinctive types of suffering (described by the prepositions *in*, *with*, and *under*) "are experienced by each and all Persons of the Trinity in relation to the cosmos."[28] Nevertheless, Schaab argues that the best description for divine suffering is that our transcendent Mother experiences sympathetic suffering (suffering "with"), the incarnation undergoes empathetic suffering (suffering "in"), and the immanent Spirit suffers protopathetically (suffering "under").[29] Understanding the nature of each manifestation of divine suffering is crucial for understanding how the creative suffering of a Triune God can help sufferers.

God, our transcendent Mother, compassionately and eternally remembers the child in her own womb. Thus, God made space within Godself for that which was not God (creation), and in doing so suffers sympathetically or *with* her creation:[30] "The transcendent Mother of the universe therefore inherently senses and intimately suffers the least bit of distress that afflicts the growing life within Her. Moreover, the transcendent Mother suffers her own travail in the eternal birthing process."[31] Hence, God, as transcendent Creator, suffers sympathetically with the cosmos: "She is sickened morning and evening by the violence, oppression, and exploitation that ravages the developing life within her, the offspring of her love."[32] This perspective undermines prevalent visions of God as inflicting suffering as punishment from afar or an impassable God unmoved by the suffering of God's creatures. This model of divine compassion is helpful for some sufferers who experience alienation, loneliness, and feelings of unworthiness. This manner of interpreting divine suffering will help those who take solace from, and derive strength from, a personal God who suffers *with* them.

Shekhinah (the feminine Hebrew noun denoting the indwelling of God in the world) and the incarnation suffer empathetically *in* the developing universe and oppressed of the cosmos.[33] The cost of our continually creative and often unjust world is suffering, oppression, and death. Consequently, the suffering and rejected servant of God experiences firsthand the omnipresence of pain, suffering, and death in our evolutionary world and as a result, liberation for sufferers comes "from the realization that they can identify their suffering with that of another and that another identifies with them in their pain."[34] Christ suffered both the inherent suffering associated with his willing participation *in* the cosmic kenotic-kinetic and inflicted anthropogenic (human-caused) suffering manifest *in* his passion and crucifixion.

Since Christ chose to be fully human—in all the joyfulness and suffering this entails—and Christ is the second person of the Trinity, then our Triune God has intimate and affective knowledge of suffering and is truly empathetic to the suffering experienced in our world. God knows and feels the pain of individual sufferers, so we are never alone in our struggles. This vision of divine love as empathetic compassion can also remind believers of the healing power lying hidden in their relationships with family members, friends, school, work, and the church community, which today are often overlooked or disregarded in the pursuit of a purely technological fix for all suffering. Christ, as part of a triune family who chose to be in an intimate relationship with all of creation, took on suffering but ultimately transformed this suffering into new life.

Christ's empathetic suffering *in* the developing universe and *in* the experiences of the oppressed elicited powerful responses from those in relationships with him; both at the foot of the cross and at the hiatus of the cross and burial, women were courageously present and prophetically resisting suffering by companioning God's suffering servant at great cost to themselves. They remained present and their compassionate companionship witnessed to the darkness of Christ's crucifixion that love will prevail despite their utter powerlessness to alleviate what Jesus was enduring. They said to the darkness, we beg to differ.[35] Divine empathy can empower human sufferers to embrace, endure, and transform the physical reality of suffering, and cultivate communities of compassionate companions whose steadfast love helps to bring forth newness of life in spite of suffering and death. This way of approaching suffering, modelled on Christ's suffering *in* the cosmos, challenges the modern trend of insulating ourselves via displacement or institutionalization of anyone who uncomfortably reminds us of our invitation to be empathetic fellow sufferers (e.g., the elderly, the sick, the dead, and the disabled). Hence, for sufferers who experience oppression and marginalization, the Incarnate One who suffers empathetically brings comfort not only because God knows what they are going through, but also because of the witness to solidarity that such divine suffering demands from the communities in which sufferers dwell.

The third component of Schaab's vision of divine suffering is immanent protopathy, which describes the experience of the Spirit who suffers *under* the immediate travail of an evolving world. This mode of suffering "is *not* a suffering with another or a suffering in union with another. It is a primal and immediate suffering that wells up under and through the passions of those who yearn and strive for the full flourishing of human and cosmic being whenever that full flourishing is at risk of frustration or demise."[36] Schaab argues that it is the Holy Spirit as Sophia who experiences, "with unparalleled immediacy," that which frustrates creation's movement toward completion and wholeness in God. This includes that which obstructs creativity or abundant life such as violent and destructive evolutionary processes, exploitation, violence, injustice, and despair. This mode of divine suffering can give sufferers a new way of understanding the Holy Spirit who can fuel their own resistance to whatever is frustrating their fullness of life. Sophia can reconnect all who suffer as a communion of suffering subjects:

> The Spirit...is the life of the life of all creatures; the way in which everything is penetrated with connectedness and relatedness; a burning fire who sparks, ignites, inflames, kindles hearts; a guide in the fog; a balm for wounds; a shining serenity; an overflowing fountain that spreads to all sides. The Spirit is life, movement, color, radiance, restorative stillness in the din....Her power makes dry twigs and withered souls green again with the juice of life.[37]

This vision of cosmic transformation powered by an immanent and interior Spirit counters purely militaristic understandings of resistance offered to sufferers today; a manifestation of this is the slogans offered by many cancer institutes, such as "We Will Conquer Cancer in Our Lifetime" (Princess Margaret Hospital) or "Fight hard, fight tough...Fight Like a Girl!" (Choose Hope Cancer Awareness Campaign). These images of resistance are necessary and meaningful to many sufferers; however, in "battles," there is no place for failure—*either* you win the battle against cancer *or* you lose to this more powerful, foreign entity.

Schaab's expression of immanent protopathy can empower sufferers to resist that which thwarts their well-being without alienating their material bodies (or dysfunctional elements of their bodies) so that they can holistically and creatively participate in their healing process that does not deny the reality of death. This model allows for a fullness of life and personhood in spite of death, diminishment, or disability rather than a life devoid of suffering or death.

The creative suffering of God as suffering "under" the kenotic-kinetic reminds believers that life is not about either/or but mysteriously it is both/and. Our world, our lives, and the nature of our Creator can be *both* cruciform *and* creative. This helps sufferers to appreciate their active participation in the transformation of their suffering as a manifestation of the powerful and immanent presence of Sophia-God, who brings new life out of death and sustains our evolutionary world's movement toward ultimate wholeness and healing in God.

Gloria Schaab's exploration of the creative suffering of the Triune God offers many ways to understand divine suffering that can help believers when they experience suffering. Another area in need of elaboration is the concept of the emergent compassion in the incarnate and risen Christ.

The Incarnate and Risen Christ as Emergent Compassion

Christ of Chalcedon affirms that Christ was fully human and fully divine. This means that the historical and biological life, ministry, death, and resurrection of Jesus Christ can never be completely separate entities. This is the foundation of the argument this section makes; namely, that the experience of suffering of the incarnate Christ and the rebirth proclaimed by the risen Christ reveal the eternal and ongoing compassion of God. However, this love can be described in new ways because we have learned so much more about our ancient, dynamic, and unfinished world. A better way to articulate God's ongoing loving desire to be and suffer with us (*com*passion) over our 13.8-billion-year family history is "emergent compassion." This is the manifestation and sharing of divine, suffering love with creation through Christ who emerged from Earth's creative processes two thousand years ago.

Ecotheologians have offered new images and metaphors for advancing our understanding of the incarnation as emergence. James Nash, within his reflection on the "Incarnation as Cosmic Representation," explores the deep material connectivity of the incarnation and creation in new ways:

> We are embodiments of biotic history on this planet, incorporating all simpler systems in evolution....We carry within ourselves "the signature of the supernovas and the geology and life history of the Earth." ...Humans are representatives of the earth, interdependent parts of nature—and this totality is what God became immersed in through association with the Representative of Humanity in the Incarnation.[38]

He argues that since we know that humanity has emerged from Earth's creative processes, then Jesus the Cosmic Christ can be described simultaneously as a representation of humanity and the cosmos.[39] Nash's understanding of Christ's deep connectivity with creation is likewise articulated by Norman Habel in his understanding of "deep incarnation":

> If we recognize Earth as a living organism, can we also say that God became 'incarnate' in Earth? Does Jesus the creature represent all creation? The answer, I believe, is yes! Jesus is animated dust from the ground, is that piece of Earth where God's presence is concentrated in the incarnation. God becomes flesh, clay, Earth.[40]

Gloria Schaab develops the understanding of "deep incarnation" further by connecting the term *emergence* from evolutionary theory with the doctrine of the incarnation. She indicates that we live in a world designed to create novel forms of life from preceding, less complex forms, but these emerging forms are not "reducible or explainable solely in terms of the form that preceded them."[41] Christ did not disrupt this principle but worked within these parameters to become incarnate. Thus, Schaab argues that "the most suitable context through which to consider the Incarnation is through the dynamic of emergence."[42] She creatively integrates the principle of emergence with Karl Rahner's belief that the incarnation was both the *present* fulfillment of creation (the unity of the divine and human natures of Christ) and the *future* promise for the unity and integrity of the whole cosmos in God. She indicates that Rahner emphasized incarnation as both God's definitive self-communication to the cosmos, but also "the definite acceptance of the self-communication by the cosmos in Jesus Christ."[43] Humanity (and Christ) emerged from the continuously creative and unfinished cosmos, and as such, all creation is groaning as it awaits completion.[44] Accordingly, in the incarnation, God as creative, suffering Love is "forever woven into the fabric of matter and history and continues to share in the sufferings of creation ontologically and experientially."[45] One way to picture this is to envision God's suffering love as extending backwards from Bethlehem to the Big Bang—an energetic moment when God decided to freely endow matter with "diverse potentialities" and empowered the cosmos to create itself.[46] God respected its integrity and freedom, and in an ongoing act of great suffering love, God let creation be itself. Bethlehem represents the moment when Jesus emerged from these creative processes and freely and unconditionally embraced the kenotic-kinetic that included all the associated anxieties, limitations, and physical hardships embedded in truly biological existence. God's loving desire to be unreservedly incarnate or "with us" began at the moment that the celestial furnace brought forth the matter that would eventually complexify into the materials, processes, and webs of life that facilitated Christ's conception in the womb of Mary. The many manifestations of God's compassion emerged as the cosmos complexified and was ultimately concentrated into the Word made flesh, Jesus Christ.[47] This dynamic vision of emergent compassion liberates the incarnation from being narrowly confined to a singular event (i.e., the birth of Christ or the crucifixion) or to the singular doctrine of atonement for sin; Earth's violent and creative processes were at work long before the existence of humans who could sin.[48]

However, God's compassion did not stop in the stable at Bethlehem, during the ministry of Christ, or on the cross at Golgotha, but carries forward to the end of time. This new perception of the incarnation draws theological attention to the necessity of embracing the idea of "deep" resurrection: the saving and healing power of the resurrection being offered to all of creation.[49] The outpouring of divine compassion in the life, ministry, death, and resurrection of Christ models how God's compassion can extend forward from Golgotha to our lives today, and ultimately, to the end-time. This idea unites the risen Jesus with the entire cosmos laboring under the kenotic-kinetic to bring forth newness out of disintegration and suffering. The risen Jesus is neither separate from the materiality of the evolutionary world, nor from cosmic history. Rather, in a way that we will never completely comprehend, "the risen Christ is to be found at the very heart of creation as the concrete and effective promise that creation is indeed going somewhere, that it is already always oriented toward an eschatological end that endows the whole of it with the future promise of a definitive and redemptive 'yes.'"[50]

Our Earth literacy allows for a more expansive appreciation of both the incarnation and the resurrection; deep incarnation and resurrection speaks anew of how the creative power of divine, suffering love triumphs over both inflicted suffering and biological death. But how does this help those who suffer? Ilia Delio hints at the answer to this: "In the suffering and death of Jesus we find the power to love in the midst of suffering because love is stronger than death."[51] Gloria Schaab concurs: "In his emergence in cosmic history, Jesus has revealed to us the divine plan for the fullness of time, the summation of all things in the Christ-mystery, the mystery of the nature of the cosmos which has God as its evolutionary goal and completion."[52] Thus, appreciating the incarnation and resurrection as manifestations of emergent compassion inspires human sufferers to envision divine love or *eros* as a magnetic force drawing human sufferers and all of creation toward a fullness of life—a "new creation"—in the sacred heart of the risen Christ.

The coupling of the incarnation and resurrection by Earth-literate believers can proclaim anew the transformative power laying hidden in vulnerability and suffering, and empower people living with broken bodies, domestic abuse, or within the chaos of a fractured world to place their hope for future health and wholeness in the incarnate and risen Christ. Elizabeth Johnson indicates that our Easter *Alleluias* are not proclaimed only because of the good fortune of Jesus as an individual, but because of the realization that the destiny of Jesus is not only meant for him but for all of creation:

> [Christ's] destiny means that our hope does not merely clutch at a possibility but stands on an irrevocable ground of what has already transpired in him. Life in all fullness awaits. Unimaginable as it may be, this means that salvation is not the escape of the human spirit from an existence embedded in matter, but resurrection of the body, the whole body-person, dust and breath together.[53]

Sufferers today require powerful symbols to evoke the energies within themselves and their communion of compassionate subjects to embrace, resist, and transform their suffering into new life in Christ. Let us now investigate ways that Christianity's most powerful symbol, the cross, prophetically proclaims God's eternal compassion in an evolving world.

The Cosmic Cross

Leo J. Donovan wrote, "Some images are so powerful that, if we take time for them, they can alter our lives. The spirit hovering over the waters, the Lord who is our shepherd, the mountain on which every tear will be wiped away are such images."[54] The cross as both a symbol and historical reality is another transformative image with many associated meanings. Historically, the cross has been appropriated by imperial powers and sovereigns to justify the conquering of whomever is considered the "other" (e.g., non-Christians, the poor, indigenous people). For example, Douglas John Hall explores the use of the cross by French explorer Jacques Cartier to bespeak of ownership of indigenous land and peoples in Canada rather than as a symbol of divine *agape* or love.[55] The cross has also been appropriated by patriarchal cultures to justify submission and self-abnegation of women, and by the contemporary pop music culture to express various meanings (e.g., power, wealth, fame, spirituality). Despite many abusive and distorted interpretations, the symbol of the cross remains a living symbol, one open to novel interpretations.

The Cosmic Cross: Compassion through the Ages

The emergence of Earth literacy and the construction of an ETA pour new meaning into the symbol of the cross. Teilhard de Chardin spoke eloquently of the value of the cross in an ancient evolutionary world:

> Under our very eyes, and in our hearts, I am convinced Christ-the-Redeemer is fulfilling himself and unfolding himself in the figure of Christ-the-Evolver. Thereby, too, the meaning of the Cross is taking on greater breadth and dynamism for us: the Cross which is the symbol not merely of the dark retrogressive side of the universe in genesis, but also and, even more, of its triumphant and luminous side; the Cross which

> is the symbol of progress and victory won through mistakes, disappointments and hard work; the only Cross, in very truth, that we can honestly, proudly and passionately offer for the worship of a world that has become conscious of what it was yesterday and what awaits it tomorrow.[56]

Holmes Rolston III also indicates how Earth literacy critiques the prevailing ideas that the cross was only valuable because it offered atonement for human sin: "Long before humans arrived, the way of nature was already a *via dolorosa*. In that sense, the aura of the cross is cast backward across the whole global story, and it forever outlines the future."[57] Through the lens of an ETA, the cross is a concrete, real, historical monument of God's unconditional, suffering love for both humanity *and* the entirety of creation: past, present, and future. Douglas John Hall argues that "God is as firmly committed to the life of this world as that cross was planted in the ground at Golgotha, that is, (symbolically) at the very center of death's apparent sovereignty."[58] The cross as a historical event was not part of a divine plan to extort guilt, nor should it be interpreted as a manifestation of God's vindictiveness or coerciveness. To do so negates the positive dimension of the cross, namely Christ's labor of supporting our cruciform and creative evolving world, and reconciling the world with God.[59] The cross was part of a human act (crucifixion) but it became an opportunity for God to make present and real God's unfathomable depth of love for the world since the beginning of time. It was one of many moments (albeit a unique and vital one) in creation that shows God's commitment to bring eternal life, unity, and peace out of death and destruction.

There are many transformations from death to new life in the sacred cosmic story and these "narratives" must be appreciated to invigorate theological imaginations to see the cross with new eyes. For example, without the sacrifice of the leaves, deciduous trees would die during the winter. However, in this process of eliminating the leaves, the tree exhibits great beauty. Biochemical reactions cause the production of the green pigment in the leaves to decline and when the green color fades, other pigments previously hidden emerge. Thus, the carotene pigments in birch and hickory trees and the anthocyanins of red maples, red oaks, and sumacs are unveiled as the leaves die, causing the symphony of brilliant yellow, red, and purple hues of an autumn landscape. This is just one vivid expression of Earth's kenotic-kinetic, and it speaks boldly to the emergence of new life from suffering and death. It also reminds believers that there can be beauty in some moments of great sacrifice. Human theological imaginations need to be cultivated by a vibrant Earth literacy in order for us to be able to appreciate cosmic moments of sacrifice and grace, including the cross. The costly and creative sacred universe story reminds believers that new life does arise from the ashes of diminishment and death, and these are concrete, but partial, expressions of the hope for new life symbolized by the cross. A robust Earth literacy allows believers to imagine God's presence, love, and commitment in new ways without losing sight of how, on the cross, Christ suffered as a human and bore the sins of the world.

Astute believers should ask how this cosmic cross helps the Christian community and human sufferers. Pierre Teilhard de Chardin wrestled with this question in his retreats, journals, letters, and texts (and some of this will be revealed in chapter 13). He believed that using an evolutionary model to express the mystery of the cross did not minimize or displace the place of the cross in theology, but rather, it amplified "the truth, the power, and the irresistible appeal of the Cross."[60] He was clear that "once we have fully grasped the meaning of the cross, we are no longer in danger of finding life sad and ugly. We shall simply have become more attentive to its barely comprehensible solemnity."[61] Hence, the cosmic cross incites hope in an unfinished and tragic world.

Contemporary ecotheologian Ilia Delio has further developed Teilhard's perspective, stating that the cross reveals God's unconditional love for the world manifest as "powerful, transforming energy that heals reconciles, unites and makes whole."[62] She argues that "with arms outstretched Christ crucified embraces a sinful world disrupted by human violence, disconnected, and incomplete—a God who is radically in love with the world."[63] Consequently, the formation of biospiritual theological imaginations can aid sufferers because they will possess a deep appreciation of the breadth and depth of God's compassionate presence and love that spans all of cosmic history.

The Cosmic Cross: Reconnecting Human and Cosmic Suffering

By appreciating nature's *via dolorosa* or kenotic-kinetic as the way of the cross, sufferers will also appreciate the cosmic dimension of the cross.[64] Thus, human suffering is resituated within the kenotic-kinetic that animates the sacred cosmic story. This repositioning will remind sufferers who are overwhelmed by the highly industrialized (and individualized) approach to alleviating suffering, that their suffering can also be characterized by the same beauty and transformation from death to new life inherent in deciduous trees and the cross. The divine love symbolized by the cross invites humanity (and all of creation) to respond to God's love with great love and to participate in the painful and joyful unfolding of the cosmos. This reconnection with the cruciform Earth as a way to understand one's own suffering is fostered by a theology of faith, hope, and love grounded in an ETA. A theology of faith resonates the truth that God who created the world brings life out of death again and again; a theology of *hope* is one that ultimately places our trust in the activity of serendipitous creativity, the Holy Spirit working in and through Earth's creativity; and a theology of *love* recognizes that the compassionate heart of Jesus is the beating heart of the universe.

For some sufferers held prisoner by their overwhelming experience of silence, pain, loneliness, or unworthiness, this approach pays serious theological attention to the concrete experiences of suffering in the world and yet also cultivates hope in transformation. Embracing the kenotic-kinetic does not reduce a sufferer's life to meaninglessness;[65] rather it enables human persons who are laboring under the cruciformity of being part of a finite world (e.g., sickness or diminishment) and those oppressed by inflicted suffering (e.g., racism or sexism) to know that God is with them and working to heal and liberate them. Believing this can evoke a response to suffering far greater than merely accepting it; it can evoke feelings of gratitude, peace, outrage, hope, and meaningfulness that shatter apathy and paralysis and empower transformation. Their awakening to concrete moments of transformation and grace in Earth's communion of suffering subjects can inspire sufferers to interpret their pain as a manifestation of the same kenotic-kinetic that continually responds to violence, destruction, and death in unexpectedly creative ways. Hence, the symbol of the cosmic cross can bring solace in their darkest hour by reconnecting sufferers to Earth as primary healer and source of the sacred transformative Spirit who is continually present and active in the world.

In an evolutionary world, the cross does not lose its expiatory function but it is given another layer of meaning; Earth's evolutionary processes can be an expression (albeit partial) of the transformation symbolized by the cross. Consequently, the cross can become, as Teilhard asserts, the symbol and the expression of "evolution" in its fullest sense. The cosmic cross is not only a "consolation" for the world's miseries but a "stimulant" moving all of creation toward fullness of life in the crucified and risen Christ.[66]

The Cosmic Cross: Empowering Compassion

A final way in which the cosmic cross aids sufferers is through its critique of modern understandings of power as domination. The cosmic cross reveals how great power resides in vulnerability and brokenness. Wisdom revealed in the cosmos, such as the symbiotic (and thus vulnerable) tendencies inherent in evolutionary processes offered by Lynn Margulis or the powerful nature of smallness and vulnerability to build communion witnessed by Jean Vanier, adds depth to our understanding of God's power manifested in vulnerability on the cross:

> Power and strength can separate people; whereas weakness and recognition of weakness and the cry for help brings people together. When you are weak, you need people. It's very easy. When you are strong you don't need people, you can do everything on your own. So, somewhere the weak person calls people together. And when the weak call forth the strong, what happens is they awaken what is most beautiful in a human person—compassion, goodness, openness to another and so on. Our weakness brings people together.[67]

The scandalous message of divine power in powerlessness is necessary to evaluate contemporary understandings of power as oppressive and coercive. The latter understanding of power only inspires apathy, fosters narrow, self-satisfying expectations, and breeds intolerance of any form of suffering and of sufferers themselves. In other words, suffering and death have no place in this world.

Hall indicates that "when an entire culture is held in the grip of a worldview in which death is allowed no voice, death's power over life is immensely increased."[68] At Golgotha, the cross symbolized an act of a religiously and politically motivated group to dominate and silence another. Nevertheless, God still responded powerfully, as Ilia Delio suggests: "The power of God is the powerlessness of God's unconditional love shown to us in the cross."[69] In her text *The Unbearable Wholeness of Being*, she elaborates: "As divine love empties itself into the other, it empowers the other by withdrawing its own power and allowing the other to flourish as other."[70] Accordingly, God's true transforming power was power in relation—*com*passion—and laid hidden in vulnerability and suffering. The cosmic cross can offer human sufferers hope via God's powerful compassion, even in the midst of a modern world that disembodies and disconnects.[71]

SUMMARY

Understanding divine suffering as compassion inspires human persons to describe their own suffering as a sharing in the kenotic disposition inherent in our evolutionary world and our Creator. It addresses the denial of suffering and delusions of mastery that are rampant in contemporary human consciousness. In prophetic ways, Earth literacy has awakened theological imaginations to the interconnectivity and interdependency, challenging the central images affiliated with the matrix of power as domination, such as the exclusivity of the circle of God's beloved children, the conquest of all suffering via technological intervention, and the intolerance of vulnerability. New images of divine power as mutual em*power*ment will cultivate new ways of living and loving, and in turn, will awaken believers to dimensions of alienation, devaluing, and marginalization that afflict sufferers today.

Hopefully, this new understanding of divine empowerment in suffering offered by the cosmic cross will evoke different, unexpected responses to suffering, vulnerability, limitation, and death. Faith in the incarnate, crucified, and risen Christ constantly reminds humanity of how vulnerability and finitude are part of any creative process and abundant life. This is the depth of faith being asked of us by belief in God of evolution. Douglas John Hall indicates that this rich faith is brought about "when the divine Spirit takes us by the hand, so to speak, and puts us in the company of the crucified one, where we are caused to face, finally, our utter vulnerability, mortality, and impermanence but in the company therefore of one who befriends us and shows us that the end is really the beginning, that *this* death is the entrance into the newness of life."[72]

12

ECOSYSTEMIC SUFFERING: A WINDOW

Thomas Berry indicates that the "universe, earth, life, and consciousness are all violent processes."[1] However, he also indicates that "the violence of the natural world was essentially creative in the larger arc of its unfolding."[2] This, he claims, illustrates the "pervasive intimacy" and "compassionate quality" written into the very fabric of the universe.[3] His deliberate phrasing comes from the empirical evidence that the cosmic forces that bond-build-develop are always in creative tension with forces that repulse-disintegrate-destroy. This dialectic is the kenotic-kinetic, and it animates our evolutionary world.

After perusing our map, looking out the window is a decisive second step in understanding the mystery of suffering because theology cannot ignore the way in which the human subject has emerged from Earth nor how we are participating in the kenotic-kinetic of Earth's life systems. Our creativity and suffering is intimately intertwined with the fecundity and suffering of all creation. Hence, we must gaze upon the cruciformity present within Earth's ecosystems to see how some of our suffering is a manifestation of the kenotic-kinetic. Looking outwards upon Earth's sacred story of kinship strengthens our acuity of inherent suffering so we can address the myopia causing humans to inflict unnecessary suffering in both our human and other-than-human communities.

ECOSYSTEMIC SUFFERING

As noted in part 1, the rise of the machine metaphor and an increasing human-centered worldview caused us to become more and more alienated from our planetary home. This has diminished humanity's appreciation of creation as an organic, living matrix and primary source of meaning for life. Thus, the organic connections between human beings and Earth have become invisible and unintelligible to the modern consciousness.[4]

One significant effect of this planetary illiteracy is that we have become convinced that the natural cycle of life, growth, suffering, and death in nature does not apply to us. Consequently, many sufferers labor under the false conception that sacrifice, limitation, and suffering is only a result of sin and hence, can and should be denied or avoided at all cost. And when believers do age, become sick, or are less than fully abled, they have few theological tools or concepts (other than suffering as punishment for sin) with which to interpret and respond to this cruciform experience. They have even less when they witness jaguars devouring their prey, or when they explore the immense loss of life during the extinction event sixty-six million years ago, or more recently, the extinction of Costa Rican golden mountain toads just over two decades ago. This theological deficiency can compound their suffering. Denis Edwards speaks to this: "In the current dialogue between science and theology, the issue of the suffering of human and nonhuman creatures takes on a new intensity, with science making it clear how predation, competition for survival, death, and extinction are built into the 3.8 billion-year-history of life on Earth."[5]

Elizabeth Johnson also indicates another side effect of our alienation from Earth; sacrifice, limitation, and suffering are imagined as something only those deemed "other" should experience. Prevailing dualistic worldviews (e.g., mind being more valuable than body, or men more valuable than women, or humans more valuable than nature, or the wealthy more valuable than the poor) allow "a man to split off the dark side from his essential self, to take his mortality and dependence and project it upon the body, nature, women, the poor which he can then attempt to conquer and control."[6] When this mind-set game was coupled with distorted visions of Darwin's "survival of the fittest" (e.g., social Darwinism), humanity's reluctance to embrace our participation in the cosmic kenotic-kinetic increased, as did our inclination to project suffering onto the most vulnerable.[7] Elizabeth Johnson notes,

> Once the fifth edition of Origin adopted the phrase "survival of the fittest," a concept coined by the English political theorist Herbert Spencer, the book's thesis was unfortunately linked with Spencer's philosophy of inevitable progress that entailed social winners and losers among human beings. By the turn of the twentieth century, a loose collection of ideologies had gathered under the label "Social Darwinism." These theories generally held that the powerful in society are innately better than the weak; that their success is proof of superiority; and that social progress requires action toward specific goals that control the less fit, or even eliminate them.[8]

When we cut ourselves off from Earth and began to deny our participation in the planetary kenotic-kinetic, our understanding of our own suffering diminished and we became numb to the suffering of our human brethren and Earth's many subjects.

When we look out the window on ecosystemic suffering, we see that a great proportion of suffering is tragic, undeserved, but necessary, and thus, outside the "theological grid of guilt and punishment."[9] Robert J. Russell is clear that theology "must respond to the enormous challenge that suffering, disease, death, and extinction in the natural world pose to Christian faith....Clearly biological death is not the consequence of the Fall (Gen. 3) at the dawn of human history; instead it is constitutive of life."[10]

By looking out the window upon the kenotic disposition of Earth's planetary communion, we hope to reawaken theological imaginations to the presence and worth of ecosystemic suffering and inspire new ways to understand the concepts of sentience, sacrifice, and hope. Furthermore, we will investigate three troublesome questions concerning ecosystemic suffering: How can other-than-humans suffer? How can a world that is good and loved by God also include predation? How can believers speak of hope in light of extinction?

Before looking into the darkness, we must look to the light. Accordingly, the following offers a beautiful tribute to the beauty and creativity of our evolutionary world:

> A spider web glistens with dew in a dark night. A dull moon rises behind flowing clouds at sunset. The satiny warm water of a luxuriant coral reef teems with life in a Tahitian atoll. Clouds form on the frozen north face of the Matterhorn. The Serengeti plain streams with numberless herds of wildebeests. Penguins nest by the thousands in the Antarctic. The melody of a parrot lilts through a tropical Hawaiian jungle. Gorillas emerge from their forest to stop and look upwards at a tremendous waterfall, seeming to experience a moment of sacred space. The blistering heat floods the Australian aboriginal peoples' sacred place, Uluru ("Ayers Rock"). As the first chapter of Genesis proclaims, all that God creates is good, even very good.[11]

Robert J. Russell wonders at the beauty and fecundity of the created world, yet in a subsequent paragraph, he recognizes how inadequate this portrait is without an engagement with the shadowy side of this same landscape:

> Still there is a "shadow side" to the world without—and within—which we also experience in daily life, and it leads us to cry out to God our Holy Redeemer. The spider web hides the terror of the trapped insect watching the impending jaws of the spider. The full moon rising might cause tidal waves that flood low-lying villages in the Pacific. The brightly-coloured coral reef is often the hunt of a reef shark, while the exquisite beauty of the jellyfish distracts us from the poison in its tentacles. Clouds forming on the face of the Matterhorn may actually come from an avalanche taking the lives of the climbers. Across the Serengeti plain, wildebeests die wrenchingly in the jaws of lions just as Antarctic penguins are sported for and then devoured by killer

> sharks as they leap an ice shelf into surrounding waters. Indeed, in the food chain that marks the history of life on earth most animals die an agonizing death in the jaws of predation. As Paul's letter to the church at Rome exclaims, "We know that the whole creation has been groaning in travail together until now" (Rom 8:22).[12]

Russell narrates how created life is prolific and magnificent as well as cruciform and tragic. His descriptions offer many manifestations of the kenotic-kinetic within Earth's ecosystems that highlight the need to look closely at the ecosystems within which we dwell to appreciate both the light and dark side of the kenotic-kinetic. This requires the formation of a robust Earth literacy and an appreciation of an ETA. The fruit of these efforts is the broadening of our understanding of sentience, sacrifice, and hope that can positively impact theological conversations concerning human suffering.

Broadening our understanding of sentience, sacrifice, and hope has already begun in ecotheology and has helped believers appreciate how the kenotic-kinetic relates to pre-sentient and sentient beings, predator-prey relations, and extinction events. The following new horizons present some of the contributions.

New Horizons for Understanding Sentience

Can one speak of the suffering of a star as it explodes as a supernova, or a rock as it disintegrates? Can one speak about the suffering of a bacterium as it swims in an acidic medium or a carrot that is consumed or a hare caught in the jaws of a fox? These are all disintegrative experiences and are manifestations of the kenotic-kinetic, but the term *suffering* is only used to describe the cruciformity of the kenotic-kinetic experienced by sentient subjects (e.g., bacteria, the carrot, and the hare). The nomenclature used to describe the kenotic-kinetic in pre-sentient subjects (e.g., star, rock) is an *entropic* experience. *Entropic* is a term used in science to represent the degree of randomness or the process of decline or disintegration within systems (including social systems). This term is apt to describe the experiences of rocks as well as humans. But, the term *suffering* can only apply to the latter. Within more complex ecological systems (including human bodies), experiences of the kenotic-kinetic that can be designated as suffering hinges on the ability to perceive and avoid that which detracts from abundant life: sentience.

Premodern understandings of suffering biased by the machine metaphor and anthropocentrism exclude other-than-human entities from being described as "sentient." Thus, as nonsentient entities, these objects could not suffer. However, thanks to the contributors to scientific and theological Earth literacy, humanity has begun to describe the ability of typically "nonsentient" entities to perceive and respond to stimuli in novel ways.

Two such contributors are Lynn Margulis and Dorion Sagan. In their essay, "Sentient Symphony," they indicate that perception, choice, and sensation do not only apply to human beings or animals, but also to all life on Earth. They indicate that life is characterized by self-maintenance (or self-production) and living purposefulness, reproduction, and adaptation. They insist that these characteristics are manifest as five kingdoms and each reveals from different angles the mystery that is life. Life, they indicate, "can be seen as an intricate pattern of growth and death, dispatch and retrenchment, transformation and decay" and as a living, playful, marvel of complexity and interrelationship. Hence, life is far "less mechanistic" than previously thought.[13] They offer many examples of sentience within unlikely places: microbes sense and avoid heat; certain bacteria detect magnetic fields; *Amoeba proteus* find *Tetrahymena* "delectable," while avoiding *Copromonas*; chemotactic bacteria will swim toward sugar and away from acid; *Spiculosiphon* will select sponge spicules to make their shell rather than general sediment.[14] Margulis and Sagan offer convincing evidence that the horizon for understanding who or what possesses sentience is much broader than previously thought:

> That bacteria are simply machines, with no sensation or consciousness, seems no more likely than Descartes' claim that dogs suffer no pain. That bacteria sense and act, but with no feeling is possible—but ultimately solipsistic.... Cells, alive, probably do feel....At even the most primordial level living seems to entail sensation, choosing, mind.[15]

Evidence indicates that the gulf between *Homo sapiens sapiens* and other organic beings is a "matter of degree, not of kind." Human sentience is a magnification and complexification of the "little purposes, wants, and goals of uncounted trillions of autopoetic predecessors who exercised choices that influenced their evolution."[16] Accordingly, our understanding of sentience can be broadly understood as the capacity to feel and react to influences or stimuli both consciously (e.g., a human feeling the sun burning her skin and responding by moving into the shade) or unconsciously (e.g., a plant moving toward the sun). Margulis and Sagan indicate that some animals, plants, and fungi no longer consciously respond to their perception of stimuli. This is not unlike the phenomenon of muscle memory when dancers practice a routine until they are no longer consciously aware of it, but their bodies "perform" when cued. "Cells, with eons of practice, do not consciously decide to respire oxygen or reproduce by mitosis" and more complex organisms have many physiological reactions (e.g., metabolic pathways) "submerged" in their permanent unconscious.[17] The inability of humans to perceive these submerged perceptions and responses to stimuli should not limit sentience to only human perception and reactions. So broadening how we understand sentience will affect how we understand who suffers.

Another contributor to this discussion is Jay McDaniel. He attempts to broaden the boundaries of sentience by including abiotic (nonliving) entities due to their ability to "feel" and react to subatomic energy events:

> With primal traditions the world over, and informed by the speculative insights from the new physics, Christians can assume that sentience, understood as the capacity of energy events to feel influences, albeit unconsciously, from their submicroscopic environments, is itself characteristic of the submicroscopic energy of which mountains, rivers, stars and wind consist. Christians can affirm that there is no sharp dichotomy between sentient and insentient matter and that so-called "dead" matter is simply less sentient—less alive—than "living" matter. That is to say that nothing is really dead.[18]

McDaniel wants to expand our understanding of sentience to include these feelings experienced by "dead" matter so that humanity will have a better understanding of how God loves creation. However, this chapter offers a more nuanced classification of this energetic experience of mountains, rivers, and stars as the participation of *presentient* subjects (not nonsentient objects) in the kenotic-kinetic via entropic (disintegrative) and syntropic (mutually creative) events.

John Haught does not expand his vision of sentience as far as McDaniel, and this is more in line with what is being presented in this chapter. Haught indicates that sentient life, in addition to possessing "centers where feeling is registered and adaptive responses initiated,"[19] also has "the capacity to strive, and therefore to achieve or fail."[20] Thus, when entities in Earth's ecosystems strive but fail to achieve fullness of being, they "suffer," and this is a manifestation of the shadow side of the kenotic-kinetic. For example, a carrot has a less complex form of perception than a human, and yet a carrot does possess an awareness of its environment; it can curve to move away from a solid impediment in the soil. It also strives to achieve its full "carrot-hood" (as inscribed within its genetic code) and pass this along to its offspring. Hence, that which thwarts its creative efforts (e.g., arid soil, nutrient deficiency) is avoided when possible (e.g., root growth toward more suitable soil conditions) to maximize its survival and flourishing.

Margulis and Sagan bring up an important point concerning the limits of this striving: "*Amoeba proteus* does not today set out to make itself into a mouse; it knows only that the swimming *Tetrahymena* it relentlessly pursues is tasty. Amoeba-knowledge at this level of sensing and moving generates a million little such willful acts."[21] The living purposefulness of the amoeba is confined within the parameters of amoeba-knowledge. This is just one example of how each organism, to varying degrees, is capable of perceiving, interpreting, and responding to stimuli and inducing change (and impacting the relationships of which they are a part).[22] Carrots and amoeba can be understood as sentient subjects, but the question remains: How does this help within theological conversations concerning suffering?

Arthur Peacocke, who was mentioned briefly in chapter 4, has explored sentience within Earth's ecosystems and connected his work to theological understandings of human suffering.[23] In his essay "Biological Evolution: A Positive Theological Appraisal," Peacocke indicated that an increased *sensitivity* inevitably heightens the experience of suffering. Hence, any augmentation in a subject's capacity to feel "accentuates awareness both of the beneficent, life-enhancing elements and of the inimical, life-diminishing elements in the world in which the organism finds itself."[24] Later, he developed this idea further by outlining how pain, suffering, and death are inevitable consequences of created life acquiring advantageous information processing and storage systems. Thus, all organisms dwelling in ecosystems can suffer due to their capacity to sense, but human suffering is an intensified form of suffering thanks to our augmented capacities to sense. In addition, we are also capable of inflicting unnecessary suffering: humans "experience pain and suffering with a heightened sensitivity and, more than any other creatures, inflict them on each other."[25]

Consequently, other-than-human entities have varying capacities for suffering due to varying degrees of sensitivity and differing abilities to process and respond to these stimuli. Peacocke argues that all living, sentient beings suffer, but he does not connect this suffering with the moments of sacrifice and disintegration that pre-sentient beings endure. Despite this space for other-than-human suffering, Peacocke holds that the term *suffering* is more appropriately applied to self-conscious beings (rather than all sentient beings) because of our capacity to be empathetic.[26]

The aforementioned contributions show how ecotheology has embarked on new conversations concerning sentience and ecosystemic suffering. The interconnectivity of our universe story, as demonstrated in the pillars of an ETA, has allowed modern theological mindscapes to see human sentience as an unique extension of a cosmic form of consciousness that includes pre-sentient subjects (the first stars). Thomas Berry articulates this eloquently: "[Humans are] that being in whom the universe reflects on and celebrates *itself* in a special mode of conscious self-awareness."[27] Elizabeth Johnson also highlights this: "Human consciousness is in continuity with the energy of matter stretching back through galactic ages to the Big Bang, being a special, intense form of this energy."[28] The best way of incorporating this truth into theological conversations is via the kenotic-kinetic. The kenotic-kinetic enables a connection to be made between sentient and pre-sentient subjects because both participate (in varying degrees) in this ancient evolutionary dynamic, yet they remain differentiated from each other; the shadow side of the kenotic-kinetic manifests as entropic experiences for pre-sentient entities and as suffering for sentient subjects. Believers and co-sufferers need to be reacquainted with ecosystemic suffering via the kenotic-kinetic so that they can have more tools to help describe, interpret, and respond faithfully to suffering in an evolutionary world and reimagine God's care for, redemption of, all created entities.

New Horizons for Understanding Sacrifice

When theological imaginations have been schooled by the new descriptions of suffering offered in the fourth category, then the fourth pillar—kenotic-kinetic—can be understood as a "give and take" process that involves both creativity (self-actualization/self-affirmation) and cruciformity (self-sacrifice/self-emptying). It is a sacrificial dialectic of receptivity that demands that there be an openness to (or making space for) the other in oneself. This concurrent process involves a building up of your identity (a creative process of self-actualization) and a loss or giving up of your identity (a cruciform process of self-emptying) because you are receptive to that which is not you. Both of these tendencies are held in tension within this sacrificial dialectic.

The Merriam-Webster dictionary defines *sacrifice* as "the act of giving up something that you want to keep especially in order to get or do something else or to help someone." In light of the kenotic-kinetic, sacrifice can be understood in new ways. The kenotic-kinetic appreciates the sacrifice and struggle inherent in our unfolding universe story alongside its beauty and ability to flourish. This appreciation however, does not trivialize traditional perceptions of sacrifice as something only human's do, nor diminish the agony of this sacrifice, nor erode the redemptive efficacy of Christ. Rather, cosmogenesis reveals that Earth's immensely transformative processes are enabled by the dialectic of sacrifice and genesis, that human sacrifice is a manifestation of this larger sacrificial dynamic, and Christ is continually present to our sacred cosmic story, luring our unfinished narrative to completion and peace in the loving embrace of God. Looking out the window on creation can lead humanity to a new appreciation of sacrifice in its many forms, such as the sacrifice inherent within the emerging cosmos (e.g., interpersonal sacrifice in predator-prey relationships), the sacrifice innate to human life (e.g., intrapersonal and interpersonal sacrifice), and the sacrifice of Christ on the cross.

In the 1950s, J. H. Fabre outlined how laboring to bring forth new life was the "sublime law of sacrifice."[29] More recently, ecotheologians Elizabeth Johnson and Gloria Schaab have developed the idea of cosmic sacrificial labor using the experiences of women and the experience of midwifery to describe the travail of evolutionary emergence.[30] They do this to ensure that the concept of sacrificial labor associated with procreation is not used to oppress women.[31] One formidable danger of connecting theological understandings of sacrifice with the labor associated with female procreative processes is that it will be misused to sanctify the unjust, inflicted suffering that women experience due to their unique procreative capabilities; indeed, the necessary inherent suffering offered by a woman giving birth should not be treated as the same as the suffering experienced by an abused woman. The latter should not be tolerated as would be the case for the abuse of a child or man. Johnson's description of cosmic labor helps to ensure that the sacrificial process of bringing forth newness is not shouldered by women alone and actively engages all of creation. This expands theological interpretations of sacrifice beyond human pregnancy and childbirth, and connects the sacrifice women experience throughout their lives with the sacrifice inherent within Earth's ecosystems. It also connects them with the powerful transformative forces working in creation.

Thomas Berry expands this understanding of sacrifice even further when he outlines the new spatial and temporal dimensions of ecosystemic sacrifice and cosmic receptivity:

> Everything feeds on other beings and nourishes other beings. The grass is fed by the sun and the sun is fed by energies inherent in the supernova explosion of the star, whence our sun is derived, and so back to the primordial blazing forth. All this enables us to feed on grass. Fed by each other, we nourish each other. The universe is caught up in this reciprocity.[32]

The reciprocity Berry is describing requires readers to link together the gift being received (e.g., grass for us to eat; energy for grass to capture; materials from the supernova that made up the sun) and the prior experience of sacrifice that enabled the creation of the gift. This places the concept of sacrifice within a larger, 13.8-billion-year context. The costly, creative dance of our unfolding universe is a springboard for exploring the barbarous and complex form of sacrifice in Earth's ecosystems, and can help resituate human experiences of sacrifice within a broader horizon of cosmic sacrificial receptivity.

Johnson and Schaab offer readers a perception of cosmic sacrifice as the labor involved in the emergence of newness in the universe. When something is created, something is lost or sacrificed. *Pre-sentient* entropic experiences involve the disintegration and sacrifice of a subjects present state of self-hood (e.g., star or rock) in the process of creating newness (e.g., new elements or sediment). Some would be uncomfortable with saying that the disintegration of a rock into stream sediment is sacrifice since rocks lack the ability to choose. However, despite their lack of ability to actively choose a different fate, rocks can be seen as passive agents who, by their interior structural forces (part of their "self-hood" as particular created beings), resist the forces of disintegration. Rocks sacrifice being rocks in order to become sediment thanks to the entropic forces of the environment. However, *sentient* subjects also participate in the kenotic-kinetic. They strive to become that which accords to its nature (written in their genetic coding and behavioral prompts) and undergo the cruciform forces of our evolutionary world. Paramecia, plants, and animals resist that which thwarts well-being but, as participants in the kenotic-kinetic, they sacrifice whether via molecular degradation, hurricane force winds, or predation. Since, predator-prey relations are particularly challenging experiences of sacrifice in Earth's ecosystems, they need further exploration.

Cosmogenesis reveals that, from the beginning there was only a limited amount of materials on Earth, so recycling and engulfing/claiming/taking other organisms or materials was adopted early on. For example, worm-sucking anomalocaridids evolved 540 million years ago, predatory microbes that drilled their way through defensive armor of Amoeba emerged 740 million years ago, eukaryotic predators who engulfed other cells arose 2 billion years ago, parasitic prokaryotes developed 3.5 billion years ago, and catalytic nucleic acids that broke down other nucleic molecules to fuel their own growth evolved prior to 3.5 billion years.[33] These processes were good survival strategies (stimulating the emergence of an immense variety of biological and structural complexity) and brought forth a host of intricate feeding relationships.[34]

With the advent of vertebrate life and the central nervous system over 500 million years ago and the emergence of complex behaviors among organisms (e.g., increased parental care and cooperative social organizations) approximately 65 million years ago, there arose an even greater need to recycle and reclaim materials. One way to meet this need was by ingesting already fairly complex materials. Thus, even more intense forms of predator-prey relations manifested the sacrificial dynamic inherent in the kenotic-kinetic. Let us now explore how this manifestation works.

The Creatively Cruciform Dance of the Spider and the Fly

A good case study to examine is the predator-prey relationship between the spider and fly. They are participants in the kenotic-kinetic and their fates are deeply connected within the dynamic flow of fecundity and cruciformity inherent within Earth's ecosystems. Flies act as pollinators and decomposers, as well as food sources for many organisms, and spiders have an important role of controlling insect populations and create intricate (and beautiful) webbing to facilitate this purpose. Both spider and fly participate in the kenotic-kinetic not by choice but by a spontaneous response to their genetic coding. Because they are living finite beings, they experience both self-affirmation (the desire for self-preservation) and self-emptying (disintegration, loss of identity, or death). In striving to be most "fly like," a fly can be caught in the web of a spider that is striving to be as fully "spider like" as possible. Both fly-ness and spider-ness are eruptions of Earth's creativity but they come at a cost. Being participants in the kenotic-kinetic means that the fly will be vulnerable to the spider and in certain circumstances (e.g., when it flies into the web), it will have to sacrifice its selfhood. The vulnerability of the spider may not be recognized at first but, if seen through a different lens, it becomes apparent; within their food web, spiders are vulnerable to their natural predators such as frogs or lizards and, within their species population, they are vulnerable to the fly population because if there are not enough flies, spiders will die.

Thus their origin, lives, and fates are intertwined. And the creativity that brought forth such complexity (fly-ness and spider-ness) comes at great individual cost; even though the fly vigorously resists dying to nourish the spider, the fly is consumed as a consequence of Earth's movement toward greater creativity and complexity. This way of articulating this complex relationship is no comfort to the fly, and even a perfect understanding of this sacrifice will never lessen this suffering. Nevertheless, both predator and prey are unique expressions of cosmic creativity and each participates in *both* the self-actualizing drive to survive and flourish, and the self-emptying dynamic involving sacrifice, vulnerability, and death.

Recalling Robert J. Russell's double-edged portrait of creation outlined earlier in this chapter, we are reminded of the cost or sacrifice inherent in the Earth's creativity, which includes human creativity and flourishing. Becoming fully human is a costly but worthwhile undertaking. However, when a spider feeds on the fly trapped in its web, or wildebeests, penguins, or rabbits fall prey to their natural predators, there is an affective inclination in a human observer to describe and interpret (and judge) this experience by way of the human lens; in our minds and hearts, an innocent creature seems to be unjustly sacrificed to the ferocious predator and hence, it is only living a futile life at the whim of a cruel world "red in tooth and claw."[35]

The reality of violence and destruction in the cruciform world is not in dispute here; what is being proposed is that by cultivating a robust Earth literacy and embracing an ETA, believers can better appreciate sacrifice inherent in life and the false forms of sacrifice that are oppressive. It does not, however, negate or alleviate the suffering experienced by a rabbit in the jaws of the fox nor explain why this cruciform reality evolved instead of another more benign reality. Nevertheless, a realistic appreciation of Earth's kenotic-kinetic will contribute to "our most profound understanding of our human situation, even if it does not bring it within reach of our rational processes."[36] When Earth is embraced as a communion of suffering subjects rather than a collection of inert objects, then the sacrifice present in human ecologies can be understood in new ways.

New Meaning of Sacrifice and Justice

One benefit of exploring ecosystemic suffering as sacrifice or sacrificial receptivity is the challenge it makes to the radical individualism prevalent today that narrows how people see sacrifice contributing to the common good.

A second benefit is that it gives the biblical tenet "No one has greater love than this, to lay down one's life for one's friends" (John 15:13) new meaning. By appreciating the many forms of the kenotic-kinetic in our cosmic family history, some, who are being constantly reminded to "sacrifice" or negate their own self-actualization due to their gender or socioeconomic class, will be reminded that they are called to cultivate their own lives in order to have an abundant life to lay down for their friend.

A third benefit is that Earth-literate believers can root out and address unnecessary and unjust suffering hidden under the pretense of being just the way life is meant to be or a form of divinely sanctioned sacrifice. Ivone Gebara indicates that Jesus's suffering or sacrifice often serves as justification for the misery imposed on the poor and women, and that women's submission to males is predicated upon Christ's submission to the Father. This way of understanding sacrifice intensifies the suffering of women (and those deemed "other" by their race, creed, gender, or species) because it promotes mute resignation or passive tolerance of suffering as the only acceptable response. Consequently, sacrifice as only silent submission and self-abnegation is perceived to be virtuous.[37] However, if we look to the kenotic-kinetic, this overemphasis on self-emptying is corrected by a concurrent movement of self-affirmation.

Looking out the window on the cosmos reminds sufferers that the sacred universe story narrates a tale of active resistance to that which thwarts well-being. The sacrificial dimension of the kenotic-kinetic can help aid believers to strive to become who we are called to be but never forget we are part of a cosmos where sacrifice and self-emptying also play a role—for all of creation, even the most powerful. Earth speaks poignantly that when the sacrificial-creative dialectic is unbalanced, Earth's ecosystems and human ecologies languish. For example, when rabbits in Australia had no predators, the entire ecosystem (including human economies) became threatened; when, too, mosquito populations were sacrificed by the human shortsighted and indiscriminate use of DDT, the health of entire ecosystems, including that of humans, suffered; and when women and the poor are unable to have abundant life, societies are less vibrant and resilient.

The kenotic-kinetic as sacrificial receptivity or the labor to bring forth newness does not uncouple creative forces from destructive ones and can help affirm a connection between self-actualization and self-sacrifice—rather than merely promoting self-abnegation alone. Thus, sacrifice can have a self-affirming dimension that manifests at the level of the individual, the ecosystem, a planet, or a massive star.

As will be seen in the lives of Pierre Teilhard de Chardin and Audre Lorde in the next chapter, as well as in the Book of Job and the hemorrhagic woman (Mark 5:25–34), the act of lament or self-affirming resistance to that which compromises self-worth and well-being can be a deeply faithful response to the invitation to sacrifice and suffering encoded into our finite world. The universe narrative does not advocate that humanity must passively sacrifice our lives for the furthering of another form of life (e.g., HIV, shark). Rather, it supports creative acts of self-preservation. Earth teaches humanity that as participants in cosmogenesis, we can vigorously seek our self-preservation (and the resources required to do so) and learn to respond to destructive evolutionary forces in innovative ways. This worldview does not promise a life devoid of suffering; it promises a life transformed, even in the face of suffering and death.

Understanding the kenotic-kinetic as the context for engaging sacrifice experienced by humans does not magically eradicate or comprehensibly explain all instances of suffering, nor does it alleviate the excruciating pain of knowing a loved one is suffering from a terminal illness. Nevertheless, being aware of the kenotic-kinetic animating cosmogenesis can help human sufferers to be receptive to both genesis and cruciformity and, after their devastating diagnosis, be empowered to *respond*, as the cosmos does to unavoidable suffering through genesis and innovation. This can be a path to fulfillment and peace in the brokenness of our world.

Extinction and Hope

Since we live in a post-Newtonian, evolutionary world where the machine metaphor is inadequate, we can say that the cosmos (which includes Earth) is a dynamic and unfinished adventure rather than a static collection of planets with humans as its only crowning achievement. A static and mechanical vision of the world affirms what is—the current status quo—and precludes spontaneity, ambiguity, and cocreativity. It also envisions God, the ultimate Source of all potentiality or novelty, as completely separate from the world and either unable or unwilling to intervene. Both responses are incongruent with the understanding of *theos* offered by an ETA. As a result of our evolutionary world, believers need a new horizon of hope where "all creatures find hope and eternal life in God's new creation." This eschatological model envisions humans as co-sufferers and the "eschatological companion" of all created life and God as intimately present within the world, laboring to bring forth new life from death.[38] This is the message of the first pillar of an ETA. However, when believers look out of our window on the world, they see a special form of ecosystemic suffering that makes being hopeful hard: extinction. This is the litmus test for an ETA: How does extinction fit into the theological visions of hope in transformation and new life offered by an ETA?

Extinction is not merely the death of an individual organism. It is the permanent eradication of an entire species. It is the loss of life in the present and the loss of all possible future life for the species. How can this be reconciled with God who is love and the modern understanding of redemption? Today, scientific data offers a chilling vision of cosmic loss due to extinction. We know that in the Permian mass extinction 248 million years ago, more than 90 percent of the planet's species were destroyed, and the trilobites, rugose, and tabulate corals, acanthodians, placoderms, and pelycosaurs also did not survive beyond the Permian boundary.[39] The Cretaceous–Paleogene extinction event nearly 65 million years ago saw more than half of the Earth's plant and animal species, including the last nonavian dinosaurs, become extinct.[40] However, the genetic and ecosystemic lacuna created by these great experiences of loss enabled the proliferation of mammals—and eventually humans. However, the International Union for Conservation of Nature (IUCN) and the United Nations name the actions of one species as the cause of the extinction spasm we are in now: humans.[41] This is an unprecedented phenomenon that requires much reflection, but here other forms of extinction will receive serious theological attention.

A vital element of the doctrine of redemption offered in the first pillar of an ETA is hope that all of creation, especially those denied life (e.g., victims of extinction) or personhood (e.g., African American slaves or victims of domestic abuse) can experience justice, wholeness, table fellowship, and right relationship, both now and at the end-time. James H. Cone, in his article "God and Black Suffering," indicates that the theme of justice and redemption cannot be extricated from the concept of hope despite the painfulness of this commitment: "Black hope was not an easy hope. The idea of heaven was the means by which slaves affirmed their humanity in a world that did not recognize them as human beings. It was their way of saying that they were made for freedom not slavery."[42] Their hope today stemmed from the perfect community where they had a rightful place. This future time reached back and qualified the hope held in the present.

Ecosystemic suffering manifest as extinction is not the same as racism; some extinction events are inherent in an unfinished world, but racism is always inflicted suffering authored by humans. However, a similar approach can be taken. The hope we have today that the extinct golden toad has a special place in God's household requires a robust vision of the end-time that can reach back and qualify this hope. A mechanistic, static, and human-centered understanding of the world, God, and the *eschaton* cannot offer this hope but an ETA can. For example, Denis Edwards argues that, since all creation—including sparrows—is intrinsically loved by the Creator and communicates something of Godself, the Spirit of God is present to each creature today and at the end-time. Thus, each creature can find respite, healing, and ultimate redemption in Christ.[43] Edwards uses the term *redemption* in a more expansive sense by including other-than-human creatures. He addressed the inherent pain of cosmic creativity (including extinction) in his vision of redemption as well as the need to forgive and redeem inflicted suffering caused by human sin. Accordingly, redemption is liberation from injustice, suffering, and death (even extinction as the ultimate death) for all of God's creatures. For Edwards, all victims of cosmogenesis permanently abide and are treasured within "the everlasting compassionate love" of the Trinity and are remembered and celebrated in the Communion of Saints.[44] This is a provocative statement and adds meaning to St. Paul's letter to the Ephesians: "With all wisdom and insight he has made known to us the mystery of his will, according to his good pleasure that he set forth in Christ, as a plan for the fullness of time, to gather up all things in him, things in heaven and things on earth" (Eph 1:8–10).

Edwards offers a vision of God and the end-time that enables sufferers to reimagine the term *atonement*, normally a theological concept deeply intertwined with traditional understandings of suffering as expiation and punishment for sin. Instead, he inspired believers to see atonement as an "at-one-ness" that connotes both the intermediate and ultimate transition of our world and ourselves from a state of incompleteness, cruciformity, and injustice to fulfillment and peace in God. Hence, all creatures are inscribed and *re-membered* (i.e., both recollected as memories and recomposed materially) in God—even the fallen sparrows, the victims of extinction, and human sufferers.[45]

Believers dwelling in a sacred and unfinished world beckoned toward wholeness by God's transformative grace can speak faithfully about hope of transformation for the Mauritius dodo (hunted to extinction), the golden toad (a victim of climate change), and for human cancer sufferers with a terminal diagnosis. The suffering of the cancer patient is not the same as the two previous forms of ecosystemic suffering, nor does it have to be; but they are all unique expressions of the kenotic-kinetic, and hope for fullness of life comes from the same Divine Source. It is God who will satisfy and sanctify the victims of extinction and the human sufferer. Human sufferers need hope that the cruciformity of this world, painfully manifested in extinction, violence, illness, and death, does not mean that life is futile and the Creator of this world uncaring, powerless, distant, or punitive. Instead, sufferers can be empowered by the good news revealed by the Book of Creation and the Book of Scripture; the world is open-ended, unpredictable, and moving toward fulfillment, well-being, wholeness, and peace—the essence of the Hebraic term *shalom*.[46] Earth literacy allows sufferers to understand how their suffering is interconnected with the cruciformity of our 13.8-billion-year family history, and how their redemption—"a taste of eternal fellowship with God and salvific grace"—is intertwined with the redemption of all of creation.[47]

SUMMARY

Looking out the window to appreciate ecosystemic suffering offers no ultimately satisfying answers to the mystery of suffering or to the question of why this suffering world exists as it does. Nevertheless, appreciating the cruciformity inherent in our world does sharpen human acuity to the reality of suffering, including the suffering within our human family. Looking out the window invites believers to question expectations of what they think suffering is and challenges some distorted perceptions that we can find ultimate "solutions" to suffering (and live a life devoid of all suffering) via technological innovations.

By investigating suffering "on the ground," the sacred story of the cosmos speaks to a new inclusive vision of redemption where all will experience radically abundant life with God. And for some sufferers, if there is room for the golden toad in heaven, there will be room for them. Consequently, being attentive to our cruciform and creative world characterized by sacrifice, loss, growth, and transformation, empowers human sufferers to see our world as alive with the Spirit of God and come to believe, as Martha did, in Christ's consolation: "I am the resurrection and the life. The one who believes in me, even though they die, will live, and everyone who lives and believes in me will never die. Do you believe this?" (John 11:25–26).

13

HUMAN SUFFERING: LOOKING IN THE MIRROR

The previous two chapters took us from looking at divine suffering as our map to looking out the window on ecosystemic suffering. In this final chapter, we look into the mirror to explore the mystery of human suffering. Rather than a direct linear process with only three steps, exploring suffering is more a dialectical dance that moves from divine suffering to ecosystemic to human and back again, often without an intentional path, but with a rhythm as unique as the individuals taking part in this sacred cadence. Consequently, this chapter will not attempt to provide *the* interpretation of suffering to help all human sufferers. One needs only to recall the many diverse categories of suffering offered in chapters 9 and 10 to realize the futility of posing one ultimate solution for suffering. However, our awareness of the many categories of suffering will help prevent uncritical and problematical interpretations that compound the suffering of some individuals. For example, when believers proclaim that the suffering of people living in poverty is a divinely sanctioned punishment for sin, a test to endure, or an inherent part of an evolutionary world like natural selection, then good people do nothing to alleviate such suffering. Instead, they allow and often compound this unjust, inflicted suffering because they believe God or the cosmos wants it this way.

Accordingly, instead of providing a solution to suffering, this chapter tells the story of how two individuals both look to a divine map (albeit in radically different ways) and look out on the suffering inherent in our evolutionary world to help them describe, interpret, and respond to their suffering. Hearing their stories of enduring and transforming their suffering gives us a glimpse at how an evolutionary worldview can hold much promise for sufferers. But even in this attenuated form, they provide much insight. The first narrative is that of Pierre Teilhard de Chardin and his response to suffering as a Christian theologian well-versed in evolutionary science. His account will be augmented by a second voice, Audre Lorde (1934–1992), a Caribbean American poet and activist, who dwelled in a very different sphere of life from the Jesuit priest and anthropologist. She loved and suffered deeply, and embraced a robust "earthing spiritual literacy" manifested through her inspirited, embodied relationships.[1]

PIERRE TEILHARD DE CHARDIN'S REFLECTION

In his foreword to *The Divine Milieu*, Pierre Leroy outlines how Teilhard lived a great deal of his life under the shadow of crisis, perplexity, emotional depression, and physical strife, and how these experiences of suffering were mirrored in his philosophy and personal writings. He embraces a well-formed Earth but he also experienced great loss, rejection, and suffering in his life that permeated his writings.[2] Although he was more theoretical in his approach, compared to the next more personal interpretation of suffering offered by Audre Lorde, his mind, heart, and spirit were always searching for faithful ways of interpreting human suffering in light of his knowledge of God and evolution.

Many aspects of Teilhard's childhood helped to form him into an astute observer, a lover of the natural world, and a Christian. However, he always held this awe of creation in tension with his awareness of the fragility of created life; not even the iron implements he found, nor the stones that captivated the imagination of this budding geologist were as certain and enduring as God's abiding reality. Even his decision to dedicate his life to God[3] resonated with the uncertainty and fragility he saw manifested in the natural world; the anticlerical movements in the French Republic at the dawn of the twentieth century forced his order to seek refuge in England. This truth about the world was reinforced through his personal experience of great loss. First, he experienced the deaths of his eldest brother and younger sister in 1902 and 1904, followed by the death of his elder sister, a member of the Little Sisters of the Poor in Shanghai, in 1911. His experiences of the cruciformity of life intensified during the First World War; the death of another brother in battle deeply affected him as did his vocation during the war as a stretcher bearer on the frontlines (1915–19). Teilhard was "baptized in the crucible of war."[4]

When all these experiences converged with his knowledge of the pain and loss inherent in Earth's evolutionary processes, he crafted unique theological interpretations of suffering. One unique contribution was his radical optimism for the cruciform world despite the darkness he experienced. This optimism did not negate the horrors of an imperfect, unfinished world; instead, this optimism erupted from his deep conviction that God endured all things and was moving all creation toward something better, more durable, in Christ. For example, in a letter to his cousin Marguerite (August 23, 1916), he speaks of the ruined landscape of the "worst battlegrounds of Verdun," the cohabitation in the trenches with corpses, and the often sudden and grisly encounter with death. But these descriptions were the springboard for Teilhard's deeper message concerning suffering, creation, and God:

> I don't know what sort of monument the country will later put up on Froideterre hill to commemorate the great battle. There's only one that would be appropriate: a great figure of Christ. Only the image of the crucified can sum up, express and relieve all the horror, and beauty, all the hope and deep mystery in such an avalanche of conflict and sorrows. As I looked at this scene of bitter toil, I felt completely overcome by the thought that I had the honour of standing at one of the two or three spots on which, at this very moment, the whole life of the universe surges and ebbs places of pain but it is there that a great future (this I believe more and more) is taking shape.[5]

After the war, Teilhard was sent to China—out of the hub of intellectual life in France—because he embraced evolutionary ideas in his theology at a time when others would not. European and American societies' grasp of evolution was tenuous at best and volatile at worst, which was reflected in the aversion of Teilhard's superiors to his ideas. For example, Teilhard was asked to repudiate his ideas around the same time as the Scopes "Monkey Trial" (1925) in Tennessee. The resulting prohibition of teaching evolution in schools in the United States mirrors the punishment imposed on Teilhard in Europe.[6] After his censure in Europe, he went to China in 1926 and focused his energies on contributing to the disciplines of geology and anthropology where he partook in great scientific discoveries (e.g., the Peking Man). His meticulous research into evolutionary processes cultivated his Earth literacy and inspired his theological imagination, enabling him to pen his famous spiritual text *The Divine Milieu* (1929) dedicated to lovers of the natural world. He also crafted his more philosophical undertaking *The Phenomenon of Man* (1938) during his time in China. But after experiencing further intellectual and emotional rejection in Europe, Teilhard was asked to go to New York (1951–55) where "he spent his final years in a residential hotel room with a single window looking out into a sunless alley."[7] Teilhard never lived to see his books in print, nor did he experience the positive effects of his work on theological imaginations, but his contributions to those who followed were significant.[8]

It is clear that Teilhard's Earth literacy informed his theological interpretation of suffering and the cross. From his research, Teilhard knew that our planet was old, deeply interconnected, and moving toward more complex forms of life capable of consciousness and thus a more spiritual reality. But he also knew that our world was still under construction and so, it was suffering.[9] "The world…is an immense groping, an immense search, an immense attack; its progress can take place only at the expense of many failures, of many wounds."[10] It was very important to Teilhard to converge these ideas; he believed that the beauty and creativity inherent in evolution gave us hope amidst great brokenness that God is laboring with us to move our world toward its ultimate completion. His belief in God's immanence in Earth's creative processes further fueled his intense awe and wonder of the majesty of our evolutionary world. His assertion that God dwelled at the heart of the world and animated, guided, and sustained its costly movement toward abundant life inspired his description of creation as a divine milieu—a source of revelation and a dwelling place of

God: "Everything that is active, that moves or breathes, every physical, astral, or animate energy, every fragment of force, every spark of life, is equally sacred; for, in the humblest atom and the most brilliant star, in the lowest insect and the finest intelligence, there is the radiant smile and thrill of the same Absolute."[11] Hence, all aspects of life, including suffering, have significance and purpose. It is this truth that inspired Teilhard's deep reverence for creation:

> One day, I was looking out over the dreary expanse of the desert. As far as the eye could see, the purple steps of the uplands rose up in series, towards horizons of exotic wilderness; again, as I watched the empty, bottomless ocean whose waves were ceaselessly moving in their "unnumbered laughter"; or, buried in a forest whose life-laden shadows seemed to seek to absorb me in their deep, warm folds—on such occasions, maybe, I have been possessed by a great yearning to go and find…the vast forces that cradle us and possess us…for there lay matter, and matter was calling me. To me in turn, as to all the sons of man [*sic*], it was speaking as every generation hears it speak; it was begging me to surrender myself unreservedly to it, and to worship it.[12]

Teilhard saw suffering as a byproduct of our dynamic but unfinished world, and thus, creation has much to teach us about our own finitude:

> Pale, icy, moon, will those who then look on you, men [*sic*] living in the fullness of their strength on this ageing earth, will they understand the final meaning of your speechless face?…'What does your wan face, burnt-out star, hold up for all ages to see, tell us again, if not that Mankind [*sic*] grows, fettered to a corpse.'[13]

However, he also saw suffering as an energetic process that could be directed in constructive or creative ways. Consequently, he felt that sufferers often felt useless as if "cast up by the great stream of life, lying by sheer ill-luck incapable of work or activity" in a world characterized by dynamism.[14] Teilhard wanted to offer hope to sufferers by interpreting suffering as an opportunity to channel the energy associated with suffering toward a sacred activity: the construction of the kingdom of God. Teilhard understood the world as an ancient divine project that requires the participation of all who suffer, regardless of species, and he saw human sufferers as worthy participants in the creation of the better, more complete world God desires. Sufferers of any species, he declared, "are the expression of this stern but noble condition. They are not useless and dwarfed."[15] This hope resonated strongly in his writings:

> What a vast ocean of human suffering spreads over the entire earth at every moment! Of what is this mass formed? Of blackness, gaps, and rejections. No, let me repeat, of potential energy. In suffering, the ascending force of the world is concealed in a very intense form. The whole question is how to liberate it and give it a consciousness of its significance and potentialities.[16]

Teilhard's vision of suffering as potential energy illustrates the transformational power residing in suffering—as the title of Magdalena Gómez's poem suggests: "In Darkness Grows the Green." These costly, yet grace-filled moments, were providing the energy to move our unfinished world toward completion and wholeness in God. Teilhard understood evolution as the energetic process by which the natural world brought forth newness from disintegration and death, and he believed in God's immanence in our evolutionary world. Consequently, he converged these into his vision of how suffering played a role in moving individual human sufferers and our Earth community toward abundant life in God:

> The world would leap high toward God if all the sick together were to turn their pain into a common desire that the kingdom of God should come to rapid fruition through the conquest and organization of the earth. All the sufferers of the earth joining their sufferings so that the world's pain might become a great and unique act of consciousness, elevation, and union. Would not this be one of the highest forms that the mysterious work of creation could take in our sight?[17]

For Teilhard, this movement toward God started with the moment creation burst forth, but it found special expression in Christ's suffering on the cross. Jesus was "directing the intense energy of his suffering" toward the growth of love in the world.[18] Thus, a singular understanding of the cross as atonement was unsatisfactory for Teilhard, for it missed the broader significance of the cross:

> Could it not be precisely for this that the creation was completed in Christian eyes by the Passion of Jesus? We are perhaps in danger of seeing on the cross only an individual suffering, a single act of expiation. The creative power of that death escapes us. Let us take a broader glance, and we shall see that the cross is the symbol and place of an action whose intensity is beyond expression. Even from the earthly point of view, the crucified Jesus, fully understood, is not rejected or conquered. It is on the contrary he who bears the weight and draws ever higher toward God the universal march of progress. Let us act like him, in order to be in our existence united with him.[19]

Teilhard also developed this idea in *The Divine Milieu*:

> To sum up, Jesus on the Cross is both the symbol and the reality of the immense labour of the centuries which has, little by little, raised up the created spirit and brought it back to the depths of the divine milieu. He represents (and in a true sense, he is) creation, as, upheld by God, it reascends the slopes of being, sometimes clinging to things for support, sometimes tearing itself from them in order to pass beyond them, and always compensating, by physical suffering, for the setbacks caused by its moral downfalls. The Cross is therefore not inhuman but superhuman. We can now understand that from the very first, from the very origins of mankind as we know it, the Cross was placed on the crest of the road which leads to the highest peaks of creation....The Christian is not asked to swoon in the shadow, but to climb in the light, of the Cross.[20]

Consequently, Teilhard offers a "practical, productive, and creative spirituality of the cross"[21] and turned the energy of his rejection, depression, and physical suffering into "his own work for the kingdom of God."[22] However, Teilhard's vision is not without some concerns, as were outlined in chapter 3. First, his assumption of a triumphant progression to a purely spirit reality diminishes the innate worth of the material bodies of sufferers. For him, salvation and wholeness comes when all is spirit and all material life has fallen away. This reflected the popular intellectual belief during his time that favored the spiritual over the material. Also, his linear line of ascent to God (with its penultimate apex in the human consciousness, especially the European consciousness) could be seen as a form of triumphalism and superiority that is not upheld by evolutionary science nor current theology; modern scientists have shown that evolutionary trees with many branches or vast, interconnected, and sacred webs of life best describe our world. A linear system or ladder ascending to God with humans at the apex is inadequate. Modern ecotheologians, thanks to their Earth literacy, offer more complex visions of God's interaction with the world that involves chance and uncertainty.[23]

A final note of concern for Teilhard's interpretation of suffering is his radical optimism that suffering can be used to create a better world. In many cases, this may be true, but on the whole, does it hold up in light of the children of Auschwitz—the litmus test offered by Hans Jonas? When this idea is uncritically applied, it could justify grave suffering. However, despite these critiques, Teilhard's Earth literacy helps us understand human suffering in new ways.[24]

AUDRE LORDE'S REFLECTION

While Teilhard looked at the world and saw suffering as a way to move toward a more spiritual realm of existence, Audre Lorde gazed intently at the world and affirmed embodied existence for what it was: inspirited yet painfully broken. Lorde's writings offer readers an account of how one particular woman, who struggled against racism, sexism, and other forms of oppressive thought patterns and societal structures, found healing and new life in spite of suffering and dying from cancer. She wrote poignantly of her efforts to integrate her experience of suffering with cancer into her life story, and in this struggle, she revealed that her most vibrant source of resistance and healing was her deep connectivity with Earth, fellow artisans and activists, and Black women. The following offers a glimpse at how she voiced her Earth literacy in her interpretation of the suffering she endured six months after a radical mastectomy to treat her breast cancer:

> I'm not feeling very hopeful these days, about selfhood or anything else. I handle the outward motions of each day while pain fills me like a puspocket and every touch threatens to breach the taut membrane that keeps it from flowing through and poisoning my whole existence. Sometimes despair sweeps across my consciousness like luna winds across a barren moonscape. Ironshod horses rage back and forth over every nerve. Oh Seboulisa ma,[25] help me remember what I have paid so much to learn. I could die of difference, or live—myriad selves.[26]

In her cancer journals and poetry, Audre Lorde offers her personal silhouette of suffering that models a deep connectivity to Earth as the spiritual source of abundant life. Her Earth literacy was not formally schooled by the fossilized bodies of ancient ancestors; rather, it was expressed in her keen observations of her inspirited body in relation to other bodies within a cosmic community. Through her life, love, and work, this Caribbean-born feminist, activist, and poet tells her story to offer wisdom to others who are suffering:

> I have been blessed to believe passionately, to love deeply, and to be able to work out of those loves and beliefs. Accidents of privilege allowed me to gain information about holistic/biological medicine and their approach to cancers, and that information has helped keep me alive, along with my original gut feeling that said, *Stay out of my body*. For me, living and the use of that living are inseparable, and I have a responsibility to put that privilege and that life to use....If one Black woman I do not know gains hope and strength from my story, then it has been worth the difficulty in telling.[27]

Lorde's writings demonstrate how connectivity with the sacred and powerfully creative currents of the cosmos and in human communities awakened to its presence, links a sufferer to an ancient source of transformative power. In the case of Lorde, the cosmic communion is represented by the communion of women who shared Lorde's deep connection with the divine Mother, her desire for truth and justice, and her appreciation of embodied, creative power: *eros*. She used this term *eros* to describe a transformational life force within all of life, "the personification of love in all its aspects," "personifying creative power," and "creative energy empowered."[28] And like Teilhard, Lorde always held her appreciation of the brokenness of creation in tension with her wonder at the sacred healing and creative power (*eros*) of the cosmos. Even in the sterility of a hospital in Switzerland, she offers her readers a glimpse of her understanding of the creative power of the cosmos that does not shy away from the pain:

> Then at 4:30 in the morning, her little fingers of [moon] light reached under the lined window curtains, and I got up as if bidden and went out onto the terrace to greet her. The night was very very still; she was low and bright and brilliantly clear. I stood on the terrace in my robe bathed in her strong quiet light. I raised my arms then and prayed for us all, prayed for the strength for all of us who must weather this time ahead with me. My mother moon had awakened me, calling me out into her brightness, and she shone down upon me as a sign, a blessing on that terrace with the soft gurgle of flowing water in my ears, a promise of answering strength to be whoever I need to be. I felt her in my heart, in my bones, in my thin blood, and I heard Margareta's voice again: "It's going to be a hard lonely road, but remember, help is on the way."[29]

In ways similar to Teilhard, her coupling of life and death, diminishment and creativity, and appreciation of the lessons taught to us by creation magnifies how human sufferers can be liberated from their forced silences and share in the divine process of creation when they cultivate an Earth literacy. Lorde is clear that it is by reconnecting as a communion of women who are in touch with Earth and who are compassionate (e.g., who share in the experience of suffering and stand in solidarity with each other) that a sufferer can find her voice and escape the intense loneliness, invisibility, and pressures of conformity that face women in general, but especially women suffering from cancer:

> May these words serve as encouragement for other women to speak and to act out of our experiences with cancer and with other threats of death, for silence has never brought us anything of worth. Most of all, may these words underline the possibilities of self-healing and the richness of living for all women.[30]

In a speech given prior to her cancer journals, she names the many pains she has endured because of the silencing she endured due to her race, gender, and sexual orientation. To remedy this "silencing," she documents her awakening to the "source of power within [her] self,"[31] that enables her to overcome her fears, speak of her experiences, and allow herself to share her suffering within a community of fellow suffering subjects—each gifted, each broken. After being diagnosed with breast cancer, Lorde describes a compounding of the alienation she previously felt because now she was a sick, Black, lesbian woman. Once again, she was silenced and disconnected from sources of healing. However, by remembering what helped her overcome her previous experiences of alienation, she was promised liberation again, even in her diminishment and death. Her reconnection within a sacred communion of fellow sufferers liberated her from fear and inspired her transformation:

> The women who sustained me through that period [of intense agony][32] were Black and white, old and young, lesbian, bisexual, and heterosexual, and we all shared a war against the tyrannies of silence. They all gave me a strength and concern without which I could not have survived intact. Within those weeks of acute fear came the knowledge—within the war we are all waging with the forces of death, subtle and otherwise, conscious or not—I am not only a casualty, I am also a warrior.[33]

Lorde's suffering became an opportunity for "self-revelation"[34] within a community of female, co-sufferers who empowered her to voice her laments and actively resist diminishment. Her embodied spirituality, which she identified as *eros*, is the context for interpreting her suffering; this consciousness and love of her own sacred, "in-spirited" body (and the many bodies—human and other-than-human—she encountered) allowed her suffering to become a space of creativity, conversion, strength, and transformation. In her earlier prophetic article, "Uses of the Erotic: The Erotic as Power," she offers her readers a vision of the power of love not as an external, coercive force, but as an internally cultivated, creative, and harmonious force possessed by women. It is this innate power that would sustain her in her suffering:

> The very word erotic comes from the Greek word *eros*, the personification of love in all its aspects—born of Chaos, and personifying creative power and harmony. When I speak of the erotic, then I speak of it as an assertion of the life force of women, of that creative energy empowered, the knowledge and use of which we are now reclaiming in our language, our history, our dancing, our loving, our work, our lives.[35]

Lorde articulated the divine present in the universe as an African sacred goddess, Seboulisa, who was the source of all embodied life and the source of the power held by women as empowerment (power-with) not domination (power-over). This deity is not the Christian God (Father) that Teilhard espoused, but her embrace of an imminent deity can help modern Christian believers to reimagine how the animating, vivifying, creative Spirit works in light of the cruciformity, sacrifice, and labor of cosmogenesis. Lorde's work can help connect the idea of *viriditas*, offered by Hildegard of Bingen, with the inspirited bodies of human sufferers. And this offers hope for when sufferers immerse themselves deeply within Earth's vivifying current of costly creative power and trust their broken yet beautiful bodies are extensions of Earth, they can find peace, transformation, and wholeness, even in the face of death. For Lorde, "in this way alone we can survive, by taking part in a process of life that is creative and continuing."[36]

Audre Lorde worked passionately, loved ardently, felt deeply, battled unceasingly, and suffered intensely. Her journals reveal her understanding of how connected her suffering was with the cruciformity inherent in creation; she never gave cancer the last word nor let her experience of suffering alienate her from her creative life force and the mother of us all—"mother Seboulisa" or "[her] mother moon"—which sustained and healed her in spite of the impending death of her body. Instead, Lorde chose to connect with the creative power inherent in our evolutionary world and her human communities to resist and transform the tragic dimensions of her life.

Her narrative is a story of defiance and acceptance, *eros* and *agape*. She lived, loved, labored, and died as an inspirited, embodied woman, faithful to her belief in a deity that permeated and transcended all aspects of Earth, including her suffering and her pain.[37] Her deep physical and spiritual communion with Earth as a spiritual entity, whom she called Mother or Goddess, was a vibrant source of power, love, and healing for her three-year journey with cancer. She articulated honestly how her inspirited body lived antagonistically and at the same time tranquilly as a diverse unity of being (i.e., she was a Black, feminist, lesbian woman battling cancer).[38] In her dark moments, she cried out in lament to the Divine Source of life present in and through the universe, and yet within that anguished cry, she also voiced her own personal commitments and creative abilities to transform her struggles. Her Earth literacy helped her to appreciate cosmic creativity as a double-edged sword: pain and joy, tragedy and exuberance, individuality and connectivity. Lorde's consciousness of this informed her request of her Creator: "Do not let me die a coward, mother. Nor forget how to sing. Nor forget song is a part of mourning as light is a part of sun."[39]

It was her Earth-centered, embodied *eros*, the sacred magnetic force drawing her to a fullness of who she was called to be within a communion of women of color battling cancer, racism, apartheid, and sexism.[40] *Eros* grounded how she lived and loved, and ultimately, it transformed her so that her suffering and death were true extensions of her life and work.[41]

SUMMARY

This chapter gives us a glimpse at the insights into human suffering offered by two people from very different walks of life. Their interpretations of suffering emerge from a robust (and differently formed) Earth literacy that appreciated the principles of an ETA. Both incorporate descriptions of suffering from classical categories, such as lament, witness, testing, and mystery, but they also have a keen appreciation for those offered in the fourth category: cruciformity of creation, sacrifice and labor, and the kenotic-kinetic. Teilhard's and Lorde's personal narratives of healing and transformation can empower sufferers to resist unjust, inflicted suffering while still recognizing that they participate in an unfinished, broken world where inherent suffering plays a necessary part. These insights do not *solve* the problem of suffering; there will never be a satisfying solution. But the way these two individuals encountered suffering enabled them to offer life-giving responses to suffering despite continuing rejection, suffering, and death. It is my hope that their insights can help transform theological conversations concerning suffering.

The description of God as the magnetic energy of Love animating cosmogenesis invites sufferers to immerse themselves within their communion of subjectivity (e.g., women, friends, Earth, church, and family) and reconnect within the Source of life present at the heart of created matter, rather than denying or avoiding inherent suffering. Whether God's presence with us is described as the sacred reserve of energy animating the cosmos (Teilhard), or as *eros* or the life force of women emanating from the goddess mother of us all (Lorde), or as *viriditas*, a Christic greening power (Hildegard), the message is powerful: death and destruction are part of our world but they will never have the last word. God as Divine Creator, Sustainer, and Redeemer is eternally working to bring light from darkness and new life from death.

Teilhard and Lorde take this message to heart and are never passive or powerless in their struggles but active participants in their own (and the world's) transformation. Their lives and words show that when awakened to mutually empowering, embodied, and immanent Love, a sufferer has the "energy to pursue genuine change within our world" and themselves, rather than denying the existence of suffering, or dreaming of an escape from the world, or "merely settling for a shift of characters in the same weary drama."[42]

As Jesus Christ cried out in agony to the heavens from the cross at Golgotha, it was first and foremost a cry for relationship, both divine and material, in the midst of suffering.[43] Thus, acknowledging that our home is a planetary communion of suffering subjects allows the voices of those who have been silenced and burdened with self-loathing and loneliness, to be heard and their suffering transformed. Both Teilhard and Lorde affirm how a vision of cosmic connectedness can be a deep source of healing and transformation, and how unavoidable suffering can be a potential locus for personal and communal transformation. Both Teilhard and Lorde were intimately aware of the green growing in the darkness so they "sought the eyes of death as Lover, bestowing compassion as Prophet" and foretold the "uselessness of anything less than love."[44]

EPILOGUE: NEW HORIZONS

When the machine metaphor captivated our imaginations and God was seen predominantly as a distant, apathetic deity, sufferers became illiterate of the great community of suffering subjects of which they were a member. They also became alienated from a powerful and sacred source of transformation.

Cultivating a distinct Earth literacy reinvigorates theological imaginations and allows believers to embrace a distinctly ecological theological anthropology that reconnects sufferers with their ecological dwelling spaces and with their Creator and Redeemer. This does not, however, present an exhaustive answer to the problem of human suffering. Instead, it offers innovative ways of appreciating the necessary (meaning unavoidable, not intended) and "good" suffering inherent within an evolutionary world as distinct from unjust, inflicted suffering that should be eradicated. When we used divine suffering as our map and looked out the window on the suffering inherent in our dynamic cosmos, a new category to describe suffering emerged that challenged the uncritical use of retribution or atonement for sin as ways of explaining suffering. Thus, appreciating our sacred universe story as a valuable source of divine revelation offers new promise to human sufferers.

NINE DIMENSIONS OF PROMISE

1. **Human sufferers can appreciate the cosmos as a communion of compassionate subjects instead of an alienated, voiceless collection of autonomous objects.** When human sufferers feel invisible, abandoned, and worthless, our universe story articulates a powerful narrative of cosmic connectivity and remembrance on both a biological and spiritual level. Cosmic solidarity and an acknowledgment of inherent suffering throughout 13.8 billion years liberate sufferers from Western society's tendency to avoid meaningful engagement. This awakens human sufferers to their membership within an ancient cosmic family of compassionate sufferers where not even an individual sparrow is forgotten or unloved by God (cf. Matt 10:29; Luke 12:6).
2. **Human sufferers can construct a courageous model of solidarity and resistance to suffering that encourages both self-affirmation and sacrifice.** Cosmogenesis reminds sufferers how disintegration and death are integral parts of the emergence of new life. It also reminds humanity that trust and risk, order and chaos, growth and diminishment, frustration and achievement are intimately coupled in our evolutionary universe. This allows sufferers to reimagine resistance to suffering as an individual, communal, and cosmic practice rather than as a purely human model of combat where death only signals defeat.
3. **Human sufferers can address powerlessness in the face of suffering.** The sacred universe story teaches that the power demonstrated by the God of evolution is not *power-over* but *power-with*. Hence human sufferers can awaken to how they and their planetary community of fellow sufferers participate in God's creative activity in bringing forth new life as well as God's sacrifice and compassion. This connection to the power hidden in communion can address the powerlessness felt by sufferers; they can be empowered to participate in their own healing and transformation as members and planetary citizens, and see how their limitation, frustration, diminishment, and even death can be part of their (and the world's) journey to intimacy with God.

4. **Human sufferers can recognize that they are never alone in their pain.** Earth literacy addresses the myopia of humanity that has generated a distorted sense of individuality. Today's radical autonomy feeds the loneliness that many sufferers experience and has disconnected many sufferers from their own communities and families, and from Earth as a sacred source of healing. Strengthening humanity's acuity to the suffering of Earth's other-than-human subjects can awaken sufferers to our participation in the cruciformity of life. But we are never alone. This strengthened acuity will stimulate a new appreciation of the moments of grace inherent to diminishment, limitation, and death when it is an extension of an abundant life (cf. John 10:10).
5. **Human sufferers can reimagine what compassion, sacrifice, and witness mean in our planetary community.** The sacred universe story relieves sufferers from the modern delusion that a life free of sacrifice, vulnerability, or suffering is possible. This illusion prevents our human communities from being *com*passionate (people who suffer with one another) and compounds suffering by both blaming sufferers for their own suffering and using a distorted vision of "survival of the fittest" to sanction the suffering of those deemed less worthy. Cosmogenesis stimulates a new, positive appreciation of the sacrificial/affirmation dialectic that grounds all created life and can reinvigorate biblical and classical descriptions of suffering as compassion, sacrifice, and witness.
6. **Human sufferers can testify anew to our vocation as an Easter people.** Our sacred cosmic story testifies to the intrinsic worth of creation and the hope laying in the irreversible, ongoing, and unpredictably creative evolutionary processes. This addresses the fears of many sufferers that their lives are/were meaningless and they are worthless. Consequently, our evolutionary world can help ground our vocation as an Easter people and inspire hope.
7. **Human sufferers can appreciate God as Immanuel in new ways.** The sacred universe story illustrates how the creative suffering of the Triune God can be interpreted and experienced by all of creation in many ways: sympathetically, empathetically, and protopathetically. This multiform way of

understanding how our transcendent and immanent God can be present to humans in their suffering brings sufferers hope and comfort. It also offers new meaning to the words offered by the Prophet Isaiah: "Do not fear, for I am with you" (Isa 41:10).

8. **Human sufferers can understand the incarnation and risen Christ in new ways.** When our theological understanding of the incarnation and resurrection is traced backward from Bethlehem to the Big Bang and forward from Golgotha to ultimate fullness of life at the *eschaton*, sufferers can appreciate anew the love God has for all creation and how Christ is a magnetic force luring all of creation toward fullness of life. Thus, no creature ever dies "godforsaken." Human sufferers are invited to see how their pain and suffering is not the ultimate end; rather, it is a part of a bigger 13.8-billion-year journey of transformation and love modeled on the incarnate and risen Christ.
9. **Human sufferers can witness to the power of the cosmic cross.** An ETA allows the cross at Golgotha to symbolize the presence of divine compassionate love throughout the universe's entire unfolding, including the sacrificial gift of the first stars, the many extinction spasms, the rise of predation, the single mother struggling to provide for her children, the old man curled up on a hospital bed, those fighting for justice and peace in El Salvador, or the young girl, desperate for release, who takes her own life. Earth literacy and an ETA allow believers to appreciate how "the cross of Christ concentrates the suffering of God into a point of intensity and transparency that reveals this to be characteristic of God's perennial relation to creation."[1] This perspective can allow sufferers, and those courageously companioning them, to see how they are being invited to become witnesses to the power of the evolving God-in-relation, and the incarnate and risen Christ lying hidden in suffering that continually calls forth new life from death in unexpected ways.

These are nine dimensions of the *promise* offered to sufferers and those companioning them when they face the mystery of human suffering. This is not a guarantee or a solution. These final thoughts sum up how the formation of biospiritual theological imaginations that embrace an ETA can help sufferers—namely, hope for abundant life in spite of suffering and death. These various dimensions speak to "God's bottomless enthusiasm for the wet and wild" and to the powerful presence of the numinous in creation, continually laboring to transform suffering in our evolutionary world.[2]

Just as Hildegard intertwined *viriditas* with *ariditas* centuries ago, sufferers today are reminded that Earth's prolific creativity is inextricably intertwined with *pathos*; the Divine Triune community, our 13.8-billion-year universe story, and the lives and writings of Teilhard and Lorde all testify to this. Those who courageously choose to follow God of the cosmic cross and travel beyond traditional understandings of human suffering as retribution and atonement can become witnesses to the noblest greenness that grows in the darkness and is never overcome.

NOTES

FOREWORD

1. Teilhard de Chardin, *The Phenomenon of Man*, trans. Bernard Wall (New York: Harper and Row, 1959), 302.

2. St. Maximus the Confessor, *On the Cosmic Mystery of Jesus Christ*, trans. Paul M. Bowers (Yonkers, NY: St. Vladimir's Seminary Press, 2003), 55.

3. Arthur R. Peacock, *Science and the Christian Experiment* (Oxford: Oxford University Press, 1971), 137.

INTRODUCTION

1. Denis Edwards, *Made from Stardust* (North Blackburn, Victoria, Australia: CollinsDove, 1992).

2. Heidi Ann Russell, *Quantum Shift: Theological and Pastoral Implications of Contemporary Developments in Science* (Collegeville, MN: Liturgical Press, 2015), xxiii.

3. Thomas Berry, "Christianity's Role in the Earth Project," in *Christianity and Ecology: Seeking the Well-Being of Earth and Humans*, ed. Dieter T. Hessel and Rosemary Radford Ruether (Cambridge, MA: Harvard University Centre for the Study of World Religions Publications, 2000), 132–33.

4. This is an adaptation of Thomas Berry's famous statement: "Earth is a communion of subjects not a collection of objects."

5. Douglas John Hall, *The Cross in Our Context: Jesus and the Suffering World* (Minneapolis: Fortress Press, 2003), 186.

6. Pope Francis, *Laudato Si': Caring for Our Common Home* (May 24, 2015), http://w2.vatican.va/content/francesco/en/encyclicals/documents/papa-francesco_20150524_enciclica-laudato-si.html.

7. Elizabeth Johnson, "Losing and Finding Creation in the Christian Tradition," in *Christianity and Ecology: Seeking the Well-Being of Earth and Humans*, ed. Dieter T. Hessel and Rosemary Radford Ruether (Cambridge, MA: Harvard University Centre for the Study of World Religions Publications, 2000), 8.

8. Some activities include the 1995 Kobe earthquake, the 1883 eruption of Krakatau in Indonesia, and the 1980 eruption of Mount St. Helens.

9. See Brian Swimme and Thomas Berry, *The Universe Story: From the Primordial Flaring Forth to the Ecozoic Era—Celebration of the Unfolding of the Cosmos* (San Francisco, CA: Harper, 1992), 101–3.

10. Douglas John Hall at the 2013 Cousland Lecture "The Future of the Church," presented at Emmanuel College, Toronto School of Theology, October 16, 2013.

11. Christopher Southgate, *The Groaning of Creation: God, Evolution and the Problem of Evil* (Louisville, KY: Westminster John Knox Press, 2008), 15.

12. Magdalena Gómez, "In Darkness Grows the Green," in *Community of Religions: Voices and Images of the Parliament of the World Religions*, ed. W. Teasdale and G.F. Cairns (New York: Continuum, 1996), 75–76.

PART I

1. The Emergence of Scientific Earth Literacy

1. See "Task-based (conceptual) definition" in S. White and M. McCloskey, *Framework for the 2003 National Assessment of Adult Literacy* (NCES 2005-531) U.S. Department of Education (Washington, DC: National Center for Education Statistics), https://nces.ed.gov/naal/fr_definition.asp. (Emphasis added.)

2. David W. Orr, *Ecological Literacy: Education and the Transition to a Postmodern World*, SUNY Series in Constructive Postmodern Thought (Albany, NY: State University of New York Press, 1992), 86.

3. Ibid., 85–86.

4. Ibid., 94. For a fuller outline of David Orr's six defining characteristics of ecological sustainability, see pp. 29–38.

5. Ibid., 95.

6. From Sept. 24, 2003, to Jan. 16, 2004, the Hubble Telescope's Advanced Camera "observed a tiny patch of sky (one-tenth the diameter of the moon) for one million seconds (11.6 days) and found approximately 10,000 galaxies, of all sizes, shapes, and colors." NASA, "Galaxies," http://science.nasa.gov/astrophysics/focus-areas/what-are-galaxies/. Also see Hubble Site, "Hubble's Deepest View Ever of the Universe Unveils Earliest Galaxies," March 9, 2004, http://hubblesite.org/newscenter/archive/releases/2004/07/.

7. Brian Swimme and Thomas Berry, *The Universe Story: From the Primordial Flaring Forth to the Ecozoic Era—Celebration of the Unfolding of the Cosmos* (San Francisco, CA: Harper, 1992), 66.

8. Ibid., 73, 75, 77.

9. Ibid., 67.

10. Ursula King, "Earthing Spiritual Literacy: How to Link Spiritual Development and Education to a New Earth Consciousness?" *Journal of Beliefs & Values* 31, no. 3 (December 2010): 258.

11. Elizabeth Johnson, *Ask the Beasts: Darwin and the God of Love* (London: Bloomsbury, 2014), 123–24.

12. As quoted in John Feehan, *The Singing Heart of the World: Creation, Evolution and Faith* (New York: Orbis Books, 2012), 11.

13. Sandra Harding, *Whose Science? Whose Knowledge? Thinking from Women's Lives* (Ithaca, NY: Cornell University Press, 1991), 179, 185–86.

14. Ian Barbour, *When Science Meets Religion: Enemies, Strangers or Partners?* (San Francisco, CA: HarperSanFrancisco, 2000), 26.

15. Carolyn Merchant, *The Death of Nature: Women, Ecology and the Scientific Revolution* (San Francisco, CA: Harper & Row, 1980).

16. Peninah Neimark and Peter Rhoades Mott, *The Environmental Debate: A Documentary History*, Primary Documents in American History and Contemporary Issues Series (Westport, CO: Greenwood Press, 1999), 10–14.

17. Brian Swimme, "How to Heal a Lobotomy," in *Reweaving the World: The Emergence of Ecofeminism*, ed. Irene Diamond

and Gloria Feman Orestein (San Francisco, CA: Sierra Club Books, 1990), 17.

18. Charles Richard Elrington, *The Whole Works of the Most Rev. James Ussher, D.D.* (Dublin: Hodges and Smith, 1847), see http://archive.org/details/lifeofjamesusshe03elriuoft.

19. Charles Darwin, *On the Origin of Species by Means of Natural Selection, or, the Preservation of Favoured Races in the Struggle for Life*, 4th ed. (London: J. Murray, 1866), xiii. Buffon published his observations in *Histoire naturelle, générale et particulière* (36 vols. published between 1749 and 1788).

20. In 1859, Gustav Kirchoff and Robert Bunsen found that each element, when heated, has its own characteristic set of spectral lines. This is its "fingerprint." In 1863, William Huggins in England observed many of these same lines in the spectra of the stars. From this he deduced that the visible universe is made of the same chemical elements as those found on Earth.

21. Dieter B. Herrmann, *The History of Astronomy from Herschel to Hertzsprung*, trans. Kevin Krisciunas (Cambridge: Cambridge University Press, 1984), 69–114.

22. Sean McDonagh, *To Care for the Earth: A Call to a New Theology* (London: Geoffrey Chapman, 1986), 65. Of the five years, Darwin spent three years and three months on land studying the flora and fauna and eighteen months on the Beagle.

23. Anning was an exceptional scientist with an extensive knowledge of Earth and the skills to extract more wisdom. But this was long before women (especially poor women) were accepted in this profession in England. See Hugh Torrens, "The Greatest Fossilist the world ever knew," *British Journal of the History of Science* 28, no. 3 (1995): 257–84.

24. Darwin's research data came from his travels on the HMS Beagle when he circumnavigated the globe (1831–36).

25. The data offered by Wallace came from his journals concerning the Malay Archipelago voyage (1854–62). The paper offering his data and theories on evolution presented to the Linnean Society was titled "On the Tendency of Varieties to depart indefinitely from the Original Type."

26. Darwin's theory of natural selection was greatly influenced by Malthus. It is noteworthy that, persuaded by Alfred Wallace among others, Darwin included the term "survival of the fittest" only in the

fifth edition of his text. He took the phrase from the philosopher Henry Spencer's idea about social progress among human beings and incorporated it into his own discussion of the biological "struggle for existence." Also Darwin only first used the term "evolution" in the sixth (and last) edition published in 1872. Johnson, *Ask the Beasts*, 25.

27. Stanley Dodson et al., eds., *Ecology* (Oxford: Oxford University Press, 1998), 2.

28. *Atmosphere* was coined much earlier in 1638. Allysyn Kiplinger, "Naming a New Geological Era: The Ecozoic Era, Its Meaning and Historical Antecedents," *The Ecozoic: Reflections on Life in an Ecological-Cultural Age* 3 (2013): 19.

29. Robert Clarke, *Ellen Swallow: The Woman Who Founded Ecology* (Chicago, IL: Follett Publishing, 1973), 113–20.

30. Donald Worster, *Nature's Economy: History of Ecological Thought*, 2nd ed. (Cambridge: Cambridge University Press, 1995, c1977), 196–98.

31. This text germinated after Emerson read the Bhagavad Gita in 1831 and his voracious appetite for rhetoric, oration, philosophy, science, physics, Gothic tales, and poetry. Emerson, in the summer of 1833, spent a great amount of time at the Jardins des Plants and the Cabinet of Natural History in Paris and this revealed to him in a concrete way the intricate interconnectivity of all of nature. This truth impacted his future literary work. Paul Hawken, *Blessed Unrest: How the Largest Movement in the World Came into Being and Why No One Saw It Coming* (New York: Penguin Group, 2007), 34, 72–73.

32. "The Early Lectures of Ralph Waldo Emerson" as quoted in Robert D. Richardson, *Emerson: The Mind on Fire: A Biography* (Berkeley, CA: University of California Press, 1995), 155.

33. Roderick Nash, *Wilderness and the American Mind* (New Haven, CT: Yale University Press, 1967), 84. Also see Thoreau's essay "Resistance to Civil Government" (1849), which was later titled "Civil Disobedience."

34. When Burroughs was a clerk in the Treasury Department in Washington, DC, during the Civil War, he spent his idle moments writing about what he loved, nature, and this became his popular first book *Wake-Robin* (1871). He returned to the Hudson River Valley in 1873 to fruit farm and write. Some of his other writings in the late nineteenth century include *Winter Sunshine* (1875–76), *Birds and*

Poets (1877), *Signs and Seasons* (1886), and many others that spanned the first decades of the twentieth century.

35. This discovery was rearticulated again in 1883 by Belgium embryologist Édouard Van Beneden (1846–1910) in the eggs of intestinal worms found in horses.

2. The Development of Scientific Earth Literacy

1. Douglas John Hall, *Imaging God: Dominion as Stewardship* (Grand Rapids, MI: W.B. Eerdmans, 1986), 124.

2. Physicist George Gamow tells of a conversation he had with Einstein where the latter admits that the cosmological constant idea was the "biggest blunder" of his life. See George Gamow, *My World Line: An Informal Autobiography* (New York: Viking Press, 1970), 44.

3. Stephen W. Hawking, *A Brief History of Time: From the Big Bang to Black Holes* (London: Bantam Press, 1988), 40, 42.

4. Georges Lemaître, "A Homogeneous Universe of Constant Mass and Increasing Radius Accounting for the Radial Velocity of Extra-Galactic Nebulae," *Monthly Notices of the Royal Astronomical Society* 91 (1931): 483–501; "The Beginning of the World from the Point of View of Quantum Theory," *Nature* 127, no. 3210 (1931): 706. Scientists following Lemaître postulated that science could still observe the radiation from the early stages of the birth of the universe, but physicists Arno Penzias and Robert Woodrow Wilson were the first to record this cosmic microwave background radiation in 1965.

5. J. J. O'Connor and E. F. Robertson, "Georges Henri-Joseph-Edouard Lemaître," University of St. Andrews and School of Mathematics and Statistics, accessed January 2013, http://www-history.mcs.st-andrews.ac.uk/Biographies/Lemaitre.html.

6. Hawking, *A Brief History of Time*, 41–42.

7. Bernard Lovell, *The Individual and the Universe*, 1st American ed., The BBC Reith Lectures (New York: Harper, 1959). Also Hawking, *A Brief History of Time*, 50–51, 121–22.

8. As stated by Arthur Peacocke in Gloria Schaab, *The Creative Suffering of the Triune God: An Evolutionary Theology*, AAR Academy Series (Oxford: Oxford University Press, 2007), 113.

9. Hawking, *A Brief History of Time*, 11.

10. Linda Bennett, "What Dalton Discovered", accessed May 2016, http://edtech2.boisestate.edu/lindabennett1/502/dalton.html.

11. Purdue University, "J. J. Thompson," accessed May 2016, http://chemed.chem.purdue.edu/genchem/history/raisin.html.

12. James Schombert, University of Oregon (web page lectures), accessed May 2016, http://abyss.uoregon.edu/~js/glossary/bohr_atom.html.

13. Hawking, *A Brief History of Time*, 55. See also John Feehan, *The Singing Heart of the World: Creation, Evolution and Faith* (New York: Orbis Books, 2012), 38.

14. Ian Barbour, *When Science Meets Religion: Enemies, Strangers or Partners?* (San Francisco, CA: HarperSanFrancisco, 2000), 82.

15. CERN stands for "Conseil Européen pour la Recherche Nucléaire." For information about the Higgs Boson, see CERN, "The Higgs Boson," accessed May 2016, http://home.cern/topics/higgs-boson.

16. Shaun Maguire, October 23, 2013, "The Ten Biggest Breakthroughs in Physics over the Past 25 Years, According to Us," *Quantum Frontiers Blog*, Institute for Quantum Information and Matter @ Caltech, http://quantumfrontiers.com/2013/10/23/the-10-biggest-breakthroughs-in-physics-over-the-past-25-years-according-to-us/.

17. As cited by Linda J. Lear, *Lost Woods: The Discovered Writing of Rachel Carson* (Boston, MA: Beacon Press, 1998), 148. See http://www.public-domain-poetry.com/emily-elizabeth-dickinson/i-never-saw-a-moor-13596.

18. He also indicates that in the 1700s, only five cities in the world had over 500,000 people; in 1997, over 400 cities had over 1 million and by 2000, twenty-one cities will be classified as mega cities with a population of over 10 million. Tim C. Wieskel, "Notes from Balshaz'zar's Feast," in *The Greening of Faith: God, the Environment, and the Good Life*, ed. John E. Carrol, Paul T. Brockelman, and Mary Westfall (Hanover, NH: University Press of New England, 1997), 18–19.

19. Peninah Neimark and Peter Rhoades Mott, *The Environmental Debate: A Documentary History*, Primary Documents in American History and Contemporary Issues Series (Westport, CO: Greenwood Press, 1999), 144.

20. This is an invocation of Shiva (the destroyer god in Hinduism) from the Bhagavad Gita. See Paul Hawken, *Blessed Unrest: How*

the Largest Movement in the World Came into Being and Why No One Saw It Coming (New York: Penguin Group, 2007), 29n1.

21. Henry Nelson Wieman, *The Source of Human Good* (Chicago, IL: University of Chicago Press, 1946), 37, as quoted in Gordon D. Kaufman, *Theology for a Nuclear Age* (Manchester: Manchester University Press, 1985), 15n3.

22. Stephen Wheeler and Timothy Beatley, *The Sustainable Urban Development Reader*, The Routledge Urban Reader Series (London; New York: Routledge, 2004), 113.

23. Hawken, *Blessed Unrest*, 183.

24. Laurel Kearns, "The Context of Eco-Theology," in *The Blackwell Companion to Modern Theology*, ed. Gareth Jones (New York: Blackwell, 2004), 473.

25. The Space Age came with the launch of Sputnik in 1957 and when Russian cosmonaut Yuri Gagarin took flight in space 1961. NASA, *Yuri Gagarin: First Man in Space*, accessed December 2015, http://www.nasa.gov/mission_pages/shuttle/sts1/gagarin_anniversary.html.

26. NASA, *July 20, 1969: One Giant Leap for Mankind* [*sic*], accessed December 2015, http://www.nasa.gov/mission_pages/apollo/apollo11_40th.html.

27. Lynn Margulis and Dorion Sagan, "Sentient Symphony," in *The Nature of Life: Classical and Contemporary Perspectives from Philosophy and Science*, ed. Mark A. Bedau and Carol E. Cleland (Cambridge, MA: Cambridge University Press, 2010), 350.

28. Carolyn Merchant, *Major Problems in American Environmental History: Documents and Essays* (Lexington, MA: D.C. Heath, 1993), 444ff.

29. Richards was termed as the "first lady" of science and human sanitation, and she fleshed out the foundation of Haekel's vision of ecology within her own context of the chemistry of human communities. Robert Clarke, *Ellen Swallow: The Woman Who Founded Ecology* (Chicago, IL: Follett Publishing, 1973), 113–20.

30. Donald Worster, *Nature's Economy: History of Ecological Thought*, 2nd ed. (Cambridge: Cambridge University Press, 1995, c1977), 196–98.

31. Frederic E. Clements, "Plant Succession; an Analysis of the Development of Vegetation," ([S.l.]: [s.n.], 1916), see Biodiversity Heritage Library, http://www.biodiversitylibrary.org/title/56234.

32. Charles Elton, in 1927, published *Animal Ecology* where he laid the foundations for this new economic understanding of ecology via his vision of energy transfer within nature. Through photosynthetic conversion of energy to food, essential capital was seen in the natural economic order. Charles S. Elton, *Animal Ecology* (New York: Macmillan, 1927).

33. Arthur Tansley, "The Use and Abuse of Vegetational Concepts and Terms," *Ecology* 16, no. 3 (1935): 284–307, http://karljaspers.org/files/tansley.pdf.

34. He elaborated on Tansley's work to include economic metaphors (producers, consumers, productivity, etc.) and concepts such as food webs, "Eltonian" food pyramid, and trophic systems that entail energy transfers and transformation of materials. Raymond Lindeman, "The Trophic Dynamic Aspect of Ecology," *Ecology* 23, no. 4 (1942): 399–417.

35. "In other words, the landscape is not just a supply depot but is also the home in which we must live." Eugene P. Odum, as cited by Merchant, *Major Problems in American Environmental History*, 458. Eugene Pleasant Odum's synthetic holistic thinking within ecosystem ecology was the basis of his groundbreaking text, *Fundamentals of Ecology* (1953).

36. Donald Worster as quoted in Merchant, *Major Problems in American Environmental History*, 472–79. Also see S. T. A. Pickett and P. S. White, *The Ecology of Natural Disturbance and Patch Dynamics* (Orlando, FL: Academic Press, 1985).

37. William Morton Wheeler, "A Neglected Factor in Evolution," *Science* 15 (1902): 766–74; ibid., "The Ant-Colony as an Organism," *Journal of Morphology* 22 (1911): 307–25. Also see George Howard Parker, *Biographical Memoir of William Morton Wheeler (1865–1937)*, National Academy of Sciences of the United States of America Biographical Memoirs Volume XIX - Sixth Memoir (1938), accessed March 2013, http://www.nasonline.org/publications/biographical-memoirs/memoir-pdfs/wheeler-william.pdf.

38. His texts include *The Light of Day* (1900), *Ways of Nature* (1905), *Leaf and Tendrill* (1908), *Time and Change* (1912), *The Breath of Life* (1915), *Under the Apple-Trees* (1916), *Accepting the Universe* (1920), and *The Last Harvest* (1922).

39. J. Howard Moore's *The Universal Kinship* (Chicago: Charles H. Kerr & Co., 1918; c1906) references a specific planetary kinship,

and Rosa Luxembourg's text articulated the importance of fostering local, indigenous, natural economies that had been destroyed by industrial development. Rosa Luxembourg, *Die Akkumulation des Kapitals*, 1913; *The Accumulation of Capital*, Eng. ed. (London: Routledge & Kegan Paul, 1951), http://libcom.org/files/luxemburg%20the%20accumulation%20of%20capital.pdf.

40. H. M. Tomlinson, "The Lost Woods," in H. M. Tomlinson, *Out of Soundings* (New York: Harper & Brothers Publishers, 1931), 82–100, http://www.eldritchpress.org/hmt/lostwood.htm.

41. Freddie Whitefield and Satish Kumar, *Visionaries of the 20th Century: A Resurgence Anthology* (Cambridge: Green Books, 2006), 117.

42. George R. Tilton, "Clair Cameron Patterson (1922–1995)" (Washington, DC: National Academies Press, 1998), 8, http://www.nasonline.org/publications/biographical-memoirs/memoir-pdfs/patterson-clair-c.pdf.

43. Health Canada, "Final Human Health State of the Science Report on Lead" (February 2013), http://www.hc-sc.gc.ca/ewh-semt/pubs/contaminants/dhhssrl-rpecscepsh/index-eng.php.

44. Farley Mowat, *People of the Deer* (Boston: Little, Brown & Co., 1952); ibid., *Never Cry Wolf: The Amazing True Story of Life among Arctic Wolves* (Boston: Little, Brown & Co., 1963); ibid., *Sea of Slaughter* (Boston: Atlantic Monthly Press, 1984).

45. Linda Lear, *Rachel Carson: Witness for Nature* (New York: First Mariner Books, 2009, c1997), 4. Lear is Carson's auto biographer and is referring to her appearance before a special subcommittee on environmental hazards. The next day, she appeared before the Senate Committee on Commerce (June 1963). Her book *Silent Spring* (1962) outlined the indiscriminate use of DDT and its devastating effects on all ecosystems. Her data caused the world to look more closely at the use of pesticides (especially DDT) and call these hearings.

46. Rachel Carson, "The Pollution of Our Environment," reprinted in Lear, *Lost Woods*, 231.

47. Hawken, *Blessed Unrest*, 58.

48. G. Harlem Brundtland, "How to Secure Our Common Future," *Scientific American* 261, no. 3 (1989): 190. (Italics are author's.)

49. Comments in the *New York Times*, December 31, 1969, reprinted in David Spring and Eileen Spring, *Ecology and Religion in History* (New York: Harper & Row, 1974), 2.

3. Scientific Earth Literacy in Theology

1. Giorgio De Santillana, *The Crime of Galileo* (Chicago: University of Chicago Press, 1955), 306–10.

2. Sean McDonagh, *To Care for the Earth: A Call to a New Theology* (London: Geoffrey Chapman, 1986), 110.

3. Donald Worster, *Nature's Economy: History of Ecological Thought*, 2nd ed. (Cambridge: Cambridge University Press, 1995, c1977), 5.

4. Ibid., 11.

5. As quoted in ibid., 7. His work was groundbreaking because it looked at the entirety of the microcosm, not atomizing its parts, and his observations were local and not undertaken in exotic locales.

6. Carolyn Merchant, *The Death of Nature: Women, Ecology and the Scientific Revolution* (San Francisco, CA: Harper & Row, 1980).

7. Worster, *Nature's Economy*, 10.

8. Ibid., 8.

9. Ibid., 14.

10. Robert Bernard Martin, *Gerard Manley Hopkins: A Very Private Life*, 1st American ed. (New York: G. P. Putnam's Sons, 1991), 21.

11. Journal Entry Sept 24, 1870, in Gerard Manley Hopkins, Humphry House, and Graham Storey, *The Journals and Papers of Gerard Manley Hopkins* (London: Oxford University Press, 1959), 200. As quoted in Martin, *Gerard Manley Hopkins*, 202.

12. Martin, *Gerard Manley Hopkins*, 203.

13. Ibid., 203.

14. Ibid., 30.

15. "The Wreck of the Deutschland" (1876), "The Windhover" (1877), "Spring and Fall: To a Young Child" (1880), "To Seem the Stranger" (1885), "I Wake and Feel the Fell of Dark, not Day" (1885), "Carrion Comfort" (1885).

16. Neville F. Newman, "Hopkins Ribbendale," *The Explicator* 57, no. 4 (1999): 214–15.

17. Martin, *Gerard Manley Hopkins*, 348.

18. Ibid., 26.

19. Ibid., 306.

20. Gerard Manley Hopkins, "Inversnaid," accessed June 2016, http://www.bartleby.com/122/33.html.

21. Martin., *Gerard Manley Hopkins*, 203.

22. Ibid., 208.

23. Gerard Manley Hopkins, "As Kingfishers Catch Fire," accessed June 2016, http://www.poetryfoundation.org/poem/173654.

24. Martin., *Gerard Manley Hopkins*, 203.

25. Ibid., 205, 206.

26. Ibid., 202.

27. Pierre Teilhard de Chardin, *The Phenomenon of Man*, trans. Bernard Wall (New York: Harper & Row, 1955).

28. Pierre Teilhard de Chardin, *The Divine Milieu: An Essay on the Interior Life* (London: William Collins Sons and Co., 1960), xxii.

29. Ibid., 50.

30. Ursula King, *Pierre Teilhard De Chardin: Writings*, Modern Spiritual Masters Series (Maryknoll, NY: Orbis Books, 1999), 50.

31. Pierre Teilhard de Chardin, *Man's Place in Nature: The Human Zoological Group* (London: William Collins Sons & Co., 1966), 121.

32. Pierre Teilhard de Chardin, *The Heart of Matter* (London: William Collins Sons & Co., 1978), 181.

33. Teilhard de Chardin, *The Divine Milieu*, xi.

34. Ibid., xiv.

35. Teilhard de Chardin, *Hymn of the Universe* (London: William Collins Sons & Co., 1965), 65.

36. August 7, 1950. Pierre Teilhard de Chardin, *The Making of a Mind: Letters from a Soldier-Priest, 1914–1919*, 1st ed. (New York: Harper & Row, 1965), 302n2.

37. Teilhard de Chardin, *The Making of a Mind*, 302; see also *The Heart of Matter*, 38.

38. Teilhard de Chardin, *The Phenomenon of Man*, 260.

39. Teilhard de Chardin, *Science and Christ*, trans. Rene Hague (New York: Harper and Row, 1969), 84–85.

40. John Feehan, *The Singing Heart of the World: Creation, Evolution and Faith* (New York: Orbis Books, 2012), 89.

41. Albert Schweitzer, *Out of My Life and Thought: An Autobiography* (New York: Holt, Rinehart, and Winston, 1949), 188.

42. Joseph Sittler, *The Care of the Earth and Other University Sermons* (Philadelphia: Fortress Press, 1964).

43. Joseph A. Sittler, Address delivered to the Third Assembly, World Council of Churches, New Delhi, India, on November 21,

1961. Joseph Sittler, "Called to Unity," *The Ecumenical Review* 14 (1962): 181.

44. Sittler, "Called to Unity," 183.

45. Ibid.

46. Ibid., 187.

47. Forward in Joseph Sittler, Steven Bouma-Prediger, and Peter W. Bakken, *Evocations of Grace: The Writings of Joseph Sittler on Ecology, Theology, and Ethics* (Grand Rapids, MI: W.B. Eerdmans, 2000), xi.

48. Richard A. Baer Jr., "Land Misuse: A Theological Concern," *Christian Century* 83 (1966): 1239–41; see also his "Conservation: An Arena for the Church's Action," *Christian Century* 86 (1969): 40–43.

49. John B. Cobb, *A Christian Natural Theology, Based on the Thought of Alfred North Whitehead* (Philadelphia: Westminster Press, 1965); John B. Cobb, *Is It Too Late? A Theology of Ecology*, Faith and Life Series (Beverly Hills, CA: Bruce, 1972); John B. Cobb and David Ray Griffin, *Process Theology: An Introductory Exposition* (Philadelphia: Westminster Press, 1976).

50. Ian G. Barbour, *Ethics in an Age of Technology*, 1st ed., Gifford Lectures (San Francisco: HarperSanFrancisco, 1993), 72.

51. John F. Haught, *The Cosmic Adventure: Science, Religion and the Quest for Purpose* (Ramsey, NJ: Paulist Press, 1984), 117.

52. Barbour, *Ethics in an Age of Technology*, 71.

53. Max Weber, *The Protestant Ethic and the Spirit of Capitalism* (New York; London: Scribner; G. Allen & Unwin, 1930). Originally published in 1904–5. Also see Laurel Kearns, "The Context of Eco-Theology," in *The Blackwell Companion to Modern Theology*, ed. Gareth Jones (New York: Blackwell, 2004), 470.

54. Langdon Gilkey, *Reaping the Whirlwind: A Christian Interpretation of History* (New York: Seabury Press, 1976), 185.

55. H. Paul Santmire, *The Travail of Nature: The Ambiguous Ecological Promise of Christian Theology* (Minneapolis: Fortress Press, 1985), 126, 137.

56. Harvey Gallagher Cox and Northrop Frye, *The Secular City: Secularization and Urbanization in Theological Perspective* (New York: Macmillan, 1965). He also wrote *God's Revolution and Man's Responsibilities* (1966) and *The Seduction of the Spirit: The Use and Misuse of People's Religion* (1973).

57. Lynn Townsend White Jr., "The Historical Roots of Our Ecologic Crisis," *Science* 155 (1967): 1205.

58. Ibid., 1207.

59. See Ian L. McHaig, "The Place of Nature in the City of Man," in Ian G. Barbour, *Western Man and Environmental Ethics: Attitudes toward Nature and Technology* (Reading, MA: Addison-Wesley, 1973), 175.

60. H. Paul Santmire, *Brother Earth: Nature, God and Ecology in Time of Crisis* (New York: Thomas Nelson, 1970).

61. H. Paul Santmire, "Reflections on the Alleged Ecological Bankruptcy of Western Theology," in *Ethics for Environment: Three Religious Strategies: The Proceedings of a National Conference Held at the University of Wisconsin-Green Bay, June 11-13, 1973*, ed. David Steffenson, Walter J. Herrscher, and Robert S. Cook (Green Bay, WI: UWGB Ecumenical Center, 1973), 36.

62. Ibid.

63. Ibid., 31.

4. The Birth of Ecotheology

1. Many areas of the ecotheological tapestry had to be omitted and others treated somewhat superficially. For example, groundbreaking ecumenical and multidisciplinary work was done by the contributors to the anthology *Cry of the Environment: Rebuilding the Christian Creation Tradition* (1984). In addition, non-Christian contributions to Earth literacy are not explored but are important in understanding Earth literacy. Also other threads manifest at this time (or shortly after) and include the domains of biblical, sacramental, Trinitarian, pastoral, and ecclesial theology.

2. Thomas Berry, "Foreword," in Anne Marie Dalton, *A Theology for the Earth: The Contributions of Thomas Berry and Bernard Lonergan* (Ottawa, ON: University of Ottawa Press, 1999), vi–vii.

3. Thomas Berry, "The New Story: Comments on the Origin and Transmission of Values," vol. 5 of *Riverdale Papers*. It was also published as the first volume of the *Teilhard Studies* series (*Teilhard Studies* 1 (1978):1–13) and as "The New Cosmic Story," in *Warm Wind: Journal of the Chinook Learning Center* 2 (1979): 21–26.

4. Thomas Berry, "The New Story: Comments on the Origin and Transmission of Values," and "Twelve Principles for Reflecting

on the Universe," *Cross Currents* 37, nos. 2–3 (Summer/Fall 1987): 178–217.

5. Ibid., 216–17.

6. Thomas Berry, *The Great Work: Our Way into the Future*, 1st ed. (New York: Bell Tower, 1999), 13.

7. The term "Ecozoic" arises in Berry's work in 1989 and it was incorporated into the title of the book he cowrote with Brian Swimme (1992). Allysyn Kiplinger, "Naming a New Geological Era: The Ecozoic Era, Its Meaning and Historical Antecedents," *The Ecozoic: Reflections on Life in an Ecological-Cultural Age* 3 (2013): 10–11. Herman Greene calls this era a new "geo-bio-logical era." From Herman Greene, "Ecozoic Ideas for the 21st Century," *The Ecozoic: Reflections on Life in an Ecological-Cultural Age* 3 (2013): 41.

8. John F. Haught, *Nature and Purpose* (Lanham, MD: University Press of America, 1980).

9. Ibid., 2.

10. John F. Haught, *The Cosmic Adventure: Science, Religion and the Quest for Purpose* (Ramsey, NJ: Paulist Press, 1984), 166.

11. Haught, *Nature and Purpose*, 2.

12. Jürgen Moltmann, *God in Creation: A New Theology of Creation and the Spirit of God* (San Francisco: Harper & Row, c1985; Fortress Press, 1993), xi.

13. Ibid., 2.

14. Ibid.

15. Ibid., 4.

16. Ibid., xiv.

17. Ibid., 3.

18. Ibid., xiv.

19. Gordon D. Kaufman, *Theology for a Nuclear Age* (Manchester: Manchester University Press, 1985), 44.

20. Ibid., 37.

21. Ibid., 39.

22. Ibid., 41. He develops this idea further in the following texts: *In Face of Mystery: A Constructive Theology* (1993); *In the Beginning…Creativity* (2004). See also "Re-conceiving God and Humanity in Light of Today's Evolutionary-Ecological Consciousness," *Zygon* 36, no. 2 (June 2001): 341–47. In all of these, he describes God using the nomenclature "serendipitous creativity."

23. Kaufman, *Theology for a Nuclear Age*, 45.

24. Ibid., 53.

25. Ibid., 57.

26. Ibid., 61.

27. Ibid., 22, 26.

28. Sallie McFague, *Models of God: Theology for an Ecological, Nuclear Age* (Philadelphia: Fortress Press, 1987); Sallie McFague, "The World as God's Body," *Christian Century* 105, no. 22 (July 20, 1988): 671–73.

29. These include the dialectical theology of Karl Barth, the principles of process philosophy of Charles Hartshorne, and her mentor H. Richard Niebuhr's appreciation of relativity, symbolic imagination, and affection in the doing of theology. All these mentors influenced *Metaphorical Theology: Models of God in Religious Language* (Philadelphia: Fortress Press, 1982).

30. McFague, "The World as God's Body," accessed June 14, 2016, http://www.religion-online.org/showarticle.asp?title=56.

31. Ibid., 672.

32. Ibid.

33. Sallie McFague, *The Body of God: An Ecological Theology* (Minneapolis: Fortress Press, 1993), 166.

34. McFague, "The World as God's Body," 672.

35. Douglas J. Hall, *Imaging God: Dominion as Stewardship* (Grand Rapids, MI: Wm. B. Eerdmans/National Council of the Churches of Christ, 1986), 91.

36. Ibid.

37. Ibid., 66.

38. Ibid., 13.

39. Ibid., 10, 13.

40. Ibid., 10.

41. Martin Luther King Jr., "Remaining Awake Through a Great Revolution," Commencement Address for Oberlin College, accessed April 2016, http://www.oberlin.edu/external/EOG/BlackHistoryMonth/MLK/CommAddress.html.

42. Hall, *Imaging God: Dominion as Stewardship*, 148. Hall indicated that this takes ontic priority, meaning all the other relations are dependent on this relationship, but after a person actually exists, all three distinctions are coequal.

43. Ibid., 124.

44. Ibid., 144.

45. See Raimundo Panikkar, "The Invisible Harmony: A Universal Theory of Religion or a Cosmic Confidence in Reality," in *Toward a Universal Theology of Religion*, ed. Leonard Swidler (New York: Orbis Books, 1987), 137.

46. Ibid., 138.

47. Raimon Panikkar, "The Cosmotheandric Intuition," *Jeevadhara* 14, no. 79 (January 1984): 27–35. He develops the ideas he presents here more fully in his later text *The Cosmotheandric Experience: Emerging Religious Consciousness* (Maryknoll, NY: Orbis Books, 1993).

48. Panikkar, *The Cosmotheandric Experience*, 58.

49. Ibid., 137.

50. Panikkar, "The Cosmotheandric Intuition," 29.

51. Panikkar, *The Cosmotheandric Experience*, 75–76.

52. Panikkar, "The Cosmotheandric Intuition," 35.

53. Ibid.

54. Panikkar, *The Cosmotheandric Experience*, 34.

55. Drew Dellinger, "Martin Luther King Jr.: Ecological Thinker," in *Common Ground Magazine* (April 2014), 49–50, http://www.commongroundmag.org.

56. Jay B. McDaniel, *Of God and Pelicans: A Theology of Reverence for Life*, 1st ed. (Louisville, KY: Westminster John Knox Press, 1989), 52.

57. Rosemary Radford Ruether, *To Change the World: Christology and Cultural Criticism* (London: SCM Press, 1981), 57–70.

58. Chapter 3 in Rosemary Radford Ruether, *Sexism and God-Talk: Toward a Feminist Theology* (Boston: Beacon Press, 1983), 72–92.

59. Rosemary Radford Ruether, *Disputed Questions: On Being a Christian*, rev. ed. (Maryknoll, NY: Orbis Books, 1989), 2.

60. Rosemary Radford Ruether, *New Woman/New Earth: Sexist Ideologies and Human Liberation* (New York: Seabury Press, 1975), 204.

61. Rosemary Radford Ruether, *Women Healing Earth: Third World Women on Ecology, Feminism and Religion* (Maryknoll, NY: Orbis Books, 1996), 5.

62. Sean McDonagh, *To Care for the Earth: A Call to a New Theology* (London: Geoffrey Chapman, 1986), 214.

63. Ibid., 203.

64. Ibid., 200.

65. Dorothee Sölle and Shirley Cloyes, *To Work and to Love: A Theology of Creation* (Philadelphia: Fortress Press, 1984), 3.

66. Ibid., 2, 5.

67. Ibid., 29.

68. Ibid., 33.

69. Ibid., 20, 34.

70. Ibid., 17–18.

71. Ibid., 18–19. See also Carter Heyward, "Blessing the Bread: A Litany," in *Our Passion for Justice: Images of Power, Sexuality, and Liberation* (New York: Pilgrim Press, 1984).

72. Sölle and Cloyes, *To Work and to Love*, 13, 19. Sakokwenonkwas was a Native American sub-chief of the Mohawk nation.

73. Ibid., 25.

74. Ibid., 34. See also Ernesto Cardenal, *The Gospel of Solentiname* (Maryknoll, NY: Orbis Books, 2010).

75. Sölle and Cloyes, *To Work and to Love*, 42–43, 50.

76. Ibid., 63.

77. Jean Vanier, *Community and Growth: Our Pilgrimage Together* (Toronto: Griffin House, 1979), 196.

78. This was taken from the two lectures offered by Vanier in November 1988 at Harvard Divinity School (Harold M. Wit Lecture Series on Living a Spiritual life in the Contemporary Age). These were later published in Jean Vanier, *From Brokenness to Community* (New York: Paulist Press, 1992), 15–16.

79. Ibid., 20.

80. Vanier, *Community and Growth*, 102.

81. Many L'Arche communities have become eco-leaders in their greater communities. See www.larche.ca.

82. Vanier, *From Brokenness to Community*, 27.

83. John Polkinghorne, "The New Natural Theology," *Studies in World Christianity* 1, no. 1 (1995): 42.

84. Chapters 2 and 4 in John Polkinghorne, *Science and Christian Belief: Theological Reflections of a Bottom-up Thinker*, Gifford Lectures from 1993–94 (London: SPCK, 1994). Also see Ian Barbour, *When Science Meets Religion: Enemies, Strangers or Partners?* (San Francisco, CA: HarperSanFrancisco, 2000), 167.

85. Polkinghorne, "The New Natural Theology," 45.

86. Ibid.

87. Arthur Peacocke, *Paths from Science towards God: The End of All Our Exploring* (2001); *Evolution: The Disguised Friend of Faith? Selected Essays* (2004); *All That Is: A Naturalistic Faith for the Twenty-First Century* (2007).

88. Arthur Peacocke, *Intimations of Reality: Critical Realism in Science and Religion* (Notre Dame, IN: University of Notre Dame Press, 1984). These metaphors give humanity access to the symbolic world, but it should be noted that metaphors are ambiguous and can be both empowering and dysfunctional.

89. Peacocke, *Intimations of Reality*, 63. Also see Arthur Peacocke, *Creation and the World of Science*, Bampton Lectures (Oxford: Oxford University Press, 1979).

90. Ian G. Barbour, *Religion in an Age of Science*, 1st ed., The Gifford Lectures (San Francisco: HarperSanFrancisco, 1990), 114.

91. See Denis Edwards, "Incarnation as Basis for Ecological Conversion" (paper presented at the annual Catholic Theological Society of America Conference Miami Florida, June 2013); Gloria Schaab, "Incarnation as Emergence: A Transformative Vision of God and the Cosmos," *The Heythrop Journal* 54 (2013): 631–44.

92. Matthew Fox, *A Spirituality Named Compassion and the Healing of the Global Village, Humpty Dumpty and Us* (Minneapolis: Winston Press, 1979).

93. The first two books were *On Becoming a Musical, Mystical Bear: Spirituality American Style* (1976) and *Whee! We, Wee All the Way Home: A Guide to the New Sensual Spirituality* (1976).

94. Fox, *A Spirituality Named Compassion*, iv.

95. Ibid.

96. Matthew Fox, *Original Blessing: A Primer in Creation Spirituality Presented in Four Paths, Twenty-Six Themes, and Two Questions* (Santa Fe, NM: Bear and Company, 1983), 113.

97. Colleen Carpenter, "These Strawberries are Divine: Catholic Sisters as Midwives of a Practical Spirituality of Living on Earth," *Review for Religious: A Journal of Catholic Spirituality* 65, no. 3 (2006): 304–18; Sarah McFarland Taylor, *Green Sisters: A Spiritual Ecology* (Cambridge, MA: Harvard University Press, 2007).

PART II

5. First Pillar: Eschatological Hope

1. Denis Edwards, "Every Sparrow That Falls to the Ground: The Cost of Evolution and the Christ-Event," *Ecotheology* 11, no. 1 (2006): 103–23.

2. Robert Faricy, *The Spirituality of Teilhard De Chardin* (Minneapolis: Winston Press, 1981), 35.

3. However, Irenaeus was not eager to explore "speculation," namely, the essence of God's eternity before God's first creative act, which he saw was preoccupying and fueling the Gnostic movement. Santmire, *The Travail of Nature*, 36.

4. Irenaeus of Lyons, *Against Heresies*, 5.36.1., http://www.ccel.org/ccel/schaff/anf01.toc.html (accessed September 12, 2011).

5. Ibid., 2.9.1.

6. H. Paul Santmire, *The Travail of Nature: The Ambiguous Ecological Promise of Christian Theology* (Minneapolis: Fortress Press, 1985), 39.

7. Irenaeus, *Against the Heresies*, 3.16.6.

8. Hans Urs von Balthasar, *Cosmic Liturgy: The Universe according to Maximus the Confessor*, trans. Brian E. Daley (San Francisco: Ignatius Press, 1988).

9. Ibid., 27–28, 256.

10. Balthasar indicated that *Pseudo-Dionysius's* optimism of the world had a lasting effect on Maximus. Ibid., 58.

11. See: Maximus, *Orationis Dominicae expositio* (Exposition of the Lord's Prayer), in J.P. Migne, *Patrologia Graeca* (PG) 90, 877AB., accessed February 9, 2012, http://graeca.patristica.net. English translation offered by Balthasar, *Cosmic Liturgy*, 273.

12. It is important to note that Balthasar's interpretation of reciprocity and receptivity is infused with androcentrism (male centeredness) and some feminists, such as Michelle Gonzalez, have critiqued this distortion. Michelle A. Gonzalez, "Hans Urs von Balthasar and Contemporary Feminist Theology," *Theological Studies* 65, no. 3 (2004): 566–95.

13. See *Ambigua*, PG 91, 1288; and *Exposition of the Lord's Prayer*, PG 90, 877A, in Balthasar, *Cosmic Liturgy*, 283.

14. Irenaeus, *Quaestiones ad Thalassium* 51, PG 90, 477A.

15. "The material, that is, intellectual dwells in the material in the mode of images; but the result of both is a single world." *Mystagogia* (chap. 2), PG 91, 669BC, in Balthasar, *Cosmic Liturgy*, 173.

16. Teilhard de Chardin, *The Divine Milieu* (New York: Perennial, 2001), xl.

17. It is in his devotion to the Sacred Heart that Teilhard de Chardin united his faith and his love of the world, long before his formal theological articulation (i.e., "Universal-Christ"). Pierre Teilhard de Chardin, *The Heart of Matter* (London: William Collins Sons & Co., 1978), 43. See also Faricy, *The Spirituality of Teilhard De Chardin*, 13–23.

18. Teilhard de Chardin, *Hymn of the Universe* (London: William Collins Sons & Co., 1965), 29.

19. Teilhard de Chardin, *The Heart of Matter*, 54–55.

20. Pierre Teilhard de Chardin, *Man's Place in Nature: The Human Zoological Group* (London: William Collins Sons & Co., 1966), 121.

21. Teilhard de Chardin, *The Divine Milieu*, xxii.

22. Ibid., xxvi.

23. Teilhard de Chardin, *Hymn of the Universe*, 65.

24. Catherine Keller, "No More Sea: The Lost Chaos of the Eschaton," in *Christianity and Ecology: Seeking the Well-Being of Earth and Humans*, ed. Dieter T. Hessel and Rosemary Radford Ruether (Cambridge, MA: Harvard University Press, 2000), 195.

25. Jürgen Moltmann, "Hope and the Biomedical Future of Man," in *Hope and the Future of Man*, ed. Ewert H. Cousins and American Teilhard de Chardin Association (Philadelphia: Fortress Press, 1972), 9.

26. Arthur Peacocke, *Creation and the World of Science*, Bampton Lectures (Oxford: Oxford University Press, 1979), 319.

27. Ibid., 320.

28. Catherine Keller, "No More Sea: The Lost Chaos of the Eschaton," in *Christianity and Ecology: Seeking the Well-Being of Earth and Humans*, ed. Dieter T. Hessel and Rosemary Radford Ruether (Cambridge, MA: Harvard University Press, 2000), 189. Also see Catherine Keller, "Women against Wasting the World: Notes on Eschatology and Ecology," in *Reweaving the World: The Emergence of Ecofeminism*,

ed. Irene Diamond and Gloria Feman Orenstein (San Francisco: Sierra Club Books, 1990), 255.

29. Keller, "No More Sea," 196.

30. Ibid., 185.

31. Robert J. Russell, "Natural Sciences," in *The Blackwell Companion to Christian Spirituality*, ed. Arthur Holder (Malden, MA: Blackwell Pub., 2005), 335.

32. See Ruether, "The Politics of God in the Christian Tradition," *Feminist Theology* 17, no. 3 (2009): 337.

33. Richard Jefferies, *The Old House at Coate* (1948) as quoted in John Feehan, *The Singing Heart of the World: Creation, Evolution and Faith* (New York: Orbis Books, 2012), 154.

34. Keller, "No More Sea," 195.

35. Ibid.

36. Werner Heisenberg, *Physics and Philosophy: The Revolution in Modern Science* (1958) and *Physics and Beyond: Encounters and Conversations* (1971); David Bohm, *Wholeness and the Implicate Order* (1980) and David Bohm and F. David Peat, *Science, Order, and Creativity* (2000); Stuart A. Kauffman, *The Origins of Order: Self Organization and Selection in Evolution* (1993) and *At Home in the Universe: The Search for Laws of Self-Organization and Complexity* (1995).

37. Carl Zimmer, *At the Water's Edge: Macroevolution and the Transformation of Life* (New York: Free Press, 1990).

38. F. Leron Shults, Nancy Murphy, and Robert J. Russell, *Philosophy, Science and Divine Action* (2009); Philip Clayton, *Adventures in the Spirit: God, World, Divine Action* (2009); and Elizabeth Johnson, "Creator Spirit in an Evolving World," in *The Quest for the Living God: Mapping Frontiers in the Theology of God* (New York: Continuum, 2011).

39. Gloria Schaab, "Incarnation as Emergence: A Transformative Vision of God and the Cosmos," *The Heythrop Journal* 54 (2013): 631–44.

40. Carolyn Merchant, *The Death of Nature: Women, Ecology and the Scientific Revolution* (San Francisco, CA: Harper & Row, 1980), 80–87.

6. Second Pillar: The Intrinsic Worth of Creation

1. Denis Edwards, *Jesus and the Cosmos* (2004); *Ecology at the Heart of Faith* (2006); Ilia Delio *Christ in Evolution* (2008).

2. Hans Urs von Balthasar, *Cosmic Liturgy: The Universe according to Maximus the Confessor*, trans. Brian E. Daley (San Francisco: Ignatius Press, 1988), 71.

3. Maximus, Paul M. Blowers, and Robert Louis Wilken, *On the Cosmic Mystery of Jesus Christ: Selected Writings from St. Maximus the Confessor*, Popular Patristics Series (Crestwood, NY: St. Vladimir's Seminary Press, 2003), 17.

4. Maximus, *Ambiguum* 7, in J.P. Migne, *Patrologia Latina* (PL) 91, 1080B. As quoted by ibid., 55.

5. Maximus, *Opuscule* 7, 84D–85B, in Andrew Louth and Maximus, *Maximus the Confessor*, Early Church Fathers (London; New York: Routledge, 1996), 188–89.

6. Maximus, *Quaestiones ad Thalassium* 48, in J.P. Migne, *Patrologia Graeca* (PG) 90, 436A. As cited in Balthasar, *Cosmic Liturgy*, 273.

7. Ibid.

8. Regis J. Armstrong and Ignatius C. Brady, *Francis and Clare: The Complete Works*, Classics of Western Spirituality (New York: Paulist Press, 1982), 18.

9. Francis, *The Early Rule*, 23.7, in ibid., 132.

10. Francis, *The Canticle of Brother Sun*, in Armstrong and Brady, *Francis and Clare*, 38–39.

11. H. Paul Santmire, *The Travail of Nature: The Ambiguous Ecological Promise of Christian Theology* (Minneapolis: Fortress Press, 1985), 109.

12. Thomas Aquinas, *Summa Contra Gentiles*, trans. James F. Anderson (New York: Hanover House, 1955–57), II.44, http://dhspriory.org/thomas/ContraGentiles.htm.

13. Thomas Aquinas, *Summa Theologica*, trans. Fathers of the English Dominican Province (Benziger Bros. edition, 1947), Ia.47.1, http://dhspriory.org/thomas/summa/FP/FP047.html#FPQ47OUTP1.

14. Rohan Curnow, "Theos, Cosmos and Anthropos: Trinity, Incarnation and Creation in the Framework of Raimon Panikkar's

Cosmotheandric Vision," *Australian ejournal of Theology* (February 2006): 13–14, http://aejt.com.au/__data/assets/pdf_file/0009/395190/AEJT_6.7_Curnow.pdf.

15. John Feehan, *The Singing Heart of the World: Creation, Evolution and Faith* (New York: Orbis Books, 2012), 62.

16. Ibid., 66.

17. Colin Tudge, "Evensong at St. Paul's Cathedral: Why Nature Is Ultimately Unfathomable—and Why Reverence Towards It Is the Only Sensible Attitude" (February 27, 2007), http://www.colintudge.com/articles/article09.php.

18. Robert J. Russell, "Natural Sciences," in *The Blackwell Companion to Christian Spirituality*, ed. Arthur Holder (Malden, MA: Blackwell Pub., 2005), 334.

19. Elizabeth A. Johnson, "Creator Spirit in the Evolving World" and "Trinity: The Living God of Love," chaps. in *The Quest for the Living God: Mapping Frontiers in the Theology of God* (New York: Continuum, 2011), 181–201; 202–24; Elizabeth Johnson, *Ask the Beasts: Darwin and the God of Love* (London: Bloomsbury, 2014), 222; Gloria Schaab, *The Creative Suffering of the Triune God: An Evolutionary Theology*, AAR Academy Series (Oxford: Oxford University Press, 2007); Gloria Schaab, "Incarnation as Emergence: A Transformative Vision of God and the Cosmos," *The Heythrop Journal* 54 (2013): 631–44; Mark I. Wallace, "The Green Face of God: Christianity in the Age of Ecocide," *Cross Currents* 50, no. 3 (Fall 2000): 310–31.

20. Sean McDonagh, *To Care for the Earth: A Call to a New Theology* (London: Geoffrey Chapman, 1986), 117.

21. Ibid., 118–19.

22. Jack Harris, "Four Scientists—four visions," *Interdisciplinary Science Reviews* 22, no. 2 (1997): 94–95, http://www.tandfonline.com/doi/pdf/10.1179/isr.1997.22.2.89.

23. See "Vandana Shiva Explains Clearly Why GMOs Are a Death Knell to Biodiversity and Farming," accessed March 3, 2017, at https://www.youtube.com/watch?v=o_r6tHdZdhI.

24. See Sean McDonagh, *Passion for the Earth: The Christian Vocation to Promote Justice, Peace and the Integrity of Creation* (1994); *Patenting Life? Stop: Is Corporate Greed Forcing Us to Eat Genetically Engineered Food?* (2003) as well as his "Open Letter to the Holy See" requesting that it does not support genetically engineered food (2004), accessed March 20, 2014, http://www.gmwatch.org/index.php/news/

archive/2004/695-open-letter-to-the-holy-see-requesting-that-it-does-not-support-genetically-engineered-food-28112004.

25. McDonagh, *To Care for the Earth*, 212.

26. Aquinas, *Summa Theologica*, 1a 47.1.

27. James A. Nash, *Loving Nature: Ecological Integrity and Christian Responsibility*, Churches' Center for Theology and Public Policy (Nashville, TN: Abingdon Press, 1991), 56.

28. Ibid., 54–67.

29. Jay B. McDaniel, *Of God and Pelicans: A Theology of Reverence for Life*, 1st ed. (Louisville, KY: Westminster John Knox Press, 1989), 73.

30. Stephen Scharper succinctly categorizes these voices as follows: (1) those who critique male/female, mind/body dualisms in classical philosophy and Judeo-Christian heritage (e.g., Rosemary Radford Ruether and E. Dodson Gray); (2) those who critique European mechanistic thought and the Enlightenment focus on autonomy and objectivity (e.g., Carolyn Merchant and Vandana Shiva); (3) those who critique the evisceration of Earth's sacredness in light of a transcendent "Sky God" (e.g., Charlene Spretnak, Starhawk, and Sallie McFague). Stephen B. Scharper, *For Earth's Sake: Toward a Compassionate Ecology*, ed. Simon Appolloni (Toronto, ON: Novalis Press, 2013), 87. See also Leonardo Boff, *Cry of the Earth, Cry of the Poor* (Maryknoll, NY: Orbis Books, 2001).

31. Feehan, *The Singing Heart of the World*, 67.

32. Ruth Page, *God and the Web of Creation* (London: SCM Press, 1996), xix.

7. Third Pillar: Our Sacred Cosmic Communion

1. See the following website compiling statements from people of many faiths reclaiming Earth as sacred, accessed June 7, 2016, http://sacredearth2016.org/video. See also "Our Voices" Facebook page for more insights, accessed June 7, 2016, https://www.facebook.com/ourvoices2015/.

2. Lord Byron, "Childe Harold's Pilgrimage," *Canto the Fourth*, 178 (1818), in John Feehan, *The Singing Heart of the World: Creation, Evolution and Faith* (New York: Orbis Books, 2012), 121.

3. D. H. S. Nicholson and A. H. E. Lee, *The Oxford Book of English Mystical Verse* (Oxford: Clarendon Press, 1917), http://www.bartleby.com/236/86.html.

4. Thomas Berry, *The Dream of the Earth* (San Francisco: Sierra Club Books, 1988), 117.

5. Vision 2:13, "On the Construction of the World," in Hildegard of Bingen, *Hildegard of Bingen's Book of Divine Works: With Letters and Songs*, ed. Matthew Fox (Santa Fe, NM: Bear & Company, 1987), 33. In Hildegard's earlier work *Scivias*, her use of *viriditas* was less pronounced but she did use it to describe "the Holy Spirit's sweet freshness." Book II, Vision 1.3 in Hildegard, *Scivias*, Classics of Western Spirituality, ed. Columba Hart and Jane Bishop (New York: Paulist Press, 1990), 151.

6. Hildegard, *Divine Works*, 374–75.

7. Ibid., 379.

8. Ibid., 391.

9. Vision 1:2 in Hildegard, *Scivias*, 8, 10. Hildegard also indicated that "the soul is the green life force of the flesh." Vision 4:21 in ibid., 97.

10. See Matthew Fox's commentary, "*Viriditas:* Greening Power," in Matthew Fox and Hildegard, *Illuminations of Hildegard of Bingen* (Santa Fe, NM: Bear & Company, 1985), 30, 30–33.

11. Renate Craine, "Hildegard of Bingen: The Earth Hungers for the Fullness of Justice," *Cistercian Studies Quarterly* 26 (1991): 121.

12. Vision 4:1 in Hildegard, *Divine Works*, 80. See also Craine, "Hildegard of Bingen," 121.

13. Marsha Newman, "Christian Cosmology in Hildegard of Bingen's Illumination," *Logos: A Journal of Catholic Thought and Culture* 5, no. 1 (Winter 2002): 42.

14. Hildegard, *Scivia*, bk 2., Vision 1.3, 151.

15. Barbara Newman, *Sister of Wisdom: St. Hildegard's Theology of the Feminine* (Berkeley: University California Press, 1987), 64–65.

16. Ilse N. Bulhof, "Experiencing Nature: A Comparison between Early Medieval and Modern Encounters with Nature," *Diogenes* 21, no. 3 (March 1, 1973): 30. See also Vision 4:59 in Hildegard, *Divine Works*, 112.

17. Pierre Teilhard de Chardin, *Christianity and Evolution*, trans. R. Hague (New York: Harcourt Brace Jovanovich, 1971), 169.

18. Teilhard de Chardin, *Pierre Teilhard De Chardin: Writings Selected*, Modern Spiritual Masters (Maryknoll, NY: Orbis Books, 1999), 50.

19. Pierre Teilhard de Chardin, *The Heart of Matter* (London: William Collins Sons & Co., 1978), 48.

20. Pierre Teilhard de Chardin, *Letters from a Traveller* (New York: Harper Brothers Publishers, 1962), 303.

21. NASA, "The Big Bang," accessed May 2, 2016, http://science.nasa.gov/astrophysics/focus-areas/what-powered-the-big-bang/.

22. Carl Sagan, *The Dragons of Eden: Speculations on the Evolution of Human Intelligence* (New York: Random House, 1977), 14–17.

23. Ann Druyan and Steven Soter, "Standing Up in the Milky Way," *Cosmos: A Spacetime Odyssey*, episode 1, directed by Brannon Braga and Ann Druyan, aired March 9, 2014 (Culver City, CA: *National Geographic*, 2014), TV miniseries.

24. Thomas Berry, *The Sacred Universe: Earth Spirituality and Religion in the Twenty-first Century* (New York: Columbia University Press, 2009), 72.

25. Robert C. Hilborn, "Sea Gulls, Butterflies, and Grasshoppers: A Brief History of the Butterfly Effect in Nonlinear Dynamics," *American Journal of Physics* 72, no. 4 (2004): 425–27.

26. Bette Hileman, "Chemicals Can Turn Genes On and Off: New Tests Needed, Scientists Say," *Environmental Health News*, August 3, 2009, http://www.environmentalhealthnews.org/ehs/news/epigenetics-workshop.

27. University of Cambridge, "Planck Captures Portrait of the Young Universe, Revealing Earliest Light," March 2013, http://www.cam.ac.uk/research/news/planck-captures-portrait-of-the-young-universe-revealing-earliest-light. This data from the European space agency is confirmed by the data offered by NASA. NASA Science (Astrophysics), *Dark Energy Dark Matter*, accessed June 4, 2014, http://science.nasa.gov/astrophysics/focus-areas/what-is-dark-energy/.

28. Mark I. Wallace, *Finding God in the Singing River: Christianity, Spirit, Nature* (Minneapolis: Fortress Press, 2005), 82.

29. Matthew Fox, *Original Blessing: A Primer in Creation Spirituality Presented in Four Paths, Twenty-Six Themes, and Two Questions* (Santa Fe, NM: Bear and Company, 1983), 38. Fox employs Gerhard von Rad's terminology "voluptuous" to make this point.

30. Elizabeth A. Johnson, *Women, Earth, and Creator Spirit*, Madeleva Lecture in Spirituality (Mahwah, NJ: Paulist Press, 1993), 2.

31. W. H. Hudson, *Idle Days in Patagonia* (London: Dent, 1923), 218.

32. Feehan, *The Singing Heart of the World*, 68.

33. Ibid.

34. John Muir, *The Mountains of California* (1961, c1894) as quoted in ibid., 81.

35. Feehan, *The Singing Heart of the World*, 124.

36. Anthony D. Barnosky et al., "Has the Earth's Sixth Mass Extinction Already Arrived?" *Nature* 471 (March 3, 2011): 51–57.

37. Robert J. Russell, "Natural Sciences," in *The Blackwell Companion to Christian Spirituality*, ed. Arthur Holder (Malden, MA: Blackwell Pub., 2005), 326.

8. Fourth Pillar: Kenosis as the Kinetic of Creation

1. Holmes Rolston III, "Kenosis and Nature," in *The Work of Love: Creation as Kenosis*, ed. J. C. Polkinghorne (Grand Rapids, MI: William B. Eerdmans, 2001), 58–59.

2. Ursula Goodenough, *The Sacred Depths of Nature* (Oxford: Oxford University Press, 1998), 151.

3. Lynn Margulis and Dorion Sagan, "Sentient Symphony," in *The Nature of Life: Classical and Contemporary Perspectives from Philosophy and Science*, ed. Mark A. Bedau and Carol E. Cleland (Cambridge, MA: Cambridge University Press, 2010), 350.

4. Niels Henrik Gregersen, "The Cross of Christ in an Evolutionary World," *Dialog: A Journal of Theology* 40, no. 3 (Fall 2001): 198.

5. Gloria Schaab, "Midwifery as a Model for Ecological Ethics: Expanding Arthur Peacocke's Models of 'Man-in-Creation,'" *Zygon* 42, no. 2 (June 2007): 491.

6. Jürgen Moltmann, "God's Kenosis in the Creation and Consummation of the World," in *The Work of Love: Creation as Kenosis*, ed. J. C. Polkinghorne (Grand Rapids, MI: William B. Eerdmans, 2001), 140.

7. Ibid. Moltmann indicates that "in his Christmas hymn, Luther sees in 'the self-emptying Christ' the Creator of the world, while Vanstone sees in the sustainer of the world 'the crucified God.'"

8. Ian G. Barbour, "God's Power: A Process View," in *The Work of Love: Creation as Kenosis*, ed. J. C. Polkinghorne (Grand Rapids, MI: William B. Eerdmans, 2001), 7.

9. Robin Ryan, *God and the Mystery of Human Suffering: A Theological Conversation across the Ages* (New York: Paulist Press, 2011), 287.

10. Denis Edwards, *God of Evolution: A Trinitarian Theology* (New York: Paulist Press, 1999), 30–32.

11. Rolston, "Kenosis and Nature," 63.

12. Elizabeth Johnson, *Ask the Beasts: Darwin and the God of Love* (London: Bloomsbury, 2014), 174.

13. Ibid., 175.

14. Letter 1.13, in Regis J. Armstrong and Ignatius C. Brady, *Francis and Clare: The Complete Works*, Classics of Western Spirituality (New York: Paulist Press, 1982), 191; St. Clare, Letter 3.26, in ibid., 201.

15. St. Clare, Letter 3.6, in ibid., 200.

16. St. Clare, Letter 1.29, in ibid., 193.

17. St. Clare, Letter 3.7, in ibid., 200.

18. Amma Syncletica 22, in Laura Swan, *The Forgotten Desert Mothers: Sayings, Lives, and Stories of Early Christian Women* (Mahwah, NJ: Paulist Press, 2001), 60.

19. Ibid., 21.

20. St. Clare, Letter 3.7, in Armstrong and Brady, *Francis and Clare*, 200.

21. Swan, *The Forgotten Desert Mothers*, 129.

22. Amma Syncletica 8, in ibid., 49, 52.

23. Amma Sarah 7 and 8, in ibid., 40.

24. Amma Sarah 9, in ibid., 41.

25. Amma Matrona 2, in ibid., 35.

26. Amma Syncletica 2, in ibid., 44.

27. Amma Syncletica 15, in ibid., 55.

28. Ibid., 36–37.

29. Visions 2:23 and 4:11, in Hildegard of Bingen, *Hildegard of Bingen's Book of Divine Works: With Letters and Songs*, ed. Matthew Fox (Santa Fe, NM: Bear & Company, 1987), 86. See also Renate

Craine, "Hildegard of Bingen: The Earth Hungers for the Fullness of Justice," *Cistercian Studies Quarterly* 26 (1991): 51.

30. Vision 2:2, in Hildegard, *Divine Works*, 26.

31. Vision 3:1, in ibid., 56.

32. Matthew Fox and Hildegard, *Illuminations of Hildegard of Bingen* (Santa Fe, NM: Bear & Company., 1985), 47.

33. Craine, "Hildegard of Bingen," 56.

34. Vision 4:16, in Fox and Hildegard, *Illuminations*, 91.

35. Vision 4:11, in Hildegard, *Divine Works*, 86.

36. Vision 2:2, in ibid., 26. Italics added.

37. Fox and Hildegard, *Illuminations*, 40. Matthew Fox indicates that "it is significant in Hildegard's theology that of the three rings—Divinity, humanity and creation—humanity is placed in the center.... Humanity is meant to be a bridge, a link, a bonding force such as a marriage ring symbolizes between Divinity and nature." Ibid., 112–13.

38. Vision 2:22, in Hildegard, *Divine Works*, 41.

PART III

9. How Suffering Is Understood

1. Robert Faricy, "Teilhard de Chardin's Theology of the Cross," in *The Cross Today: An Evaluation of Current Theological Reflections on the Cross of Christ*, ed. Gerald O'Collins, Robert Faricy, Maurizio Flick (New York: Paulist Press, 1977), 14.

2. The categories I use are not the only way suffering can be categorized and studied. For example, Herwig Arts, SJ, delineates three kinds of suffering: physical, psychological, and social. Herwig Arts, *God, the Christian, and Human Suffering* (Collegeville, MN: Liturgical Press, 1993). Elizabeth Dreyer offers four broad categories of suffering: (1) suffering that causes minor inconveniences (scraped knees, rejection letter, fender bender); (2) more severe suffering (hip replacement, loss of friendship); (3) death of loved one, losing job, flood destroying home, battling cancer, addiction; and (4) catastrophic suffering as the total destruction of a human being (torture, murder, genocide, systematic rape as military strategy, enslavement). Elizabeth Dreyer, "Suffering in Christian Life and Experience," in *Suffering and the Christian Life*, ed. Richard W. Miller (New York: Orbis Publishing,

2013), 132. Kristine Rankka offers two classifications: voluntary (individuals or groups that chose the painful experience [consequence] in order to accomplish greater good—even in the face of oppression) and involuntary (the infliction of power over another that never serves the greater good because it is inflicted by one on another against his or her will). Kristine M. Rankka, *Women and the Value of Suffering: An Aw(e)ful Rowing toward God* (Collegeville, MN: Liturgical Press, 1998), 105.

3. John Westerdale Bowker, *Problems of Suffering in Religions of the World* (Cambridge: Cambridge University Press, 1970), 9.

4. Kenneth Overberg, *Into the Abyss of Suffering: A Catholic View* (Cincinnati: St. Anthony Messenger Press, 2003), 19–21.

5. Ibid., 21–22.

6. Bowker, *Problems of Suffering*, 12.

7. Ibid., 36–38.

8. Daniel J. Harrington, "Old Testament Approaches to Suffering," in *Suffering and the Christian Life*, ed. Richard W. Miller (New York: Orbis Books, 2013), 7.

9. Overberg, *Into the Abyss of Suffering*, 65.

10. Ibid., 57.

11. M. Dennis Hamm, "Sharing in His Suffering: The Social Cost of Following Jesus," in *Suffering and the Christian Life*, ed. Richard W. Miller (New York: Orbis Books, 2013), 33.

12. Ibid., 36.

13. Bowker, *Problems of Suffering*, 50, 54.

14. Ibid., 28.

15. Ibid., 56.

16. Robin Ryan, *God and the Mystery of Human Suffering: A Theological Conversation across the Ages* (New York: Paulist Press, 2011), 33.

17. Ibid., 34.

18. Ibid.

19. See also Wis 2—5, Pss 34:19, 20; 16:8–11; 31:5; 101:2–4, 6, 8; 2 Macc 7, in Bowker, *Problems of Suffering*, 15.

20. See 2 Cor 1:3–7; 2 Cor 12:10; Rev 1:9–11; 2 Tim 1:8–14; Luke 24; Josh 1:9; Ps 59:17; Isa 12:2; 1 Pet 5:10.

21. Harrington, "Old Testament Approaches to Suffering," 7–8.

22. This is also undertaken by Ecclesiastes (see 5:14, 9:5–6; 12:5–7).

23. This dimension is also exposed in Isaiah (see 40:3–5, 49:7; 53:4–7, 11).

24. For his understanding of the "taint of sin" and how it affected his life and the life of his mother Monica, see St. Augustine, *Confessions*, trans. R. S. Pine Coffin (New York: Dorset Press, 1986), Book I, 7; Book V, 8. This theme of the fall, sin of disobedience, and the transmission of the corruption of sin also occupies his imagination in *On the City of God* (e.g., St. Augustine, *On the City of God*, Book XII, 1, 6, 22; Book XIII, 1; Book XIV, 13), accessed December 12, 2012, http://www.logoslibrary.org/augustine/city/.

25. "God arranged everything from the first with a view to the perfection of man, in order to deify him and reveal His own dispensations, so that goodness may be made manifest, justice made perfect and the Church may be fashioned after the image of His Son. Thus, man may eventually reach maturity, and, being ripened by such privileges, may see and comprehend God." Irenaeus, *Against Heresies*, 4.37.7., accessed August 10, 2013, http://www.ccel.org/ccel/schaff/anf01.toc.html.

26. Ryan, *God and the Mystery of Human Suffering*, 104.

27. Amma Syncletica 19, in Laura Swan, *The Forgotten Desert Mothers: Sayings, Lives, and Stories of Early Christian Women* (Mahwah, NJ: Paulist Press, 2001), 58.

28. Augustine, "De natura et gratia," 3.3, in *Saint Augustine: Anti Pelagian Writings*, in *A Select Library of the Nicene and Post-Nicene Fathers of the Christian Church*, ed. Philip Schaff, trans. Peter Holmes, Robert Ernest Wallis, Benjamin B. Warfield (New York: Christian Literature Company, 1887), 5:121–54, http://www.romancatholicism.org/pdf/augustineantipelagianwritings.pdf.

29. William Harmless, *Augustine in His Own Words* (Washington, DC: Catholic University of America Press, 2010), 377–78.

30. Aquinas, *Summa Theologica* I.48.1.

31. Aquinas inherited *culpa* and *poena* from Augustine. Romanus Cessario, *The Godly Image: Christ & Salvation in Catholic Thought from St. Anselm to Aquinas* (Petersham, ME: St. Bede's Publications, 1990), 85–86.

32. Nicholas E. Lombardo, *The Logic of Desire: Aquinas on Emotion* (Washington, DC: Catholic University of America Press, 2011), 121.

33. Aquinas, *Summa Theologica* I-II.81.1 Aquinas follows this question with an engagement with original sin in ibid., 82.1 ad 1.

34. Peter Hess, "Evolution and the God of Hope in Roman Catholic Thought after Darwin," in *The Evolution of Evil*, ed. Gaymon Bennett et al. (Göttingen: Vandenhoeck & Ruprecht, 2008), 234n3.

35. Ryan, *God and the Mystery of Human Suffering*, 132.

36. St. Cyprian, in ibid., 105.

37. John Chryssavgis, *In the Heart of the Desert: The Spirituality of Desert Fathers and Mothers* (China: World Wisdom Inc., 2003), 1.

38. See Swan, *The Forgotten Desert Mothers*, 37–38.

39. Patricia A. Williams, "How Evil Entered the World: An Explanation through Deep Time," in *The Evolution of Evil*, ed. Gaymon Bennett et al. (Göttingen: Vandenhoeck and Ruprecht, 2008), 204.

40. Ryan, *God and the Mystery of Human Suffering*, 106.

41. Ibid.

42. Ibid., 108–9.

43. Ibid., 109.

44. Prosper of Aquitaine, in ibid., 110.

45. Augustine, *Confessions* iv, in ibid., 12.

46. See Swan, *The Forgotten Desert Mothers*, 62.

47. Susan A. Calef, "Taking Up the Cross: Suffering and Discipleship in the Gospel of Mark," in *Suffering and the Christian Life*, ed. Richard W. Miller (New York: Orbis Books), 49.

48. Lynn Margulis and Dorion Sagan, "Sentient Symphony," in *The Nature of Life: Classical and Contemporary Perspectives from Philosophy and Science*, ed. Mark A. Bedau and Carol E. Cleland (Cambridge, MA: Cambridge University Press, 2010), 343.

49. Douglas John Hall, *The Cross in Our Context: Jesus and the Suffering World* (Minneapolis: Fortress Press, 2003), 48.

50. Ibid., 154.

51. Carol J. Adams, "Battery," in *The Dictionary of Feminist Theologies* (Louisville: Westminster John Knox Press, 1996), 24.

52. Joanne Carlson Brown and Rebecca Parker, "For God So Loved the World?" in *Christianity, Patriarchy and Abuse: A Feminist Critique*, ed. Joanne Carlson Brown and Carole R. Bohn (New York: Pilgrim, 1989), 26.

53. Calef, "Taking up the Cross," 51.

54. Hall, *The Cross in Our Context*, 72.

55. Rosemary Radford Ruether, *Sexism and God-Talk: Toward a Feminist Theology* (Boston: Beacon Press, 1983), 181.

56. Gustavo Gutiérrez, *On Job: God Talk and Suffering of the Innocent* (Maryknoll, NY: Orbis Books, 1987), 22. Hence sin, for Gutiérrez, is a breach of communion with God and one's fellow human beings and this is the true cause of poverty, injustice, and oppression. Gustavo Gutiérrez, *A Theology of Liberation: History, Politics, and Salvation* (Maryknoll, NY: Orbis Books, 1973), 35.

57. Dorothee Sölle, *Suffering*, trans. Everett R. Kalin (Philadelphia: Fortress Press, 1975), 16.

58. Dorothee Sölle, "Suffering," in *New Handbook of Christian Theology*, ed. Donald W. Muser and Joseph L. Price (Nashville: Abingdon Press, 1992), 465.

59. Ryan, *God and the Mystery of Human Suffering*, 426–27.

60. Calef, "Taking up the Cross," 67.

61. Marjorie Suchocki, *The Fall to Violence: Original Sin in Relational Theology* (New York: Continuum, 1994), 16.

62. Ibid., 13, 129.

63. Mary Rose D'Angelo, "Gender and Power in the Gospel of Mark: The Daughter of Jairus and the Woman with the Flow of Blood," in *Miracles in Jewish and Christian Antiquity*, ed. John C. Cavadini (Notre Dame, IN: University of Notre Dame Press, 1999), 101. Also cited in Calef, "Taking up the Cross," 62.

64. Ibid., 60.

65. Ibid., 61.

66. Rankka, *Women and the Value of Suffering*, 222.

67. Ibid., 8.

68. Ibid., 126.

69. Ibid., 136.

70. Ibid., 135–36.

71. Wendy Farley, *Tragic Vision and Divine Compassion: A Contemporary Theodicy* (Louisville, KY: Westminster John Knox Press, 1990), 55. As cited in Rankka in her exploration of radical suffering. Rankka, *Women and the Value of Suffering*, 136.

72. Ibid., 135–36.

73. Ibid., 165.

74. Sölle, *Suffering*, 68.

75. Ibid., 69.

76. Ibid., 68, 76.

77. Ibid., 68.

10. Suffering in an Evolutionary World

1. John Haught, "Evolution and the Suffering of Sentient Life," in *The Evolution of Evil*, ed. Gaymon Bennett, Robert J. Russell, Ted Peters, and Martinez J. Hewlett (Göttingen: Vandenhoeck & Ruprecht, 2008), 203.

2. Matthew Fox and Hildegard, *Illuminations of Hildegard of Bingen* (Santa Fe, NM: Bear & Company, 1985), 66–70.

3. Brian Swimme and Thomas Berry, *The Universe Story: From the Primordial Flaring Forth to the Ecozoic Era—Celebration of the Unfolding of the Cosmos* (San Francisco, CA: Harper, 1992), 66–77.

4. Hillel J. Hoffman, "The Permian Extinction—When Life Nearly Came to an End," *National Geographic*, accessed April 4, 2014, http://science.nationalgeographic.com/science/prehistoric-world/permian-extinction/.

5. Denis Edwards, "Every Sparrow That Falls to the Ground: The Cost of Evolution and the Christ-Event," *Ecotheology* 11, no. 1 (2006): 106.

6. Christopher Southgate, "God and Evolutionary Evil: Theodicy in the Light of Darwinism," *Zygon* 37, no. 4 (2002): 820. For scientific data affirming this ecocrisis, see the International Panel on Climate Change's (IPCC) Fifth Assessment Report (Working Group I: The Physical Science Basis), accessed May 6, 2014, https://www.ipcc.ch/report/ar5/.

7. Haught, "Evolution and the Suffering of Sentient Life," 190; Elizabeth Johnson, however, outlines a more personal reason for Darwin's rejection of divine design and faith in God. "More powerful yet as a dissuasion to faith was the death of [Darwin's] beloved daughter Annie. The tragedy of her innocent suffering and his loss muted any attraction he might have for a caring, beneficent God." Elizabeth Johnson, *Ask the Beasts: Darwin and the God of Love* (London: Bloomsbury, 2014), 39.

8. Patricia A. Williams, "How Evil Entered the World: An Explanation through Deep Time," in *The Evolution of Evil*, ed. Gaymon Bennett et al. (Göttingen: Vandenhoeck and Ruprecht, 2008), 212.

9. Holmes Rolston III, *Science and Religion: A Critical Survey* (New York: Random House, 1987), 144–46, 289–93.

10. Holmes Rolston III, *Genes, Genesis, and God: Values and Their Origins in Natural and Human History* (Cambridge: Cambridge University Press, 1999), 303.

11. John F. Haught, *God after Darwin: A Theology of Evolution* (Boulder, CO: Westview Press, 2001), 56.

12. Edwards, "Every Sparrow that Falls to the Ground," 107.

13. Thomas Berry, *The Dream of the Earth* (San Francisco: Sierra Club Books, 1988), 132.

14. Ibid., 136.

15. Gloria Schaab, *The Creative Suffering of the Triune God: An Evolutionary Theology*, AAR Academy Series (Oxford: Oxford University Press, 2007), 180.

16. Robert J. Russell, "Natural Sciences," in *The Blackwell Companion to Christian Spirituality*, ed. Arthur Holder (Malden, MA: Blackwell Pub., 2005), 337. John Polkinghorne edited a text called *The Work of Love: Creation as Kenosis* (2001) that was dedicated to exploring all aspects of creation (including suffering) with respect to kenosis.

17. Berry, *Dream of the Earth*, 217.

18. Southgate, "God and Evolutionary Evil," 806.

19. For example, the feeling or emotion that a human feels in response to the suffering of others that often motivates a desire to help.

20. This mirror-window-map metaphorical framework was initially imagined by social innovator Carolyn Taylor as a way to understand human existence in the twenty-first century and has graciously agreed to me employing it as my organizational schema here.

11. Divine Suffering: A Map

1. Hans Jonas as quoted in Christopher Southgate, "God and Evolutionary Evil: Theodicy in the Light of Darwinism," *Zygon* 37, no. 4 (2002): 810.

2. Thomas Weinandy indicates that God cannot suffer. See Thomas Weinandy, "Does God Suffer?" *First Things* 117 (November 2001): 35–41. Weinandy's main argument is that since God is immutable and impassable, then God does not suffer and to claim this is untenable and religiously devastating. Those who offer rebuttals include John Haught, Arthur Peacocke, John Polkinghorne, Elizabeth Johnson, Ilia Delio, Jon Sobrino, Jürgen Moltmann, and Dietrich Bonhoeffer.

See also a recent systematic overview by Christopher Southgate, *The Groaning of Creation: God, Evolution and the Problem of Evil* (Louisville, KY: Westminster John Knox Press, 2008).

3. Bonhoeffer, "Letters and Papers from Prison," in Dietrich Bonhoeffer and Wayne W. Floyd, *Dietrich Bonhoeffer Works*, 1st Eng. ed., Dietrich Bonhoeffer Works (Minneapolis: Fortress Press, 1996), 8:479.

4. Elie Wiesel and Marion Wiesel, *Night* (New York: Hill and Wang, 2006), 65.

5. Wiesel and Wiesel, *Night*, xxi.

6. There are more dimensions of divine suffering that cannot be addressed here. One important area that Mark Wallace, Elizabeth Johnson, Denis Edwards, and Gordon Kaufmann explore is the suffering of the Holy Spirit.

7. Robin Ryan, *God and the Mystery of Human Suffering: A Theological Conversation across the Ages* (New York: Paulist Press, 2011), 47.

8. Ibid., 49.

9. Arthur Chute McGill, *Suffering: A Test of Theological Method* (Philadelphia: Westminster Press, 1982), 61.

10. Ryan, *God and the Mystery of Human Suffering*, 46.

11. Erhard Gerstenberger and Wolfgang Schrage, *Suffering*, Biblical Encounters Series (Nashville, TN: Abingdon, 1980), 98–102. See also Terence E. Fretheim, *The Suffering of God: An Old Testament Perspective, Overtures to Biblical Theology* (Philadelphia: Fortress Press, 1984).

12. Gerstenberger and Schrage, *Suffering*, 107–48.

13. Ibid., 99.

14. Elizabeth Johnson, *She Who Is: The Mystery of God in Feminist Theological Discourse* (New York: Crossroads, 1992), 254–64.

15. Jay B. McDaniel, *Of God and Pelicans: A Theology of Reverence for Life*, 1st ed. (Louisville, KY: Westminster John Knox Press, 1989), 28.

16. John Haught, "Darwin's Gift to Theology," in *Evolution and Molecular Biology: Scientific Perspectives on Divine Action*, ed. Robert J. Russell, William R. Stoeger, and Francisco J. Ayala (Rome: Vatican Observatory Publications, 1998), 401.

17. Ibid., 404.

18. Ibid.

19. Ilia Delio, *The Humility of God: A Franciscan Perspective* (Cincinnati: St. Anthony Messenger Press, 2005), 98. The storm she is referring to is from Holmes Rolston III who describes life as "a blessed tragedy, lived in grace through a besetting storm." See Holmes Rolston III, "Kenosis and Nature," in *The Work of Love: Creation as Kenosis*, ed. J. C. Polkinghorne (Grand Rapids, MI: William B. Eerdmans, 2001), 59.

20. Delio, *The Humility of God*, 93.

21. Ibid.

22. Ibid., 95–96, 99.

23. Ibid., 166. Schaab indicated that Peacocke's own relational distinctions, the Incarnate, Transcendent, and Immanent God "may be said to suffer in, with, and under the suffering of the cosmos and its creatures." Ibid.

24. Ibid., 169. See also Gloria Schaab, "A Procreative Paradigm of the Creative Suffering of the Triune God: Implications of Arthur Peacocke's Evolutionary Theology," *Theological Studies* 67 (2006): 545.

25. Gloria Schaab, *The Creative Suffering of the Triune God: An Evolutionary Theology*, AAR Academy Series (Oxford: Oxford University Press, 2007), 166.

26. Schaab affirms Peacocke's argument, based on the Nicene Creed, that "if members of the Trinity are distinguishable in terms of their modes of *creativity*, they are also distinguishable in terms of their modes of suffering." Ibid., 187.

27. Schaab, *The Creative Suffering of the Triune God*, 171–78, 187.

28. Ibid., 188. For example, Schaab describes transcendent sympathy as suffering *with* the cosmos (Ibid., 171) but later describes how "the Transcendent Mother" suffers protopathetically *under* the pangs of labor. Ibid., 188.

29. Schaab defines protopathy as "a primary suffering that is immediately produced, one that is not consequent or produced by another's suffering." Ibid., 190.

30. Ibid., 132. Schaab offers a definition of sympathy: "Quality or state of Being…affected by the suffering or sorrow of another; feeling of compassion or commiseration." Ibid., 188.

31. Ibid., 172.

32. Ibid.

33. Schaab offers a description of empathy: "Understanding, being aware of, being sensitive to, and vicariously experiencing the feelings, thoughts and experiences of another...[past or present] without having the feelings, thoughts and experiences fully communicated in an objectively explicit manner." Ibid., 189.

34. Ibid.

35. See Mary Jo Leddy's text *Say to the Darkness, We Beg to Differ* (Toronto, ON: Lester & Orpen Dennys Ltd., 1990).

36. Schaab, *The Creative Suffering of the Triune God*, 189.

37. Elizabeth A. Johnson, *Women, Earth, and Creator Spirit*, Madeleva Lecture in Spirituality (Mahwah, NJ: Paulist Press, 1993), 51.

38. James A. Nash, *Loving Nature: Ecological Integrity and Christian Responsibility*. Churches' Center for Theology and Public Policy (Nashville, TN: Abingdon Press, 1991), 109.

39. Ibid., 110.

40. Norman Habel, "A Theology of Deep Incarnation and Reconciliation," 3, accessed May 16, 2012, http://seasonofcreation.com/wp-content/uploads/2010/04/a-theology-of-deep-incarnation-and-reconciliation.pdf. (Removal of italics mine.)

41. Gloria Schaab, "Incarnation as Emergence: A Transformative Vision of God and the Cosmos," *The Heythrop Journal* 54 (2013): 631.

42. Ibid.

43. Thus, this movement of God toward the cosmos and of the cosmos toward God constitutes a definitive, irrevocable unity. Ibid., 634.

44. Ibid., 634–35.

45. Ibid., 638–39.

46. Ian Barbour, *When Science Meets Religion: Enemies, Strangers or Partners?* (San Francisco, CA: HarperSanFrancisco, 2000), 113.

47. Schaab, "Incarnation as Emergence," 639.

48. Douglas John Hall, *The Cross in Our Context: Jesus and the Suffering World* (Minneapolis: Fortress Press, 2003), 7.

49. Elizabeth Johnson, *Ask the Beasts: Darwin and the God of Love* (London: Bloomsbury, 2014), 208.

50. Brian Robinette, "Heraclitan Nature and the Comfort of the Resurrection," *Logos* 14, no. 4 (Fall 2011): 25–26.

51. Delio, *The Humility of God*, 98.

52. Schaab, "Incarnation as Emergence," 642.

53. Johnson, *Ask the Beasts*, 208.

54. Leo J. O'Donovan, "Suffering Tenderness," *America* 187, no. 18 (December 2, 2002): 14.

55. Hall, *The Cross in Our Context*, 36.

56. Pierre Teilhard de Chardin, *Christianity and Evolution*, trans. R. Hague (New York: Harcourt Brace Jovanovich, 1971), 163.

57. Rolston III, "Kenosis and Nature," 60.

58. Hall, *The Cross in Our Context*, 36.

59. Ibid.

60. Teilhard de Chardin, *Toward the Future*, trans. René Hague (Wilmington, MA: Mariner Books, 2002), 53. A more thorough analysis of how his Earth literacy impacted his interpretation of human suffering will take place in the final chapter.

61. Teilhard de Chardin, *Le Milieu Divin* (Paris: Editions du Seuil, 1957), 73.

62. Ilia Delio, *The Unbearable Wholeness of Being: God, Evolution and the Power of Love* (Maryknoll, NY: Orbis Books, 2013), 85.

63. Ibid., 86.

64. *Via naturae est via crucis*: Holmes Rolston III, *Science and Religion: A Critical Survey* (New York: Random House, 1987), 146.

65. Hall, *The Cross in Our Context*, 30.

66. Pierre Teilhard de Chardin, Letter written on Good Friday 1955 to Father Ravier. As quoted in Robert Faricy, "Teilhard de Chardin's Theology of the Cross," in *The Cross Today: An Evaluation of Current Theological Reflections on the Cross of Christ*, ed. Gerald O'Collins, Robert Faricy, Maurizio Flick (New York: Paulist Press, 1977), 23.

67. In an interview given in the video *Belonging: The Search for Acceptance*, directed by Karen Pascal (Markham, ON: Windborne Productions, 2002), DVD.

68. Hall, *The Cross in Our Context*, 148.

69. Delio, *The Humility of God*, 96.

70. Delio, *The Unbearable Wholeness of Being*, 80.

71. For example, some religious ideas that disembody and disconnect are the uncritical application of the idea of suffering as punishment for sin and salvation as an escape from the material world. Cultural ideas that disconnect and disembody are those that blame the poor for their own suffering or technocratic healthcare systems that deny the value of holistic, patient-centered, community care models. See Tracy E. Ore, *The Social Construction of Difference and*

Inequality: Race, Class, Gender, and Sexuality (Mountain View, CA: Mayfield Publishing Company, 2000), 18.

72. Hall, *The Cross in Our Context*, 149.

12. Ecosystemic Suffering: A Window

1. Thomas Berry, *The Dream of the Earth* (San Francisco: Sierra Club Books, 1988), 216.

2. Ibid., 217. Berry also indicates that "this binding curve that draws all things together simultaneously produces with the inner forces of matter that expansive tension whereby the universe and the earth continue its creative emergence into the future." Ibid., 220.

3. Ibid., 20.

4. Elizabeth A. Johnson, *Women, Earth, and Creator Spirit*, Madeleva Lecture in Spirituality (Mahwah, NJ: Paulist Press, 1993), 30.

5. Denis Edwards, "Resurrection and the Costs of Evolution: A Dialogue with Rahner on Noninterventionist Theology," *Theological Studies* 67 (2006): 816.

6. Johnson, *Women, Earth, and Creator Spirit*, 16–17.

7. See sections 5–8 in Diane B. Paul, "Darwin, Social Darwinism, and Eugenics," in J. Hodge and G. Radick, eds., *The Cambridge Companion to Darwin*, 2nd ed. (Cambridge: Cambridge University Press, 2009), 219–45.

8. Elizabeth Johnson, *Ask the Beasts: Darwin and the God of Love* (London: Bloomsbury, 2014), 103.

9. John Haught, "Evolution and the Suffering of Sentient Life," in *The Evolution of Evil*, ed. Gaymon Bennett, Robert J. Russell, Ted Peters, and Martinez J. Hewlett (Göttingen: Vandenhoeck & Ruprecht, 2008), 203.

10. Robert J. Russell, "Natural Sciences," in *The Blackwell Companion to Christian Spirituality*, ed. Arthur Holder (Malden, MA: Blackwell Pub., 2005), 336.

11. Robert J. Russell, "Groaning of Creation: Does God Suffer with All Life?" in Gaymon Bennett et al., *The Evolution of Evil* (Göttingen: Vandenhoeck & Ruprecht, 2008), 120–21. For an earlier, slightly modified version of the above quote and the paragraph quoted below, see Russell, "Natural Sciences," 326–27, 333.

12. Ibid., 121.

13. Lynn Margulis and Dorion Sagan, "Sentient Symphony," in *The Nature of Life: Classical and Contemporary Perspectives from Philosophy and Science*, ed. Mark A. Bedau and Carol E. Cleland (Cambridge, MA: Cambridge University Press, 2010), 340, 342.

14. Ibid., 342.

15. Ibid., 343.

16. Ibid., 344.

17. Ibid., 347.

18. Jay B. McDaniel, *Of God and Pelicans: A Theology of Reverence for Life*, 1st ed. (Louisville, KY: Westminster John Knox Press, 1989), 22.

19. Haught, "Evolution and the Suffering of Sentient Life," 192.

20. Ibid., 193.

21. Lynn Margulis and Dorion Sagan, *What Is Life?* New rev. ed. (Oakland, CA: Univeristy of California Press, 2000), 224.

22. Margulis and Sagan, "Sentient Symphony," 345.

23. Arthur Peacocke, *Theology for a Scientific Age: Being and Becoming-Natural, Divine and Human*, Theology and the Sciences (Grove City, OH: Augsburg Fortress Publishers, 1993), 68.

24. Ibid., 367.

25. Arthur Peacocke, "The Cost of New Life," in *The Work of Love: Creation as Kenosis*, ed. John Polkinghorne (Grand Rapids, MI: Eerdmans, 2001), 34.

26. Ibid.

27. Italic is mine. See principle 7 in Thomas Berry, "Twelve Principles: Understanding the Universe and the Role of the Human in the Universe Process," *Cross Currents* 37, nos. 2–3 (Summer/Fall 1987): 107–8.

28. Johnson, *Women, Earth, and Creator Spirit*, 37–38.

29. J. H. Fabre, *Oubreto Prouvençalo. Le Semeur*, as quoted in Charles E. Raven, *Natural Religion and Christian Theology*, Gifford Lectures (Cambridge: Cambridge University Press, 1953), 15.

30. Elizabeth Johnson, *She Who Is: The Mystery of God in Feminist Theological Discourse* (New York: Crossroads, 1992), 254–64; See also Elizabeth A. Johnson, "An Earthy Christology: 'For God So Loved the Cosmos,'" *America* 200, no. 12 (April 13, 2009): 28; Gloria Schaab, "Midwifery as a Model for Ecological Ethics: Expanding Arthur Peacocke's Models of 'Man-in-Creation,'" *Zygon* 42, no. 2 (June 2007): 487–98.

31. Johnson, *She Who Is*, 266.

32. Thomas Berry and Thomas E. Clarke, *Befriending the Earth: A Theology of Reconciliation between Humans and the Earth* (Mystic, CT: Twenty-Third Publications, 1991), 134.

33. Colin Barras, "What Was Earth's first Predator and When did It Live?" BBC Earth Series (Dec 3, 2014), http://www.bbc.com/earth/story/20141202-what-was-earths-first-predator.

34. Arthur Peacocke, "Biological Evolution—A Positive Theological Appraisal," in *Evolutionary and Molecular Biology: Scientific Perspectives on Divine Action*, ed. Robert J. Russell, W. R. Stoeger, and F. J. Ayala (Vatican Observatory and Center for Theology and the Natural Sciences; Notre Dame, IN: University of Notre Dame Press, 1998), 370.

35. From Canto 56, in Alfred Lord Tennyson's poem *In Memoriam A. H. H.*, 1850, accessed May 5, 2014, http://www.online-literature.com/tennyson/718/.

36. Berry, *The Dream of the Earth*, 220.

37. Ivone Gebara, *Out of the Depths: Women's Experience of Evil and Salvation* (Minneapolis, MN: Fortress Press, 2002), 113. See also Starhawk, "Power, Authority, and Mystery," in *Reweaving the World: The Emergence of Ecofeminism*, ed. Irene Diamond and Gloria Feman Orenstein (San Francisco: Sierra Club Books, 1990), 79.

38. Russell, "Natural Sciences," 340.

39. See Hillel J. Hoffman, "The Permian Extinction—When Life Nearly Came to an End," *National Geographic*, accessed April 4, 2014, http://science.nationalgeographic.com/science/prehistoric-world/permian-extinction/.

40. Smithsonian National Museum of Natural History, "The Cretaceous," accessed June 12, 2013, http://paleobiology.si.edu/geotime/main/htmlversion/cretaceous4.html.

41. International Union for Conservation of Nature (IUCN), "Wildlife Crisis Worse than Economic Crisis—IUCN" (July 2, 2009), http://www.iucn.org/?3460/Wildlife-crisis-worse-than-economic-crisis--IUCN; Intergovernmental Panel on Climate Change, *Emergent Risks Arising from the Effects of Degradation of Ecosystem Services by Climate Change*, accessed April 28, 2014, http://ipcc-wg2.gov/AR5/images/uploads/WGIIAR5-Chap19_FGDall.pdf.

42. James H. Cone, "God and Black Suffering," *Anglican Theological Review* 90, no. 4 (Fall 2008): 703.

43. Denis Edwards, "Every Sparrow That Falls to the Ground: The Cost of Evolution and the Christ-Event," *Ecotheology* 11, no. 1 (2006): 104.

44. Ibid., 120.

45. McDaniel, *Of God and Pelicans*, 118. Also see Ernst Conradie's articulation of material inscription in Ernest M. Conradie, *An Ecological Christian Anthropology: At Home on Earth?* (Cornwall: TJ International Ltd., 2005), 166ff.

46. In Scripture, *shalom* is used to express the well-being of others (Gen 43:27, Exod 4:18), to treaties (1 Kgs 5:12), in prayer for the well-being of cities or nations (Ps 122:6, Jer 29:7), to express wholeness and hope (Isa 9:6; Mic 5:4–5), and the time of peace (Hag 2:7–9; Isa 2:1–9, 11).

47. Conradie, *An Ecological Christian Anthropology*, 182.

13. Human Suffering: Looking in the Mirror

1. *Inspirited* makes reference to her commitment that all material bodies were a compound: matter and spirit. Thus, *inspirited* implies that the material is animated and permeated by a sacred spirit.

2. Readers are invited to see Teilhard de Chardin as *a* model not *the* model just as Audre Lorde is *a* model and not *the* model.

3. In 1899, he became a Jesuit, a member of the Society of Jesus, a Roman Catholic order of religious men founded by St. Ignatius of Loyola in 1540.

4. Mary Evelyn Tucker, "Education and Ecology: Earth Literacy and the Technological Trance," in *Teilhard in the 21st Century: The Emerging Spirit of Earth*, ed. Arthur Fabel and Donald St. John (Maryknoll, NY: Orbis Books, 2003), 3.

5. Pierre Teilhard de Chardin, *The Making of a Mind: Letters from a Soldier-Priest, 1914–1919*, 1st ed. (New York: Harper & Row, 1965), 119–20.

6. Teilhard was forbidden to teach at the Catholic Institute in Paris due to his views on God and evolution. David Grumett, "Teilhard de Chardin's Evolutionary Natural Theology," *Zygon* 42, no.2 (June 2007): 520. Teilhard also felt that the immorality attributed to evolution in the Scopes Trial was a misunderstanding of what evolution is but once it was correctly understood and grounded in Christ, it would prove that the world was not opposed to God. Pierre Teilhard

de Chardin, *The Vision of the Past* (London: William Collins Sons & Co., 1966), 136.

7. Louis M. Savary and Patricia H. Berne, *Teilhard de Chardin—Seven Stages of Suffering: A Spiritual Path for Transformation* (Mahwah, NJ: Paulist Press, 2015), 8.

8. And the controversy did not end at his death; even after his books went to press, the Holy Office rejected them, ordering, in 1957, that all of Teilhard's writings be removed from Catholic libraries and bookstores.

9. Pierre Teilhard de Chardin, "The Significance and Positive Value of Suffering," quoted in *Human Energy* (New York: HarperCollins, 1968), 48.

10. Ibid., 50.

11. Pierre Teilhard de Chardin, "Cosmic Life," in *Writings in Time of War* (London: Collins, 1968), 28.

12. Ibid., 29.

13. A reflection of a sentry during the war who sees the moon rising over the trenches. Pierre Teilhard de Chardin, *Cahiers Pierre Teilhard de Chardin* (1960), 39–48, as quoted in Henri de Lubac, *The Religion of Teilhard de Chardin* (London: William Collins Sons & Co., 1967), 58–59.

14. Teilhard de Chardin, "The Significance and Positive Value of Suffering," 48.

15. Ibid., 50.

16. Ibid., 51.

17. Ibid.

18. Savary and Berne, *Teilhard de Chardin—Seven Stages of Suffering*, 17.

19. Teilhard de Chardin, "The Significance and Positive Value of Suffering," 51–52.

20. Pierre Teilhard de Chardin, *Le Milieu Divin*, 73.

21. Savary and Berne, *Teilhard de Chardin—Seven Stages of Suffering*, 17.

22. Ibid., 9.

23. For example, see Elizabeth Johnson, "Does God Play Dice? Divine Providence and Chance," in *An Evolving Dialogue: Theological and Scientific Perspectives on Evolution*, ed. James B. Miller, rev. ed. (Harrisburg, PA: Trinity Press International, 2001), 353–70.

24. See Savary and Berne, *Teilhard de Chardin—Seven Stages of Suffering.*

25. Lorde is referring to the African goddess Seboulisa, the mother of us all, and in the first stanza of her poem "Dahomey," she intimately connects this deity with her own struggles with breast cancer. Audre Lorde, *The Collected Poems of Audre Lorde* (New York: W.W. Norton & Company, 2000), 239.

26. Audre Lorde, *The Cancer Journals Special Edition* (San Francisco: Aunt Lute Books, 1997), 9.

27. Audre Lorde, "A Burst of Light," in *The Cancer Journals Special Edition*, 130.

28. Lorde, "Uses of the Erotic: The Erotic as Power," in *Sister Outsider: Essays and Speeches by Audre Lorde* (New York: The Crossing Press 1984), 74.

29. Audre Lorde, "A Burst of Light: Living with Cancer," in *A Burst of Light: Essays* (New York: Firebrand Books, 1988), 91.

30. Lorde, *The Cancer Journals Special Edition*, 8.

31. This speech, "The Transformation of Silence into Language and Action," was originally delivered at the Lesbian and Literature panel of the Modern Language Association's December 28, 1977, meeting. It was then published in many of Lorde's books, including *Sister Outsider*, 41. (Written December 28, 1977.)

32. Lorde indicates there was a three-week period between the "telling and the actual surgery," and this was a three-week period of agony and intense "involuntary reorganization" of her life. Ibid., 40.

33. Ibid., 41.

34. Ibid., 42.

35. Lorde, "Uses of the Erotic: The Erotic as Power," 74–75.

36. Lorde, "The Transformation of Silence into Language and Action," 43.

37. Lorde, "A Burst of Light: Living with Cancer," 76, 86.

38. "I had grown angry at my right breast because I felt as if it had in some unexpected way betrayed me, as if it had become already separate from me and had turned against me by creating this tumor which might be malignant. My beloved breast had suddenly departed from the rules we had agreed upon to function by all these years." Lorde, *The Cancer Journals Special Edition*, 33.

39. Ibid., 55.

40. Ibid., 116.

41. Lorde, "A Burst of Light: Living with Cancer," 56, 62, 91, 94, 101.

42. Lorde, "Uses of the Erotic: The Erotic as Power," 77.

43. Susan A. Calef, "Taking Up the Cross: Suffering and Discipleship in the Gospel of Mark," in *Suffering and the Christian Life*, ed. Richard W. Miller (New York: Orbis Books), 69.

44. Magdelena Gómez, "In Darkness Grows the Green," in *Community of Religions: Voices and Images of the Parliament of the World Religions*, ed. W. Teasdale and G. F. Cairns, (New York: Continuum, 1996), 75.

14. Epilogue: New Horizons

1. Elizabeth Johnson, *Ask the Beasts: Darwin and the God of Love* (London: Bloomsbury, 2014), 205.

2. Catherine Keller, "No More Sea: The Lost Chaos of the Eschaton," in *Christianity and Ecology: Seeking the Well-Being of Earth and Humans*, ed. Dieter T. Hessel and Rosemary Radford Ruether (Cambridge, MA: Harvard University Press, 2000), 190.

INDEX

Index

Index